CITY OF RIVALS

CITY OF RIVALS
Restoring the Glorious Mess of American Democracy

JASON GRUMET

President, Bipartisan Policy Center
Forewords by Senator Tom Daschle and Senator Bob Dole

LYONS PRESS
Guilford, Connecticut
An imprint of Globe Pequot Press

Lyons Press is an imprint of Globe Pequot Press.

Project editor: Meredith Dias
Layout artist: Melissa Evarts

Library of Congress Cataloging-in-Publication Data is available on file.

ISBN 978-0-7627-9158-3

Printed in the United States of America

For Stephanie

CONTENTS

FOREWORD
by Senator Tom Daschle

WINSTON CHURCHILL IS OFTEN CREDITED WITH THE STATEMENT, "YOU can always count on Americans to do the right thing—after they've tried everything else." There is actually no record of Churchill ever uttering these words, but the statement captures a number of attributes that make our country unique. America does stand for doing the right thing. We are a resilient partner with our allies and nations in need. And our democratic process can be absolutely infuriating. The struggle among competing interests in our diverse society creates intense debate, frustrating delays, and occasional setbacks. But the obligation to reconcile our differences has also led to effective and durable public policy. It has never been an easy or particularly graceful process. As the Democratic leader in the Senate, I took part in many battles with my colleagues across the aisle—and occasionally with my fellow Democrats as well. On many occasions, these arguments were animated and deeply felt. But a disagreement on one issue very rarely damaged my ability to work with a colleague on another topic the very next day.

I remember sitting next to my colleague and fellow Senate leader, Trent Lott, at a Pentagon ceremony one year after the September 11 terrorist attacks. We had led the Senate together for six turbulent years. At one point, he leaned over. "You know, we have been through a lot together," he said, "and while there have been times when I've attacked you and you've attacked me, and our relationship has been strained, we have gotten through all of this together. People will never know what an accomplishment that really is."

Senator Lott and I both have the distinction of winning our first Leader elections by just one vote. Neither of us had significant latitude to commit our colleagues without an extraordinary amount of consultation with them and with each other. For that reason, we did two things that were catalytic in carrying out our responsibilities. First, we installed a "hotline" on each of our desks for whenever we thought the situation called for immediate and personal dialogue. Second, on many occasions we held joint caucus sessions where we could address whatever challenges we were facing together.

Looking back, I now regret that we didn't hold even more joint caucuses. But, that telephone got used frequently as we led the Senate through a presidential impeachment trial, the attack on September 11, the anthrax attack in my office, negotiating a governance framework for a Senate in 2001 (where both caucuses had fifty members), and countless matters regarding nominations, the enactment of legislation, and the Senate legislative schedule. But that was our job. And there was no one else who could do it.

America is certainly more divided today than it was when I left the Senate almost ten years ago. The wars in Afghanistan and Iraq, the recession, growing income inequality, and changing demographics have all deepened the political divisions in our communities. But the culture of the Congress has also changed in ways that have diminished its ability to solve hard problems.

City of Rivals explores the forces that have weakened the Congress and challenges many of the traditional notions of what is wrong with Washington. Look, for example, at the issue of transparency in government. Certainly the public must have access to the decision-making process. But the idea that Washington would work better if there were TV cameras monitoring every conversation gets it exactly wrong. We don't need smoke-filled back rooms, but we must protect the private spaces where people with different points of view are able to work through their disagreements. The lack of opportunities for honest dialogue and creative give-and-take lies at the root of today's dysfunction.

Nor is this book a nostalgic remembrance of better times past. To the contrary, Jason Grumet offers a clear-eyed account of the current polarization and presents practical ideas to get things moving despite these divisions. Politics has always been a contact sport. By embracing the critical role that constructive partisanship has played throughout history, Grumet offers a more realistic set of solutions than the traditional fix-Washington agenda.

Seven years ago, I joined with Jason, George Mitchell, Bob Dole, and Howard Baker to create the Bipartisan Policy Center. Our goal was not to take politics out of the equation or ask people to check their interests at the door. To the contrary, we have worked to create an environment in which fierce disagreements can be debated, informed by data, and thus resolved. Time and again, the BPC has developed detailed policy solutions not by splitting differences, but by combining the best ideas from the left, right, and middle. Like any good political process, there has also been plenty of hand-wringing, compromise, and the occasional horse trade. All of this has been enabled by bringing proud partisans together in an environment that builds trust and enables the exploration of new ideas.

City of Rivals traces how the elements that make the BPC so effective are being driven out of the federal government. America's leaders today don't know each other well enough and they don't trust one another deeply enough to harness the sort of collaboration we need to succeed as a nation. In addition, *City of Rivals* boldly explores how many well-intentioned and popular efforts to make government work better are doing just the opposite. If we want Congress to fix our broken immigration system, pass budgets on time, take on tax and entitlement reform, invest in infrastructure, and confront myriad other issues, we must take a hard look at the uncomfortable questions and creative solutions raised in the pages that follow.

Senator Tom Daschle
Washington, DC
April 2014

Foreword
by Senator Bob Dole

CITY OF RIVALS IS ONE OF THE FIRST BOOKS IN A WHILE THAT DOESN'T begin with the premise that Congress is irreparably broken, a necessary evil, or both. For nearly thirty-six years, I had the honor of serving in the US Congress. Things worked pretty well most of the time—but not because we all agreed about much. Indeed, those of us who endured the Great Depression and fought in the Second World War embraced a great diversity of ideas about how the government ought to be run. We argued a lot, and sometimes our disagreements got personal. But we all shared a fundamental commitment to the institution and a basic respect for our colleagues, regardless of their affiliation.

The bottom line is that we were combatants and we were friends.

I've learned from many years in Congress that it's difficult to get anything done unless you're able to compromise—not your principles but your willingness to see the other side. Those who suggest that compromise is a sign of weakness misunderstand the fundamental strength of our democracy. When I was the Republican Leader, President Reagan told me at a White House meeting that if you can't get it all, settle for 70 percent and try to get the rest next year. President Reagan was pragmatic—he felt in certain cases compromise was necessary. The progress achieved under Reagan's leadership demonstrates the wisdom of his approach, and I am proud of the many opportunities I had to support the president's agenda.

One of the most heated battles I recall from my Senate days was with Democratic senator Robert Byrd from West Virginia over a key amendment. Senator Byrd was strongly opposed to it, while I thought it was a good idea. There was some tension between Senator Byrd and me because of the importance of the amendment. He was chairman of the Appropriations Committee at the time and felt that the amendment would make his job, and the job of those who followed him, more difficult. He felt so strongly about the issue that he visited the offices of nearly fifty senators.

When the vote came in we lost, but there were no hard feelings and the next day was business as usual. We may have disagreed, but our mutual respect for one another superseded any temporary disagreement on the issues at hand.

The same holds true for working within your own party. I remember a fight over a Balanced Budget Amendment. The vote was 50–50, and we lost because one Republican voted against it. It was a very heated debate and, when we lost, a couple of my Republican colleagues wanted to ban the senator who voted against the amendment from the party. My sense was that, on the next important vote, those who were so upset over the budget vote might oppose my legislative efforts, while the lone Republican might support my position. In Congress, as in life, it always helps to have an eye for the big picture. Sure, we made some mistakes along the way, but the postwar years right through the end of the twentieth century were among some of the most dynamic and productive in the nation's history.

It wasn't easy—or even efficient—but Congress worked the way it is supposed to. We passed annual budgets; bills were developed and voted out of committees; the floor of the Senate was dynamic and often unpredictable; all senators were able to offer salient amendments and only in the rare occasion did a filibuster prevent legislation from moving to the floor for full consideration. Equally important was the time we spent together socially. Most of the tough issues were solved around small tables, over dinner at night, or in the Cloak Room between votes. Often when there was an important disagreement, I would gather the key senators into my conference room and tell them not to leave until they figured it out. Sometimes it took a few sessions, but an agreement usually emerged.

City of Rivals makes a real contribution by showing how government really works. It explains why America has been, until very recently, so good at using its diversity to its advantage. Most important, this book calls into question much of the conventional wisdom about how we got into this mess in the first place. Jason's knowledge of how to get things done in Washington shines through the pages of *City of Rivals*. I am particularly pleased that this book cuts against the grain to explain the critical and legitimate role played by lobbyists and the shortsightedness of stigmatizing congressional travel. It is convenient for politicians today to criticize Washington—but it isn't particularly courageous, and it's rarely very helpful.

The unconventional insights offered in the pages that follow provide a practical and optimistic vision of how to get America back on track. It is good reading for anyone who wants to understand what's gone wrong in the nation's capital—and required reading for anyone who wants to do something about it.

Senator Bob Dole
Washington, DC
April 2014

PROLOGUE

"I'm Not So Sure You Should Write It Down"

OUR GOVERNMENT IS MORE OPEN, MORE TRANSPARENT, AND LESS functional than ever before. If Washington doesn't get its act together soon, solvable challenges will become permanent wounds. The stakes are high and the conventional solutions simply aren't working. It is time to chart a new course and revive the world's greatest democracy.

There's nothing groundbreaking in the observation that the country is fed up with Washington, DC. While politicians preen and bicker, many Americans are struggling with unemployment, mediocre schools, lost savings, and an overwhelming sense that America is moving in the wrong direction. Add to this a Wall Street bailout and a jobless recovery and it is not hard to understand why over two-thirds of adults believe their kids won't enjoy the same opportunities that they have. The news has convinced us that the government is being run by people who seem neither to understand nor to care about the challenges facing ordinary people. Worst of all, the dysfunction feels structural and, maybe, even permanent.

While laboring in these trenches can be dispiriting at times, I see a silver lining to the story. Our conventional sense of why Washington is so broken gets a lot wrong. A closer look reveals that many of the reforms we've instituted to make government work more effectively— all of them pursued with the best of intentions—have, in practice, had the opposite effect. Through a series of bad assumptions and unintended consequences, we have weakened our government's capacity to solve problems. In the words of Pogo, "We have met the enemy and he is us."

None of that is to absolve the governing elite of their role in squandering the public's trust. They are responsible for the fact that the political system no longer seems fair and that many Americans are mad as hell. But we can acknowledge the legitimacy of popular anger, without getting caught up in it. It is time to swim sideways against this rip current. Rather than join the easy chorus of contempt promoted in recent books like Mark Liebovich's entertaining but dispiriting *This Town*, I believe that the foundation of our democracy is essentially sound and that federal employees are—by and large—sincere public servants. That may challenge the noble posture of those who see corruption lurking around every bend. But the way to get our democracy working again is to stir things up—not shut things down.

Over the past two years, I have interviewed dozens of political leaders, explained my argument, and outlined some of my ideas. Almost invariably they have responded with some version of: "I think you've got it right—but I'm not so sure you should write it down." My confidence to persevere rests on twenty years of political negotiations among highly partisan and often diametrically opposed interests. I have come to appreciate a simple truth: All public accomplishments begin with quiet conversations among people who trust each other.

In the 1990s I ran an organization created in the 1960s by a group of governors to strengthen and align the air pollution control programs in the eight northeastern states. With leaders like Mario Cuomo and Bill Weld at the helm, it became clear that no party had a monopoly on the best ideas. There was satisfaction in resolving divergent interests, and I realized the power and political influence of advocating bipartisan solutions. I did not create the Bipartisan Policy Center (BPC) because I think people should like each other or that things would be better if we just "all got along." Bipartisanship matters because it works. In a diverse and divided nation, it is the only way to get things done.

In 2001, I came to Washington to create the National Commission on Energy Policy (NCEP), a nonprofit with the goal of breaking through the stalled energy and climate change debate. The effort was inspired by the William and Flora Hewlett Foundation, whose leaders had grown increasingly concerned that the national energy discussion was careening between two extremes: the proposed restrictions in the Kyoto Climate Treaty and the environmental risks of drilling for oil in the Arctic National Wildlife Reserve (ANWR). Amid such a polarized landscape, very little was getting done.

In an effort to break the logjam, we convened an exceptionally diverse group that included former government officials, energy policy experts, corporate leaders, environmentalists, and academics. Then as now, there is little impact to agreements forged by groups of reasonable moderates—so we set out to test whether a process could succeed emphasizing the "P" as well as the "B" in bipartisanship.

One member of the commission had worked for President Clinton and another for Vice President Cheney. We had former directors of the EPA and CIA, passionate environmental leaders, and sitting CEOs from both "big oil" and nuclear power companies. (The toughest members were the economists and tenured professors who, reassured by their substantive expertise and independence, were least apt to cut a deal.) No one was asked to "check anything at the door," and everyone agreed to advocate for all consensus agreements. Rather than feigning detached objectivity, BPC embraces the idea that everyone has a special interest. Why else would they care to participate? In my experience, people claiming no special interest are either dishonest or dull.

Through the course of many discussions, political differences and vested interests eventually shifted from obstacles to inputs. The process broke down more than once, but each time we climbed out of the ditch our commitment grew stronger. It took over two years, but NCEP succeeded in developing detailed consensus agreements around climate policy, energy subsidies, domestic oil and gas production, fuel economy standards, and electric power generation. National progress on these issues had been overwhelmed by partisan and regional divisions, and our final report was aptly titled, "Ending the Energy Stalemate."

The final recommendations made everyone in the group *equally uncomfortable*—and therein lay its value. Then our good work met with good luck. After several failed attempts, Congress was determined to adopt a comprehensive energy policy. The commission's substantive analysis, political breadth, and aggressive advocacy made our proposals influential, and in 2005 Congress passed the first major overhaul of national energy policy in over twenty years.

Building on this experience, I founded the BPC in 2007, which now employs nearly one hundred staff members and works on a wide array of policy issues. Whether the topic is immigration reform, Iranian nuclear development, or offshore drilling, BPC projects all rely on the same set of principles:

- *We don't stack the deck*—Our projects are led by experts with conflicting political commitments, diverse experience, and divergent interests.
- *We respect data and conduct rigorous and transparent analysis*—BPC policy recommendations are based upon detailed studies that are broadly distributed.
- *We fight for what we believe in*—Once a project develops detailed recommendations, we work as a group to advocate for all aspects of the agreement.
- Finally, *we understand the latitude and limitations of our role*—BPC exists to advance the debate by digging deeper and pressing further and faster than is generally possible in government today.

BPC's process is unique in its simplicity. Over the course of our negotiations, we have a lot of meetings, dinners, and conference calls, and exchange thousands of e-mails. Our internal discussions are confidential, and we strive to protect our members from outside critique. The BPC staff works to ensure that all critical viewpoints are represented—even when key members are distracted—and readily throw themselves "under the bus" when helpful to speed the negotiations.

Trust is necessary, but not sufficient to overcome entrenched differences. Once earning the confidence of each new group of project leaders, BPC staff gets down to the hard work of researching issues, arguing with each other, developing option papers, engaging key interest groups, and overseeing in-depth technical analysis. While sometimes we do split these differences, more often our negotiations are propelled by new information, new ideas, and combinations of policies that enable individual positions to evolve and consensus to emerge from controversy.

While I have learned immensely from the exceptional leaders who participate in BPC activities, some of the most important insights I bring to this work come from my early experiences in college debate. To be successful in a debate, the task is to oppose whatever proposition the other side presents—regardless of what you personally believe. Debating required creativity to identify flaws and counterarguments and a willingness to explore ideas that were inconsistent with my own ideological instincts. The experience deepened my appreciation that all public policy positions provoke coherent and legitimate critiques. Moreover, I learned that the most successful arguments rarely confronted the proposition directly. Instead, they attacked the question from a different angle, co-opted their opponent's premise to offer a better solution, or simply changed the subject. The fundamental insight I carried forward into my career is that head-on collisions are rarely necessary and almost never lead to good outcomes.

Our public officials used to possess the instincts and traits that enable productive debate and collaboration. Despite heated arguments, our leaders used to pride themselves on the ability to compromise their positions, without compromising their values. Over the last few decades something fundamental has changed. But usual complaints about Washington are often bereft of practical solutions and oblivious to our nation's remarkable strengths. The hope for a return to functional government is neither naïve nor fleeting. *City of Rivals* lays out a set of seemingly unconventional ideas that promise to point the way to a more effective American democracy.

INTRODUCTION

A Tale of Two Washingtons

IN THE EARLY SPRING OF 2007, HOWARD BAKER, BOB DOLE, TOM DASCHLE, George Mitchell, and I stood in a small room at Union Station, the grand old train terminal just a few blocks from the US Capitol. In five minutes, they would walk together onto a stage to announce the founding of the Bipartisan Policy Center (BPC). It had taken nearly a year to design the organization, recruit the senators, raise some funds, and hire a small staff. Just a few final steps remained. Before the press conference could begin, we needed to decide who would speak first, remind the leaders of the key talking points, and discuss what to do if the L. Ron Hubbard devotee who had been harassing us ended up following through on his threat to disrupt the program. There was only one problem: The senators wouldn't stop telling stories.

Our pre-event briefing had begun with a joint interview granted to famed *Washington Post* columnist David Broder. As we sat down, Dole quipped that this was the first time all four senators had been in a room together "without a coffin." We had set up the meeting with Broder as a way to ensure an easy rapport among the four leaders before they took the stage—but it immediately became clear that our concerns had been misplaced. In sharp contrast to the partisan alienation that defines so much of our current politics, these former political combatants were close friends, and so the conversation quickly became extraordinarily, and surprisingly, familiar. After a few minutes spent talking about family, the banter careened past bipartisanship to a rather intimate discussion of personal health concerns.

Many might assume that the camaraderie on display that day was superficial. It is of course easier to embrace bipartisan collaboration when no longer leading a political party. However, the friendship that anchored BPC's founding was neither recent nor simply nostalgic. It was a reflection of thirty years of mutual respect, political combat, and significant accomplishment. Indeed, over the course of their careers, BPC's founders had been partisan warriors—frequently fiercer in private than on the public stage. They had battled each other over budgets, legislative initiatives, filibusters, and presidential elections. In many instances, their disagreements had been impassioned, if not downright angry.

Nevertheless, through decades of intermittent acrimony, something had bonded them together. Even at the most trying moment, they had each held to a belief that even their fiercest political adversaries shared both a love of country and a fundamental respect for the legislative process. This conviction deeply influenced the way Washington worked under their leadership. Even when championing wildly divergent agendas, they trusted one another enough to cooperate where possible, aware that greater wisdom could be gleaned from melding disparate demands.

<hr />

The four distinguished senators who came together that day at Union Station had agreed to establish the BPC because they shared a sense that the foundation of our democratic system was in real jeopardy. Traditions and institutions that had long guided America's success seemed brittle and strained. At a moment of dynamic global change, our political system was grinding to a halt. Despite their differences, the BPC's founders all agreed that the erosion of our political system was jeopardizing the American Dream.

It wasn't, to their minds, simply that Washington had become more partisan—much as that characterizes the conventional wisdom. Truth be told, Dole, Baker, Mitchell, and Daschle had *all* thrived within a political culture suffused with clashing ideologies. For them, the problem was that the impulse to negotiate, befriend a colleague, reach out to new members, or even protect an opponent, had become the exception and not the rule. It wasn't that the actual legislative process had changed. Rather, the nation's leaders had begun to abandon the traditions and methods that had historically enabled agreements. The political arena was losing the capacity to solve big problems. And something, they agreed, needed to be done.

To many observers, destructive partisanship and gridlock seem baked into the political system. But a look at even recent history demonstrates that it need not be this way. Even at moments of extreme political tension, Washington has frequently found ways to sidestep dysfunction. In late 1995, for example, Congress was seized in a month-long government shutdown generated by an impasse in budget negotiations between the Clinton White House and congressional Republicans.* Despite the intense acrimony, quiet work continued. In the midst of the shutdown, Democrat Henry Waxman and Republican Tom Bliley entered into negotiations on a controversial bill to improve food quality standards. Waxman and Bliley knew each other well. In fact, their wives had shared a Passover seder while traveling together in Prague. While Clinton and House Speaker Newt Gingrich slugged it out on national TV, Bliley and Waxman worked out a detailed agreement that would eventually sail through both houses of Congress. When President Clinton's chief of staff, Leon Panetta, was informed that "a compromise on pesticides" had been reached, Panetta responded: "If Waxman and Bliley are together on this, I don't need to know any more. We're for it."

The question is what happened over the course of the intervening years to turn things so sour. What has changed to make the system so fragile? Most important, why hasn't Washington figured out how to metabolize today's vitriol? Writing in the 1830s, Alexis de Tocqueville remarked that the "new" world seemed blessed by the unique capacity to make "repairable mistakes." It is not that he thought our leaders were any wiser than others. Instead, our system of government had an almost innate ability to right our ship of state before taking on too much water.

The fact that we're still here after some of the profound errors committed in the last two centuries argues that de Tocqueville was on to something. Unfortunately, it appears that we are testing this theory yet again. From the debt to the disappearing middle class to a broken immigration system, America faces structural challenges that won't go away on

---

* There were actually two shutdowns, the first beginning in November 1995 and the second ending in January 1996. Taken together, the government was shut down for a total of 27 days.

their own. The palpable fear across our country is that our long record of successful mid-course corrections is finally coming to an end. We've had a great run, but like all great empires, the sun is starting to set and winter is coming.

REPAIRABLE MISTAKES

Like the BPC's founders, I am fundamentally optimistic about the nation's future and believe there is a way out of our contemporary grid-lock. Otherwise, why start an organization predicated on the return of principled collaboration? But it is time for a fresh analysis of *why* we're in this current eddy of malaise. The prevailing view is that Washington has been corroded by a toxic mix of money in politics, the twenty-four-hour news cycle, and the partisan drawing of congressional districts known as gerrymandering. While the pursuit of campaign cash, cable fame, and protectionist districts have altered the political terrain, an undue focus on these factors is sending too many of us into unnecessary despair. So rather than whine about Rachel Maddow and Sean Hannity, wish for a new Supreme Court, or dream of utopian alternatives, it is time to take a hard look at what is truly different about politics in America today and to craft a new set of solutions that don't rely on nostalgia, impossible hopes, or unrealistic expectations.

When most visitors arrive in Washington, they are awed by the grand and imposing buildings that define the District of Columbia. The White House is at one end of Pennsylvania Avenue, and the Capitol is at the other. The State Department is in Foggy Bottom, and the Pentagon is across the river. It is tempting to sort out the workings of the federal government by the geography of its offices: separate buildings house distinct departments; each is responsible for some essential element of the federal mandate. It's a quick-and-easy way to get your mind around how Washington works.

But, a fuller understanding of Washington requires an understanding of the lives of the people who work in these buildings. It is common to assume that authority figures and celebrities lead alien lifestyles. (Forty years later, I still remember the shock of seeing my elementary school teacher at a grocery store.) Looking through the lens provided by the media, it is easy to imagine that politicians power-down after their evening news interviews, waiting in suspended animation for black cars to pick them up with the next morning's talking points. Until fairly recently, however, most DC politicians lived pretty ordinary lives. They lived in the suburbs with their families, sent their kids to local schools, fought the traffic to work, and went to the movies and out to dinner with friends. The old cliché that Washington is Hollywood for the less attractive got it wrong: Once the day's legislative business was over, most politicians fell back in the mundane routines of ordinary American life.

Few of us appreciate this elemental fact about the political world: The informal networks that inevitably develop between those who engage in the ungainly dance of public service have long been an essential element of Washington. In many cases the people making decisions inside the government—the powerful ones who speak to reporters and the staff who do most of the real work—are tied together by the same kinds of informal connections that characterize any community: Their spouses are social, their kids are classmates, and they've attended the same holiday parties for years. They have much richer relationships than can be portrayed in any given cable news segment, and these ties play a crucial role in determining how they behave in public life.

To no small degree, understanding these relationships and encouraging the constructive partisanship that flows from them is a unique mandate of the Bipartisan Policy Center. The vast majority of think tanks in Washington serve a defined partisan interest. The Heritage Foundation and the Center for American Progress, situated on the right and left respectively, were each founded to further the aims of a particular ideology. Even many groups that actively assert a "nonpartisan" stance—organizations like the American Petroleum Institute and People for the American Way—nurture an affinity with either the left or the right.

Ideologically driven institutions serve an essential role in the political process. Our democracy depends upon the collision between different interests and political parties. By establishing the partisan edges of an issue, these organizations help to set the boundaries for each debate.

However, zealots are rarely in the room when agreements are developed and decisions are made. In a divided nation, "all or nothing" politics have an all but certain outcome—and rarely is it "all." The challenge lies in striking the right balance between ideological extremity and feckless indifference. The answer has served our country for over two hundred years and is fundamental to any true democracy: *constructive partisanship*.

From the Reagan-era tax overhaul to the Clinton-era welfare reform effort, progress has historically been made not by those blind to partisan interests, but rather by those negotiating in good faith from their own ideological position. Our goal should be to be bipartisan with a focus on the "P." And that speaks to the critical distinction between *nonpartisanship* and *bipartisanship*. Rather than seek to cleanse our political process of partisan interests, the BPC aims to engage proud Democrats and proud Republicans in substantive negotiations that embrace political imperatives and yield pragmatic results.

FUNCTIONAL PARTISANSHIP

In 2001, President George W. Bush and Senator Ted Kennedy reached a historic agreement on No Child Left Behind (NCLB), a landmark bill designed to reform the nation's education policy. At the time, it was embraced broadly across the political spectrum (even if, in the years since, it has been subject to criticism). From a legislative standpoint, the 1990s were a very productive decade. Despite divided government and stark ideological differences (like the right's Contract with America), the Congress functioned. To some extent, NCLB marked the end of that era. There have been a few notable exceptions: the 2007 Energy Independence and Security Act passed the Senate 86–8 and the House 314–100. Congress also passed, to surprisingly little fanfare, a major patent reform bill in 2011. In 2013, the Violence Against Women Act was reauthorized, along with a bill to augment preparations for the nation's response to a chemical and biological weapons attack.

But on the whole, since NCLB, Washington's major legislative accomplishments have been almost exclusively achieved through party-line discipline. The Affordable Care Act—the Obama Administration's signature achievement—did not receive a single Republican vote. The fury and frustration stoked by this legislative breakdown has badly wounded this Congress. Since being signed into law in March 2010, the House of Representatives has voted fifty-two times to defund or otherwise dismantle the legislation—and there seems no end in sight to the frustration and protest. President Obama complained in his 2013 State of the Union Address that Washington too often jumped simply from "one manufactured crisis to the next." And no matter whom you blame for the state of perpetual bickering, it is striking to note the difference in congressional productivity between today and 1997, when President Clinton and Speaker Gingrich—who truly did not enjoy one another's company—worked out the first balanced budget in a generation.

It is tempting to wax nostalgic for better times when partisanship wasn't vitriolic, politicians were noble public servants, and the system was not corrupted by money. However this wistful vision of Washington is a lie. Poet Susan Stewart aptly describes nostalgia as a disease that pines for a time that never existed. The historic accomplishments of earlier eras weren't driven by political magnanimity or congressional equanimity.

For nearly 250 years, we have careened from controversial wars to harsh appointment battles, from presidential impeachments to contentious committee hearings, and from destructive scandals to caustic campaigns. What has changed of late is that the essential tension between partisanship and familiarity has fallen out of balance. The challenge for us, moving forward, is to rediscover that equilibrium.

The Next Sputnik Moment

In October 1957, when the Soviet Union announced the successful launch of Sputnik, the first man-made satellite to orbit the earth, many Americans went into a state of low-level panic. It wasn't that the Soviets' technological triumph sparked the sort of visceral terror that overwhelmed the nation on 9/11. But the surprise announcement from Moscow spoke to an underlying fear that framed the nation's foreign policy for the next several decades. Many thought the United States might well lose the Cold War, and the country would eventually be overrun by the menace gathering strength behind the Iron Curtain.

No one knew that night whether the United States had the wherewithal to go head-to-head with the Soviets. Totalitarianism will always be better at making plans and following through; democracies tend to get messy and distracted by the cacophony of competing voices. Many feared that Leninism would have a leg up in a world in which the sophistication of any one nation's nuclear arsenal could upend the global hierarchy. Indeed, in the weeks and months that followed the Sputnik launch, some rushed to exploit the nation's panic. Partisans on both sides of the aisle scrambled to blame the other for what seemed like a glaring example of America's failure to keep pace with Soviet technology.

From today's perspective it is easy to imagine the partisan carnage that would naturally have followed. We might have expected the Democratic leadership to bring Congress to a virtual halt with dozens of brutal hearings designed to embarrass the Eisenhower Administration for this blow to national pride and security. Frustrated by the Democratic Party's attacks on President Eisenhower, Republicans could have called for entitlement cuts, claiming that Social Security was gobbling up money better invested in the space program. Democrats, incensed that Republicans were defending an ostensibly incompetent administration, could have laid into the massive profits being made by the private arm of the military-industrial complex—making particular hay of the salaries going to executives at the helm. Each side could have made the nation's feckless efforts to out-innovate the Soviets the central focus of their political messages, vowing to block the other's agenda in the hyperbolic service of our nation's very survival. Washington might have become entirely gridlocked, leaving the Soviets with a wide-open opportunity to exploit their early lead in the space race.

Fortunately, none of that happened.

Instead, faced with a genuine crisis, politicians of all stripes banded together in support of the American space program. Of course, some Democrats (most notably Senator Stuart Symington of Missouri) tried to use Sputnik to indict Eisenhower, claiming that the president was asleep at the switch. But Symington's colleagues in the Senate, including Democratic leader Lyndon Johnson, rejected that line of attack, embracing instead "a 'let's-find-out-the-facts'" approach. And in the years that followed, the two parties worked together to take up the challenge, speeding past the Soviets in the space race and eventually, a quarter century later, winning the Cold War outright.

The issue today is whether the same ethos can again prevail in Washington. Against the backdrop of the challenges we now face in the early twenty-first century, we have to wonder whether the American political system will live up to the legacy of making "repairable mistakes" that de Tocqueville noted the better part of two centuries ago. Will, in a moment of national angst, a dysfunctional political system finally spring into action?

The answer most participants and observers give is that they hope so. They look forward to the moment when a new spirit of collaboration finally prevails in the nation's capital. They have crossed their fingers in the expectation that a new generation of leaders will inspire Washington to "do the right thing." They pray that, before some calamity—a severe disruption of global oil supply, a default on the national debt, a damaging cyberattack—the nation's collective leadership figures out a way forward.

But we can't leave it at that. We can't afford to let Washington stumble along when America's promise of opportunity and place in the world are in peril. It's wonderful to have hope—but we also need a plan to break free from this vicious cycle of self-inflicted wounds. It has taken a while to dig this hole and there is no single solution or courageous act that will turn things around. Moreover, it is neither possible nor desirable to work toward a Kumbaya moment that rids Washington of conflict and antagonism. The American story has, to this point, been defined by our ability to derive strength from our diversity. We must build upon this foundation to foster a renewed culture of functional partisanship. It is time to rediscover the dark art of principled compromise.

CHAPTER 1

The Roots of Collaboration

THOUGH IT'S NOW ENSHRINED AS THE FOUNDATION FOR HISTORY'S MOST enduring democracy, the Constitution wasn't universally embraced when it burst onto the public scene in the fall of 1787. In the years prior, concern had grown throughout the thirteen former colonies that the government established by the original "Articles of Confederation" wasn't performing up to snuff.* Having failed to provide for a chief executive, executive agencies, a judiciary, or a tax base, the newly formed country had often found itself paralyzed. But while most Americans acknowledged that *something* needed to change, there was very little consensus about which direction to head.

At the time, memories of England's King George's autocratic rule were still fresh in the public's mind. For that reason, many feared that a more centralized charter would put the nation under another oppressive regime. However, few thought the country could abide much more of the disorganized status quo. What to do was a touchy subject—particularly among those who worried about the implications of shifting more authority from the states to the federal government. It took months of discussion, collaboration, and compromise. And even after all that, it was far from a foregone conclusion that the individual states would embrace the new charter.

After the draft Constitution was released publicly, a raucous national debate whipped into high gear. On the one side were the Constitution's critics, known collectively as the "anti-Federalists." New York State

---

* After the United States declared its independence, but before the Constitution was ratified, the national government was organized under the so-called "Articles of Confederation," which provided for very little executive power.

governor George Clinton and George Mason, author of the Virginia Declaration of Rights, both expressed grave concerns that the newly proposed federal government would steal too much power away from ordinary people. Mason argued that the Constitution would lead America down the path to "a Monarchy, or a corrupt oppressive Aristocracy." The best check on abusive government, he claimed, was a direct connection to the people at the state and local level; on that front, the new charter represented a giant step backward.

On the other side were the Constitution's "Federalist" defenders. With the mission of answering the anti-Federalist critiques, two of the Federalists' most prominent leaders, Alexander Hamilton and James Madison, collaborated with John Jay on *The Federalist Papers*, a series of newspaper treatises that they hoped would answer the detractors' concerns.* The newly drafted Constitution had imperfections, they acknowledged. But they argued that the tensions enshrined in the proposed charter offered the best hope to hold true to the ideals of the Revolution. The Articles of Confederation weren't preserving liberty as much as they were sacrificing the very ideals of republican government. And the design enshrined in the Constitution, they contended, offered the best way forward.

The Federalists weren't completely insensitive to the Anti-Federalists' concerns. Many wanted to address them head on. The "Bill of Rights"— the term we generally use to describe the first ten amendments to the Constitution—was designed to mollify that criticism that the Constitution deviated too much from principles articulated in the Declaration of Independence. To placate the concerns of critics like Mason and Clinton, each amendment restricted the new federal government's authority. If the core of the Constitution offered the Federalists much of what they wanted from a new government, the Bill of Rights served as a relief valve for anti-Federalist concerns.

Whether an elegant compromise or simply a kluge of discordant ideas, the balance paved the way for ratification. But it didn't resolve the conflict between proponents of direct democracy and federal authority.

---

* Despite close collaboration, Hamilton and Madison became bitter political enemies in later years, as Hamilton remained a steadfast Federalist and Madison drifted to become more enamored of Thomas Jefferson's advocacy for direct democracy led by common citizens and responsive to their will.

The same arguments that defined the debate in the late 1700s echo in today's political battles. Partisans with various interests continue to cross swords over the proper exercise of federal power. And for that reason, it is worth taking a moment to understand more thoroughly what was behind the defining political disagreement of the post-colonial era.

THE FOUNDING GENERATION

A decade ago, the conservative political scientist Charles Kesler argued that the essential issue separating the Federalists and the anti-Federalists was their differing conception of the "proper relation between republicanism and responsibility." To the anti-Federalists, he explained, the most effective way to keep the government in line—to avoid the second coming of English-style despotism—was to guarantee that elected representatives felt forever duty-bound to reflect the opinions of those who elected them. In their view, there could be no better way to keep the nation's power brokers honest than to tie their fortunes to the will of the voters. And so the anti-Federalist's central aversion to the new Constitution was that it created *obstacles* to direct accountability.

The Federalists, however, were focused on another priority. They too embraced the concept of popular sovereignty, and sought to establish a framework responsive to the will of the people. But they simultaneously believed that an effective republican government had a responsibility to do what was right *regardless of public opinion*. They worried that a majority of voters might support a policy that victimized a minority, or that a momentary swell of passion might steer the nation in the wrong direction. They were fearful that a nation of factions would be unable to derive a coherent public policy. No doubt, they were also motivated to some degree by a desire to sustain their aristocracy and the powers of the ruling class. But their broader aim was to craft a framework capable of balancing immediate local desires and enduring national interests. They envisioned a governing structure that, like an iron rod, would bend only slightly with each blow of a hammer. Federalists sought to channel the zeal of popular opinion without becoming its servant.

This points to an underappreciated truth about the Founding Generation: The cohort who fought in the Revolution and wrote the Constitution wasn't exclusively driven by an idealistic love of liberty; rather, they struggled with how to strike a balance between the short-term demands of the average citizen and the shared wisdom of their chosen leaders.* And despite the presumptions about the views of America's most famous politicians, the hidden truth is that the pursuit of the national interest and desire for stability are as important in our governing structure as are liberty and fealty to popular will.

This truth is often awkward for those tasked with telling the story of America's founding. We were all taught in elementary school that the United States was established to free a disenfranchised nation from the oppression of "taxation without representation." To that end, textbooks suggest that the Founders were singularly focused on restricting authoritarian prerogatives, devising a system of checks and balances between the various branches of government.

But that is a simplistic narrative that does a disservice to the Founders' true intentions. As Madison wrote in *Federalist 10*:

> *A pure democracy, by which I mean a society consisting of a small number of citizens, who can assemble and administer the government in person, can admit of no cure for the mischiefs of faction . . . Hence it is that such governments have ever been spectacles of turbulence and contention; have ever been found incompatible with personal security or the rights of property; and have in general been as short in their lives as they have been violent in their deaths.*

In essence, many among the Founding Generation worried that too much obedience to public referenda would cripple the government. They were concerned that leaving too much power in the hands of the individual states—let alone to the whims of an erratic public—would leave the United States with *not enough* constructive political conflict. Indeed, it was only by constructing a governing structure diverse enough to ensure frequent competition and disagreement between a "greater variety of

---

* The term "Founding Generation" is used in lieu of "Founding Fathers" to diminish the suggestion of parental benevolence as well as the implication that these political leaders were a cohesive unit with aligned interests.

parties and interests" that they felt they could eradicate the possibility that a single faction would "invade the rights of other citizens."

Critics today might claim that the Founders were trying to craft a system that would allow the nation's elite to control the government—and those detractors aren't entirely wrong. But what's also true is that those drafting the Constitution saw collaboration—even if just among ordinary citizens—as a crucial check on the misguided whims of public opinion. They feared that like-minded legislators would seek short-term gains to the detriment of society's long-term well-being. Wider-ranging debate would help ensure that the government was *responsible* to the electorate, and not simply *responsive.*

Intuitively this made sense. If each state was able to go its own way, or if the passions of public opinion were allowed to subsume the body politic, the various and conflicting ideas swirling through the post-colonial world would never have met. Most Framers believed that the key to a well-run country was to build a political framework that forced constructive conflict and demanded collaboration. Without the alchemy to reconcile competing interests, they feared that the "United" States of America might not be sustainable under the strain of competing local interests. That foresight marked a core component of the Founders' genius. As is the case today (e.g., deep-blue Massachusetts and dark-red Texas), the individual legislatures governing the various states during the post-colonial period weren't always steeped in a great deal of internal diversity. But *across* state boundaries, the factions varied dramatically. In the late 1700s, the rural gentry that dominated Virginia were driven by political designs very different from those held by the commercial interests in New York. But the Federalists did not view this as a liability. They believed that these distinctions could be used to the country's advantage.

It is striking that the same wisdom holds today—even if we're not particularly inclined to acknowledge it. On the surface, many Americans argue that they'd prefer the government simply to reflect the popular sentiment—that majority rules. But at the same time, we tend to embrace divided government because we rightly mistrust the authoritarian quality of single party domination. We hate the dysfunction on display in Washington, but we want there to be disagreement within the legislative process. And our challenge today, as it was during the colonial period, is to capture and direct the energy that results from this fusion.

———

Designing a system to harness that fundamental tension was no easy task. Beyond the awkward dance created by spreading power between three separate branches of government, the Federalists were determined to fashion a governing architecture that compelled individual members of Congress to reconcile the short term with the long, the immediate demands of the electorate with the broader public interest. They weren't naïve; they realized elected officials who consistently voted against their constituents weren't likely to survive long in office—even if the local demands were shortsighted. But their belief that politicians could be prompted to act in the nation's broader interest was rooted in a very particular definition of political courage.

THE DEVOLUTION OF COURAGE

Throughout American history, we have defined political bravery in different and often conflicting ways. Today, gutsiness is often measured by a politician's willingness to fight the powerful interests in Washington. The "brave" politician in the twenty-first century is the one who refuses to abandon the causes prized by his or her most adamant constituents regardless of impact on the national interest. In 2011, for example, Tea Party conservatives praised politicians' refusal to pay the nation's debts—despite the fact that practically every economist and business leader feared that a default would send the economy into a tailspin. At the same time, progressive Democrats applauded those who refused to consider even modest entitlement adjustments—despite the fact that nearly every sound fiscal analysis recognized the situation to be unsustainable.

That is not the only way to define bravery; in fact, in some respects, it is pure cowardice. In contexts outside the contemporary debate, political courage is frequently understood as a willingness to follow one's conscience *despite* the demands from the loudest local voices. Former senator Trent Lott tells the story that his predecessor in the Senate, John Stennis, was regularly referred to as a "statesman." After over a dozen years in the

Senate including several years in leadership, Lott wondered, what's a guy have to do to be similarly regarded? His eventual conclusion: "Do what you think is right even when your constituents disagree and then go home and explain your vote."

The battle between those two definitions of courage is as old as the Republic. The public figures who supported the Whiskey Rebellion of the early 1790s, for example—men and women who, during the course of the Washington Administration, took up arms to avoid what they saw as an onerous tax on the fruits of their harvest—believed themselves to be brave citizens fighting for justice. But viewed through the long lens of history, the hero is President Washington himself, who sent troops to quash the insurrection and protect the fragile union.

Thomas Jefferson faced a similar dilemma in 1803, when deciding whether to take control of the Louisiana territory. The public—including many of Jefferson's own supporters—was vocally opposed. The deal was too expensive, some argued. Many also questioned the legality of the land grab, claiming that "the Constitution gave Jefferson no power to incorporate Louisiana into the union," as one historian explained. But Jefferson persevered, stating that the benefits of the treaty—gaining "'uncontrolled navigation' of the Mississippi," eradicating "all 'dangers to our peace,'" and improving "the 'fertility of the country'"—were too beneficial to be sacrificed in the name of public opinion. Once again, political courage lay in the rejection of popular opinion, rather than the repudiation of institutional Washington.

It was with just those sorts of policy challenges in mind that the Founding Generation sought to erect a governing architecture that balanced the national interest with more popular demands—or, rather, long-term with short-term heroism. It was assumed that members of the House of Representatives would heel more closely to the popular will, as its members risk dismissal every two years. But the Founders hoped the same would not be true for members of the Senate, who would more frequently vote their consciences without fear that their seat was more immediately on the line. By ensuring that senators were to stand for election only once every six years, the Founders sought to protect them from the whims of public opinion, enabling them to more easily vote their conscience.

That wasn't the only way the Founders strove to encourage the Senate to think long-term. In what is now viewed as a historical mistake, the Framers required that senators be chosen not by the public at large, but by members of the state legislatures. Fortunately, the Constitution was written to evolve, and nearly everyone today supports the direct elections mandated in 1913 by the Seventeenth Amendment. But much as we may find many of the elitist and discriminatory beliefs operating in the eighteenth century deeply offensive, we can't lose sight of the underlying intention: The Founding Generation explicitly rejected the notion that America should be governed by public referenda.

As Alexander Hamilton said:

A pure democracy, if it were practicable, would be the most perfect government. Experience has proved that no position is more false than this. The ancient democracies in which the people themselves deliberated never possessed one good feature of government. Their very character was tyranny; their figure, deformity.

Beyond the institutional checks the Founders installed to withstand the urge of popular opinion, the Federalists set up a political process to induce policymakers to engage the national interest: They created a system that would compel politicians *to get to know one another.*

Federalist 63, most likely written by Madison, addressed the importance of designing a legislative body capable of resisting public impulse:

As the cool and deliberate sense of the community ought, in all governments, and actually will, in all free governments, ultimately prevail over the views of its rulers; so there are particular moments in public affairs when the people, stimulated by some irregular passion, or some illicit advantage, or misled by the artful misrepresentations of interested men, may call for measures which they themselves will afterwards be the most ready to lament and condemn. In these critical moments, how salutary will be the interference of some temperate and respectable body of citizens, in order to check the misguided career and suspend the blow mediated by the people against themselves, until reason, justice, and truth can regain their authority over the public mind?

The Founders weren't unsophisticated. They knew that politicians would want to do what their constituents desired. It was no more popular in the late 1700s to raise taxes or slash benefits than it is today. But Madison and his colleagues were convinced that a government could be constructed to provide some counterweight against the urge to do the public's bidding.

For more than two centuries, that balance has worked to America's benefit. Time and again, those pilloried for doing what isn't politically expedient have later been lionized in the years and decades that followed for their principled bravery. Noting that very point, then-Senator John F. Kennedy documented the plight of Daniel Webster, Kennedy's distant Massachusetts Senate predecessor, in his 1957 book *Profiles in Courage*. As Kennedy detailed, Webster's support for the famous Compromise of 1850 sparked outrage among his abolition-minded constituents. The legendary nineteenth-century orator was a strong opponent of slavery, reluctant to support a plan that permitted new "slave" states into the union, as the Compromise proposed. But he simultaneously believed that a failure to balance the slave states' interests would lead almost immediately to civil war—and that the dissolution of the Union was the worse of two terrible options.

As Kennedy pointed out, the Compromise, which Henry Clay pushed through Congress with Webster's help, managed to delay the Civil War by more than a decade—time enough to allow the North to build the munitions and infrastructure it would eventually need to defeat the Confederacy. Had Webster heeded his constituents' demands, the South's secession might well have been successful, enabling slavery to persist for several more decades.

The arc of history allows us to see Webster's long-term strategy as political bravery but, at the time, that is not how his detractors interpreted his embrace of Clay's compromise. Quite the opposite: Webster, who had served in the Senate with such distinction, was attacked unmercifully by abolitionists who believed he had sold out the cause. Despite years of honorable service, the legendary senator was forced to retreat from public life in ignominy. But to Kennedy's mind, considered a century later, Webster's perseverance wasn't any kind of treachery. Quite the opposite, he laid his career down for the greater good, which Kennedy felt was an admirable expression of political courage.

That same tension is replete through the whole of American history. In every age, the great statesmen of our democracy have endeavored to strike the proper balance between heeding the public demands in the short-term, and preserving their interests down the road. Our nation's most revered leaders have been deeply pragmatic in their willingness to anger friends as well as adversaries. As Ronald Reagan explained in his autobiography, *An American Life*:

> *I'd learned while negotiating union contracts that you seldom got everything you ask for. And I agreed with FDR, who said in 1933: "I have no expectations of making a hit every time I come to bat. What I seek is the highest possible batting average." If you got seventy-five or eighty percent of what you were asking for, I say, you take it and fight for the rest later, and that's what I told these radical conservatives who never got used to it.*

And Reagan put that spirit into action. In 1983, Congress blocked his administration's proposal to scale back Social Security benefits. But rather than adopt an "all-or-nothing" attitude, he supported the recommendation of a bipartisan commission appointed jointly by the White House and Democratic House Speaker Tip O'Neill. The commission then produced a plan that, while derided from both the left and the right, managed both to limit the unsustainable growth of benefits while extending the life of the program. Fairly controversial at the time, the Greenspan Commission (named for its chairman, future Federal Reserve chairman Alan Greenspan) is now remembered as an example of pragmatic and principled compromise.

Our conflicting definitions of heroism result naturally from the tension embedded in our Constitution. "The public interest" is a mix of the immediacy of public opinion and informed deliberation about the future. It is not an easy balance to strike. In his 1936 essay, "The Crack Up," F. Scott Fitzgerald broadly describes the challenge: "The test of a first-rate intelligence is the ability to hold two opposing ideas in mind at the same time and still retain the ability to function."

If this is challenging for an individual, it's Cirque du Soleil when undertaken in unison by 535 members of Congress. For over two centuries, this discordant ballet has been successfully choreographed by a host of institutions and traditions. These are the features of our democracy that we must now work to restore.

TRULY EXCEPTIONAL

Arguments abound about what is most responsible for America's remarkable emergence as a global superpower. Some cite the nation's vast natural resources. Others point to the buffer that separates us from Europe and Asia. Still others, like the British scholar Niall Ferguson, have ascribed our rise to the confluence of a series of interwoven factors. Ferguson argues that six "killer apps" are, together, largely responsible for the West's rise to world domination: competition, scientific discovery, medicine, education, the Protestant work ethic, and the rule of law.

But what we too often fail to appreciate is that the DNA of America's governing institutions distinguishes our way of forging policy quite starkly from even our closest "free" allies. Unique to the strictures of the American Constitution, our leaders are prevented from sidestepping the obligation to collaborate with their adversaries. While the elements that distinguish our system—the separation of powers, for example—often make for a grinding process and cautious progress, they have also made for a steady, resilient, and adaptable nation. We bend but we do not break. Republican Senate leader and statesman Everett Dirksen often likened Congress to a waterlogged scow: "It doesn't move very fast, it doesn't move very far at one time, but it never sinks." And that, as much as any of the more traditional explanations, goes a long way toward explaining our exceptional place on the world stage and role as the "indispensable nation."

There's a certain irony in America's renown as the world's greatest democracy. For all the extolling of American virtues, few nations have established a government that mirrors our approach. Frankly, we don't even recommend it, fearing that these fragile and often war-torn nations are not ready to handle the divisions, tensions, and conflict embedded in American democracy. Where the United States has had a major hand in developing a new regime, we tend to promote comparably simple parliamentary structures. Consider how democracy over the past two centuries has evolved at Westminster, the seat of the British Parliament. The political coalition in power there rules largely by fiat. As in most parliaments around the globe, if there's agreement among the party that claims a majority of the House of Commons, they can outright ignore the views expressed by other legislators. And that works to powerful effect. When Margaret Thatcher's Conservative government moved to reform Britain's social safety net, she never had to consult members of the Labor Party; when Tony Blair's Labor government overhauled the country's National Health Service, he had little reason to placate Tory concerns. Unless another party is co-opted into the government, as the Liberal Democrats were in Britain's current Conservative government, they are entirely frozen out. Decisions are made entirely *inside* the coalition in power.

In the United States, by contrast, power is more thoroughly diffused. The president may be the most powerful single official, but even he has to seek the "advice and consent" of the Senate before any appointee assumes an office. Over the last two years our divided Congress has grappled with proposals to reform an immigration system all agree is broken. The majority of progressives and conservatives support an increase in the flow of legal workers who are essential to our economy. There is broad agreement that government must improve the security of our borders and a general acceptance that children should not be punished for being brought here illegally. However, the majority of Democrats in Congress believe that reform must grant law-abiding undocumented workers a path to eventual citizenship. Most congressional Republicans believe that people who have come here illegally must first acknowledge the criminality of their behavior before achieving legal status, let alone citizenship. Immigration reform will pass, but not until Congress bridges these differences. Whether it be appointing justices to the Supreme Court or resolving domestic crises or naming a post office, our system of government demands interaction across the political spectrum.

The same is not true in a parliamentary system. When the Chancellor of the Exchequer is crafting a fix to the country's retirement system, she can ignore the political opposition's ideas so long as it does not undermine the next national election. But her counterpart in the United States would make it her priority to *anticipate* what her political opponents might say and what they might want in return for their support. And that difference is the whole ballgame. Parliamentary systems compel members to tend almost exclusively to their supporters' concerns. The US Constitution demands that effective legislators mind their opponents carefully and encourages them to co-opt one another's best ideas.

That distinction is often lost on the American public. If anyone catches a broadcast of Prime Minister's Questions, where members of the British Parliament needle and prod the head of government—sometimes they outright heckle him—it seems as if the interaction in a parliamentary system is actually more robust than ours. But those charmingly aggressive displays are just that: displays. They mask the stark reality. All the major decisions have been made in advance. The quaint thrust-and-parry of British tradition obscures the truth that those catcalling the prime minister are powerless. Their yelling is not proof of their voice—it's the anger at their *lack* of one. And that harkens back to the very concerns the anti-Federalists voiced about abandoning the spirit of the Declaration of Independence. A prime minister, acting with the support of a majority in parliament, is about as close to a monarch as democracy would allow.

WATERGATE'S REVENGE

In 1974, America breathed a sigh of relief when President Ford declared from the East Room of the White House that "our long national nightmare is over." By resigning under the cloud of Watergate, Richard Nixon had curtailed what was unquestionably the most serious American political crisis to follow the Civil War. But understood in its proper context—just as Americans were beginning to appreciate the scale of Washington's incompetence in Vietnam—the most crucial impact of Watergate wasn't the criminal activity; it was the damage the scandal did to the nation's faith in public service.

Over the course of the four decades that preceded the Nixon Administration, Washington had managed, quite successfully, to steer the nation through several gargantuan challenges: the Great Depression; the Second World War; the beginnings of the nuclear age. Suddenly, however, Watergate spoiled the punch; it suggested that federal authority wasn't nearly as benign and virtuous as much of America had presumed it to be. Americans were awoken to the fact that the rough-and-tumble of politics had turned into something more nefarious. And that was a rude surprise; it suggested to many Americans that the federal government, an institution that had been respected for decades, was now much more suspect.

To be fair, Watergate didn't upend the public's faith in government in a vacuum. Decades later, former Senate Republican leader Howard Baker was asked why the political generation reared before Watergate had been so willing to work in concert, even with their colleagues across the aisle. His answer was extremely revealing: "because we had all fought the war together." He wasn't being metaphorical, either. It is hard to overestimate just how formative an experience the Second World War had been for members of the so-called "Greatest Generation." Even more, it is crucial to grasp how notably absent any similar experience was for their children, who had been reared in the relative affluence of the 1950s.

Unlike their parents who were joined together through the conflict of war, many Baby Boomers became politically aware during the divisive years surrounding the Vietnam War. Viewed through the jaundiced lens of Watergate, the Greatest Generation's presumption of good will was replaced with suspicion and loss of faith. Public service, once engrained as a noble pursuit, was suddenly affixed by a whole generation with a scarlet letter.

The ripple effects were unmistakable. To this day, enterprising young reporters aspire to become their generation's embodiment of Bob Woodward and Carl Bernstein, the wet-behind-the-ears *Washington Post* reporters most responsible for bringing the scandal to light. What "Woodstein" came to symbolize, along with peers like Seymour Hersh and Dan Rather, was a new creed centered on questioning (and doubting) the world of established authority figures. The great heroes of the era weren't the public servants who prosecuted the lawbreakers—independent prosecutor Leon Jaworski or Senate Watergate Committee chairman Sam Ervin—as much as they were the outside journalists who spoke truth to power.

But the ripples didn't end there. In the wake of Watergate and Vietnam, a cottage industry of citizen reformers rose up and seized the opportunity to shape public policy through nongovernmental organizations. The disappointments and abuses that defined the late 1960s and early 1970s served as an impetus for the emergence of nonprofits committed to the cause of "good government." And nothing better illustrates that progression than the story of John Gardner, the man who founded the movement's flagship organization.

A Republican transplant inside Lyndon Johnson's Democratic administration, John Gardner had served for several years as the Secretary of Health, Education, and Welfare, the department primarily responsible for implementing the specifics of Johnson's "Great Society." But then, in 1968, he decided to leave public life. His resignation stemmed partly from his personal opposition to the Johnson Administration's policy in Vietnam. But it was also spurred by his nascent belief that the Great Society was failing because a series of "special" interests were conspiring to ruin Washington. To his mind, LBJ's failure to win the War on Poverty was due largely to a coterie of influences that were working against it. Consequently, federal programs intended to improve lives across the board were being supplanted by the demands made by private interests whose voices resonated more forcefully along the corridors of power.

Freed from the cabinet, Gardner pondered what he might do to help turn things around. He considered whether to join the ranks of academia; Columbia University tried to recruit him as its new president. But eventually he determined that the most effective way he could address the nefarious influence of special interests was to create a voice that could respond on behalf of the public interest. And so, even before the Watergate break-in itself, he established Common Cause, an organization

25

designed "to build a true 'citizens' lobby." The American people could only hope to "revitalize politics and government [if] millions of American citizens [were] looking over [the politician's] shoulders," he argued. And so a new cast of "investigative citizens" set out to expose the inner workings of our government. Gardner wasn't alone in his mission. Ralph Nader, who founded Public Citizen in 1971, and Donald Ross, who co-authored the blueprint for the Public Interest Research Groups (PIRGs) with Nader, were driven by the same sense of outrage and suspicion. If Vietnam had laid the kindling for a new attitude toward government, Watergate lit the match.

In the months and years that followed, the ethos born in the 1960s began to inform a much wider movement. Common Cause and sister organizations began to lead intense lobbying efforts to take "action to reduce the influence of money in elections and secrecy in legislative practices." By 1975, Gardner's group had lobbyists working in every state to strengthen open-government laws, and by 1977, Common Cause's efforts had helped to spur the imposition of a new code of conduct in Washington, one which included "a set of rules for public financial disclosure, limits on outside earned income and gifts, a prohibition on using campaign funds for personal use, and other restrictions."

PAVED WITH GOOD INTENTIONS

Forty years after Watergate and Vietnam, the movement born in and around Watergate is ripe for reevaluation. At first glance, it might seem as if the abysmal conditions in Washington suggest that reformers have failed in the years since the torch was lit. But the truth is that the decades-old drive to "clean up" government has been remarkably successful. Dozens of laws have been passed increasing transparency and limiting interaction between lobbyists and legislators. While far from perfect, transparency is now required in most facets of campaign giving. If John Gardner were alive today, he'd surely be impressed by the progress his acolytes have made—if not the results.

But there's a paradox at work here: Even through several successive waves of "reform," distrust of government has only become *more* engrained as a cultural norm. Despite efforts to disinfect the halls of power, the disgust with government born in the Watergate era has only exploded. And the irony doesn't end there. The progressive alienation fomented by the Nixon era also created space for a new wave of conservative anti-government sentiment. In his first inaugural address, President Reagan set a clear marker stating, "In this present crisis, government is not the solution to our problem; government is the problem." And throughout his eight years in office, one of Reagan's favorite laugh lines was to tell audiences, "the nine most terrifying words in the English language are: I'm from the government and I'm here to help."

Their distrust wasn't new to American politics. After all, Mark Twain had said a century earlier that, "An honest man in politics shines more there than he would elsewhere." But the campaign to disinfect Washington has scrubbed both bad and good from our nation's capital. While transparency, access, and oversight are crucial to any working democracy, their unencumbered embrace has also encouraged a vicious cycle that has undermined governing effectiveness and legitimacy. It is time now that we ask a series of uncomfortable questions.

Has the reform movement inadvertently degraded our ability to govern?

Have efforts to reduce political abuse simultaneously increased political gridlock?

In sum, has the road to dysfunction been paved with good intentions?

CHAPTER 2

Howling at the Moon

BRICS IN THE WALL

Few will forget the opening ceremonies of the 2008 Summer Olympics in Beijing. By then, Chinese officials had spent years trying to convince the International Olympic Committee to select the People's Republic as a summer host, and Beijing was intent on showcasing its legitimacy as a global power. The results were spectacular. Held at a new, iconic stadium, the pyrotechnics, music, and synchronization dazzled a global audience of billions. The sophistication of the games sent a clear message to the global community: China, derided as a backwater for a great deal of the twentieth century, could no longer be denied the sort of respect due one of humanity's great civilizations.

By 2008, China's emergence was hardly a new story. The years that followed the end of the Cold War had seen the global hierarchy turned on its head. As Tom Friedman has argued, in the absence of a clearly definable division between two spheres of influence—one anchored by the United States and the other by the Soviet Union—"globalization" had emerged as the new world order. And when combined with the advances of the digital revolution, entire regions and expanses of humanity that had been marginalized throughout the twentieth century leapt quite force-fully into the twenty-first. For most students of history it was a moment filled with hope and optimism. The multi-polar world offered bold new possibilities for peace and prosperity. And by offering their cheap labor to the globe's wealthier markets, the developing world was given an oppor-tunity to flourish.

But when viewed through a US-centric lens, the Beijing Olympics carried a more ominous tone, echoing the raw feelings triggered by Sputnik a half-century before. Even without becoming an outright military menace, China's enormous population and economic potential challenged America's place as the world's only remaining superpower. And many in the United States interpreted this new dynamic as an implicit threat.

The fear that China might develop into an American antagonist had emerged gradually over the previous few decades. When George Lucas was crafting the villainous characters for the *Star Wars* prequel in 1999, he painted the bad guys—a cabal of alien fish—with a fairly transparent Chinese motif. And that signaled a significant cultural departure. Darth Vader's evil empire, like most bad guys of the previous generation, unmistakably alluded to the Soviet Union and Third Reich. But today, a quarter-century after the fall of the Berlin Wall, it is hard to find a major domestic policy agenda that doesn't lean on the rhetorical imperative to compete against China.

From promoting investments in education to cutting corporate taxes, from building the Keystone Pipeline to enacting new clean energy incentives, competition from China has become the impetus for nearly every proposed reform. The sense that we're falling behind has, both through popular culture and international dynamics, come to frame America's self-identity. Tom Friedman and Michael Mandelbaum noted in their recent book *That Used to Be Us* that it took a Chinese company a mere thirty-two weeks to build a brand new convention center, which was only eight weeks longer than it took DC's subway system to repair two escalators. The authors go on to argue:

> *[The] sense of resignation, that sense that, well, this is just how things are in America today, that sense that America's best days are behind it and China's best days are ahead of it, have become the subject of watercooler, dinner-party, grocery-line, and classroom conversations all across America today.*

For all the press the Sino-American tension receives, China hardly counts as the only country to have risen in the years following the Berlin

Wall's demise. A whole slew of nations frequently ignored through the course of the twentieth century have emerged more recently to become important players in the global economy. Goldman Sachs executive Jim O'Neill coined the term "BRICS"—an acronym for Brazil, Russia, India, China and (sometimes) South Africa—for the new global hierarchy. While the United States still sits at the head of the table, many believe that America's days as the *sole* global superpower are not just finite, but numbered.

Despite the evidence, not everyone accepts that the American era is nearing an end. For one, our competitors face daunting challenges of their own. China is already grappling with the damaging economic and social effects of its "one-child" policy. While recently eased a bit, this policy has left China with too small a workforce to support its hundreds of millions of retirees. India's internal politics are among the most dysfunctional in the world. Russia, under the authoritarian grip of Vladimir Putin, has taken a big step back from the heady days of Glasnost and Perestroika. Instructions not to drink or even wash with the water at the Sochi winter games reinforced the uncomfortable sense of a society in decline. Recent data also suggests that the BRICS are no longer growing at a meteoric pace and are likely to stumble well before they can pass the red, white, and blue.

America's optimists can point to a series of core strengths and historic precedents to support their more hopeful view of the future. As Robert Kagan and a series of other scholars have pointed out, the "daunting" problems we face today seem fairly tame when compared to what we've overcome in the past. Considered against the menace of global communism, mid-century fascism, and the Great Depression, competition from developing economies hardly seems like a cause for panic. Moreover, America's grudging but steady economic progress after the 2008 recession, recovering housing sector, fairly stable demographics, and the recent discovery of a massive new trove of exploitable oil and natural gas suggests that, far from inevitable decline, the United States is poised to claim a very bright future.

Granted, as Kagan has argued, it would be better if some of our domestic challenges weren't so stark. If only the federal deficit were smaller, or health care costs weren't exploding, it might be easier to remain sanguine. Without a doubt, the airports in Shanghai are spiffier than those in New York, and the trains connecting London and Paris are speedier than those shuffling between Boston and Washington, DC. But by the standards of the twentieth century, today's challenges appear pretty tame. After all, America's political system didn't survive nearly two and a half centuries of wars, scandals, economic and natural disasters, riots, and assassinations only to be defeated by some old bridges and not enough nursing home beds. If de Tocqueville's famous admonition still applies—if the United States has maintained its deep-seated ability to make "repairable mistakes"—it seems as if things should eventually work themselves out.

Masters of Our Own Decline

A second major critique of America's future prospects argues that we need only to look in the mirror. What if Americans aren't of the same mettle that they were in generations past? What if the opportunity and ingenuity that have powered our economy are on the wane? Morever, America will be unable to stave *anyone* off if we're incapable of solving normal, workaday challenges. A whole new literature has emerged trumpeting the nation's coming demise.

Recent books like Thomas Mann and Norman Ornstein's *It's Even Worse Than It Looks: How the American Constitutional System Collided With the New Politics of Extremism* typify the work emerging from a growing chorus who argue that the gridlock on Capitol Hill is evidence of a fundamental weakening of our ability to succeed domestically and compete abroad. Failing some intervention that finally gets our nation's leaders moving again, the pessimists worry that even the most mediocre challenge will allow the developing world to eat our collective lunch.

Spend an hour watching Fox, MSNBC, or CNN, and you're almost certain to hear some form of the "rot from within" diagnosis. Congress has not passed a balanced budget in more than a decade. Worse yet, 2013 was the first time in several years that Congress passed a budget at all. For much of the last decade, we have kept the government running through a series of last minute "kick the can" resolutions that agree to spend the same amount as the year before. Most troubling, Congress has made little progress in addressing our nation's long-term structural debt. Unless we begin to slow national spending and moderately raise taxes, our national debt will eventually overwhelm our economy. And that speaks to the larger breakdown of our political system. When substantive policy proposals come before the Senate, they're almost invariably filibustered. Indeed, it takes a small miracle to get even the most reasonable idea from the drafting table to the president's desk. And that perennial frustration has been driven by the fact that Washington has become defined by a perpetual game of political chicken. With rare exceptions like the fiscal agreement forged in late 2013, the leadership of both parties seems more inclined to let the country suffer than even *appear* to accommodate the opposition.

Look at the budget battle that led to the dreaded sequester. In the summer of 2011, the White House and Congress were grappling with the difficult challenge of reducing our nation's long-term debt without undermining our fragile economic recovery. Unable to agree on any combination of spending cuts, tax code revisions, and short-term stimulus measures, they punted responsibility to a "super-committee," which they empowered to craft a compromise that would be fast-tracked for broad congressional approval.* In an effort to encourage members to support whatever the super-committee prescribed, congressional leaders ensured that, if their colleagues rejected the super-committee's compromise, everyone would be punished. They'd be forced to endure a universally despised fallback—a broad "sequester" of the federal budget that would carelessly hack programs across the board.

It says something about the state of our government that Congress designed a process specifically to outwit itself and even *that* didn't work: The super-committee wasn't able to craft a compromise, and the Congress wasn't able to agree on an alternative. And so, a budget nearly universally considered to be horrendous public policy was delivered to the American people through inertia and wholly by default. Despite a late 2013 amendment restoring roughly half the resources and allowing agencies somewhat

---

* If the super-committee were to reach an agreement, the proposal would be brought to a vote on both the House and Senate floor, where no amendments would be permitted, and in the Senate, the measure would not be subject to a filibuster.

greater discretion, the sequester is estimated to have cost approximately six hundred thousand jobs.

D+

Columbia political scientist Ian Bremmer, recently ranking the risks facing the globe, placed Washington's paralysis as the fourth most threatening, just behind the risk of economic turmoil in the developing world, the potential disruption of Internet freedom in China, and the sectarian divisions rising in the Middle East. That is some seriously dysfunctional company. Indeed, our frightening lack of legislative productivity is so perilous that it's forcing us to squander whatever opportunities we have to solve many of our most pressing problems—economic inequality, budget deficits, entitlement spending, and infrastructure decay among them.

What's worse, it has become clear that the challenges we're facing are already having real and measurable effects on the way ordinary Americans live their lives. Between 2007 and 2012, US median income declined from $49,600 to $45,800 while median net worth plummeted from $125,000 in 2007 to $75,000 in 2010. It's no secret that we're transitioning from the industrial era into the information age—a shift that helps explain the dramatic decline in American manufacturing. But newer evidence suggests that we also appear to be losing on the economic frontier. The Information Technology and Innovation Foundation ranked the United States sixth in innovation and global competitiveness in 2009, but fortieth—dead last—in progress over the past decade. The number of new startups created in the United States each year has fallen from a high of between 12 and 13 percent of all new firms in the 1980s to a mere 7 or 8 percent in recent years. The evidence suggests that a country that was once the globe's premier beacon of innovation and opportunity is becoming just another face in the crowd.

But it's not just the economy. The American Society of Civil Engineers has awarded American infrastructure a grade of D+, estimating that we will need to invest over $3 trillion in our infrastructure to raise its quality from poor to acceptable. Our investments in human capital are equally disappointing. The nation's health care system, once considered the best in the world, has diminished in quality while becoming vastly more expensive. Although our health care bill exceeds the entire GDP of Russia, the World Health Organization ranks us twenty-seventh in life expectancy, sixteenth in diabetes, and first in obesity.

And despite generally heroic efforts by the nation's underpaid and overworked teachers, we are failing to fill the skills gaps that have emerged as America becomes more fully enmeshed in the knowledge economy. The cost of an undergraduate education has widely outpaced inflation, making degrees much more difficult to attain for those struggling to climb into the middle class. Moreover, the high school dropout rate among young Americans is getting worse, when factoring out the growth in GEDs, which are no substitute for a four-year high school education.

Roughly 30 percent of all Americans can't identify the current vice president, and over one in three can't assign the proper century to the American Revolution. The problems just keep piling up, and yet it seems as if the folks we send to Washington are just sitting on their hands. The great promise that, as Ronald Reagan articulated, "there's nothing wrong with America that together we can't fix," may well be slipping away. A political system that overcame the Great Depression, defeated fascism, and outlasted communism now seems unable to balance a simple budget or repair our creaky infrastructure.

And none of this has been lost on the public at large. The polling brings the story home. On the day of President Obama's second inauguration in 2013, Gallup released a poll showing that "Americans are as negative about the state of the country and its prospects going forward as they have been in more than three decades." Fewer than half of Americans believed that the nation would be headed in a positive direction in five years—marking only the second time Gallup has seen such negativity since it began asking the question in 1971. (The first time was 1979, when, a few years after Watergate, an oil shortage, spiking crime, and the Iranian hostage crisis had driven America's perception of itself to a new low.)

Declining confidence in our national leaders has been equally stark: In 1960, Democrats, Independents, and Republicans expressed general trust in Washington 79 percent, 75 percent, and 71 percent of the time, respectively. Today, by contrast, those figures have dropped to 28 percent,

17 percent, and 10 percent. And that's led many to conclude that the jig is up. We're lost, wandering around in a fog of our own creation. One of these days we'll stumble, fall down, and just roll downhill a while.

THE UNHOLY TRINITY

Why is the American political system so broken? Washington's dysfunction is generally attributed to the unholy trinity of "media, money, and (gerry) mandering." As the narrative goes, each day our ship of state sails into the Bermuda Triangle of gotcha politics, Super PACs, and distorted elections. Our leaders muddle about in a state of near constant mutiny, disoriented and afraid to collaborate with their peers. For most of us, that conventional and pervasive analysis makes intuitive sense; it's superficially compelling, thoroughly discouraging, and broadly embraced. Fortunately, it's wrong or, at the very least, highly exaggerated.

Take, first, the impact of the "new" media. The digitalization of print journalism, proliferation of cable news, and explosion of social networking has obviously transformed the news media and communication. During Walter Cronkite's era, the self-styled golden age of journalism, reporters sought to avoid political bias and differentiate between the public and private worlds of politicians. The difference between then and now is overwhelming. Consider that few Americans even knew that FDR was confined to a wheelchair, or that JFK was unfaithful to his wife. Unlike the reporting that predominates today, pieces were more frequently balanced, fewer were sensationalized, and the protagonists of any given story were often the legislators who moved the ball forward.

That said, there are elements of the new reality that should be celebrated. We are now empowered to pick and choose our sources of information from a much wider array: Liberals and conservatives can watch different cable news networks, listen to different radio programs, and click on different websites. By some stretch, that has been a boon to the average consumer who need no longer be exposed to stories he or she doesn't want to hear. But it has also had a qualitative effect on the field of reporting. Driven to be first on a story, journalists are often required to sacrifice nuance (and, more dangerously, accuracy) for speed. Compelled to develop a larger audience, reporters who generate insightful analysis may be respected, but those who can stir emotion are prized and highly compensated. As former senator Byron Dorgan once said to me:

> *Cable television and talk radio have had a much more profound impact than anybody understands. The political bleachers are crowded with Fox News and MSNBC brandishing microphones and waiting to cast shame on anyone who dares to reach across the aisle. They are the enforcers calling penalties on those few politicians willing to compromise.*

Despite all it has done for transparency, new media has focused legislators even more on satisfying the small but intense slice of constituents who follow their tweets. Internet activist Eli Pariser coined the term "filter bubble" to describe how Google's impressive algorithms have narrowed our windows into the world. Our news is now prioritized for us; it reinforces our existing worldview by anticipating and mirroring our reactions to current events.

However, many of the purportedly "new" rules of American media aren't actually so new. The vitriol on display today is, by some measure, a weak echo of an earlier age. *The Connecticut Courant*, a newspaper which favored John Adams's presidential candidacy during the campaign of 1800, wrote that in the event that Adams's opponent, Thomas Jefferson, were to win the presidency, "murder, robbery, rape, adultery and incest will all be openly taught and practiced, the air will be rent with the cries of the distressed, the soil will be soaked with blood, and the nation black with crimes." By turn, a propagandist on Jefferson's payroll spread word that Adams was a "hideous hermaphroditical character which has neither the force nor firmness of a man, nor the gentleness and sensibility of a woman." Against this backdrop of virulent personal attacks, Fox News and the Huffington Post seem like *PBS NewsHour*.

And this climate prevailed well past the post-colonial era. At the turn of the twentieth century, the heyday of yellow journalism, papers owned by turn-of-the-century media barons almost single-handedly propelled the United States into the Spanish-American War. William Randolph Hearst, owner of the widely read *New York Journal* (which competed voraciously with Joseph Pulitzer's *New York World*), knew that a war with Spanish-controlled Cuba would drum up readership. He directed the paper's editors to sensationalize the wretchedness of Cuban conditions under the imperial thumb of its Spanish rulers. When the USS *Maine* sunk in Havana Harbor, Hearst smelled blood: He ran unsubstantiated headlines blaming Spain for the incident. Soon thereafter, the United States took up arms against the Spanish in what many call the first "media-driven" war.

The oft-repeated complaint that the negative media is responsible for Washington's dysfunction is belied somewhat by our country's history. If our political system functioned fairly effectively in eras with a mostly unaccountable and blasphemous media, it seems unreasonable to place disproportionate blame on today's comparatively tame press. But even if it were, there's another, more compelling reason to look elsewhere for solutions: The Golden Age is gone for good. This new media model didn't just spontaneously appear. Americans have made it clear: They *want* news that is tailored to their ideological viewpoint. They *want* the entertainment factor of ideological opposites battling across a television screen. As Michael Kinsley, the legendary journalist and longtime participant on CNN's *Crossfire* once noted: No one would have wanted to watch a news program titled "Ceasefire." So, satisfying as it may be to wag our finger and shake our heads at today's news media, we ought not to spend too much of our energy blaming the messenger.

WHOLE FOODS OR CRACKER BARREL

Second in the unholy trinity is gerrymandering, as the process of manipulative redistricting has come to be known. The vast majority of incumbent House members win re-election and an overwhelming number of districts are "safe" for one party or the other. In its 2012 Redistricting Report, the Bipartisan Policy Center's Democracy Project found that the number of competitive House seats has steadily declined in the past several decades, decreasing from 152 in the 1970s to about 100 today. Moreover, the number of misaligned seats—seats held by one party even though the district typically leans toward the other party in presidential elections—has steadily declined over the past two decades. A study done by the BPC staff found that "the 93 seats held by Democrats in Republican districts dropped to 30 in 2002 and, today, sits at 9."

State legislators are often very street-savvy (literally down to the block level) about the tendencies of certain neighborhoods to vote Democratic or Republican. As a result, to press their respective party's advantage, they shape districts to influence the outcome of elections. BPC senior fellow and former congressman Dan Glickman (D-KS) is fond of noting that America is the only political system where instead of voters choosing their politicians, the politicians choose their voters.

Much like the new partisan media, gerrymandering contributes to the polarization of Congress. If a seat is essentially in the bag for one party, the real competition occurs in the primary where there is absolutely no incentive to appeal to the entire electorate. In primary elections ideological purity wins the game. A lawmaker's history of compromise— even if it led to significant accomplishment—is portrayed as a weakness in the attack ads of his opponent. As journalist Ron Brownstein wrote in 2011:

> *The overall level of congressional polarization last year was the highest the index has recorded, because the House was much more divided in 2010 than it was in 1999. Back then, more than half of the chamber's members compiled voting records between the most liberal Republican and the most conservative Democrat. In 2010, however, the overlap between the parties in the House was less than in any previous index.*

It is commonly held that the shift is, indeed, largely due to 'mandering. And, indeed, the punditry is rarely bashful about blaming the redistricting for what has gone wrong in Washington. Former New York City mayor Michael Bloomberg said that political polarization "all comes from gerrymandering" because the practice "pulls people away from the center." Charlie Cook of the Cook Political Report has argued that the current gridlock in Congress can largely be blamed on Republican state legislatures creating "safe, lily white strongholds"—districts that look like "an alternate universe . . . bear[ing] little resemblance to the rest of the country." *New York Times* columnist and acclaimed author Tom Friedman has argued that to create a "radical center" in American politics, Americans need to advocate for implementation of nonpartisan redistricting, because only then will districts become increasingly competitive and increasingly likely to elect candidates that do not cater to the political extremes. But, once again, we need to be careful not to ascribe too much blame to a phenomenon that, at first glance, looks to be responsible for today's dysfunction.

First of all, manipulative redistricting is, like partisan news media, hardly a new phenomenon. The phrase "gerrymander" originated when the *Boston Gazette* noted in 1812 that a particular legislative district in Massachusetts, a state then being led by Governor Elbridge Gerry, had been bent into the shape of a salamander. While modern technology has brought the art of selecting voters to new lows, several factors disprove the proposition that gerrymandering is a principal cause of today's polarization. At the top of that list is the US Senate. Congress's upper house is nearly as polarized as the House—and the Senate *can't* be gerrymandered, as each member represents a whole state. In the US Senate, centrists have left the building. Since 2010, the voting record of every Senate Democrat has been more liberal than every Senate Republican and vice versa. The days of the moderate Rockefeller Republicans and conservative southern Democrats are no more.

There is one form of strategic redistricting that is not only sanctioned, it is required by federal law. The Voting Rights Act, adopted in 1965, is designed to increase minority representation by drawing lines to create "majority-minority" districts. These districts often elect minorities and almost always elect progressives. The necessary result of these policies is to concentrate conservative voters in the surrounding districts.

But even to the extent that redistricting is a cause of polarization, studies suggest it's just not a dominant factor. Research done at the BPC has revealed that the growth in noncompetitive districts—namely those in which a presidential candidate won more than 55 percent of the vote—happened *before* Washington became so dysfunctional. Between the 1970s and the 2000s, the number of competitive House districts dropped from 152 to 103. But in the decade since, the number dropped only to 101,

suggesting that things were working fairly well—at least for a while—
after the nation's legislative districts became more monolithic.

Princeton's Nolan McCarty, UC–San Diego's Keith T. Poole, and
NYU's Howard Rosenthal conducted research that found that moderate
districts, with increasing frequency, were being represented by more partisan members. The data reveals that the prevalence of safe conservative
and liberal districts began to emerge in the 1960s—well before the elements of today's dysfunction began to define the nation's politics. As the
academics concluded, "the increase in the number of safe districts directly
associated with redistricting is not much larger than the rise associated
with the long-term trends."

In his groundbreaking book, *The Big Sort*, Bill Bishop found that
Americans are separating themselves into politically monolithic
enclaves, with Democrats moving to culturally progressive neighborhoods and Republicans settling among more conservative communities.
As David Wasserman, US House editor of the *Cook Political Report*, once
explained, customers of Whole Foods and Cracker Barrel rarely live near
one another anymore—and that is having a political impact. In 2008,
Barack Obama won 81 percent of counties with a Whole Foods and just
36 percent of counties with a Cracker Barrel—a record 45-point gap.
The trend continued in 2010, as 82 percent of congressional districts that
flipped from Democratic to Republican were home to a Cracker Barrel,
and just 20 percent had a Whole Foods. The effect has been to drive a
sort of *organic* gerrymander. There's no way, after all, to craft an honestly
marginal district amid a sea of northeastern progressives or southern
conservatives.

Regardless of its impact on election outcomes, the manipulation and
self-dealing in the current system just feels wrong. Responding to this
public frustration, seven states have created independent commissions to
fashion their district boundaries. These efforts present important opportunities to increase confidence in the election process and possibly even
enhance voter participation. However there is yet little evidence to indi-
cate an impact on the ideological character of candidates or ultimate election results. Former senator Slade Gorton (R-WA), who served as one of
four members of Washington State's 2011 Redistricting Committee, told

me "redistricting matters a little, but not nearly as much as most people think." (Gorton also notes that recent changes to the primary voting process, considered in chapter 8, hold greater potential to influence who runs for office and who gets elected.) And so the lesson is clear: While reforming the process of redistricting might make some improvements on the margin, there's little evidence to support that an end to gerrymandering will spark a bipartisan renaissance.

"THE WISDOM TO KNOW THE DIFFERENCE"

Which brings us to the third and most pervasive critique. Much as vitriolic media and partisan redistricting remain the bane of would-be reformers, nothing draws more ire than the influence of money. As those worried about the influence of cold hard cash often contend, nearly any politician's desire for power and campaign contributions can subsume his or her impulse to do what is in the country's best interest.

The evidence of money's pervasive influence is everywhere. Campaign spending at the federal level in presidential election years doubled from $1.5 billion to $3 billion between 1992 and 2000, having been a mere half-billion in 1968. According to the Center for Responsive Politics, spending then doubled again, to over $6 billion in 2012. The combined cost of the nation's biannual congressional races has also more than doubled in the past decade, with spending increasing most dramatically between 2008 and 2010. And so, just like partisan media and manipulative redistricting, reports of the pervasive influence of fundraising have become a focus for those intent on protecting the girders of American government.

And sad to say, there's also nothing particularly novel about electioneering on the private dime. In fact, it's been standard practice from well before the Constitution's ratification. Looking to defeat a candidate who had emerged on top in a previous election for a seat in Virginia's House of Burgesses, a young George Washington decided that the best way to woo prospective voters in 1758 was to "lubricate the thirsty throats of [those] who may have trudged many miles to make it to the polls"—and so he did. The same dynamic persisted through the nineteenth century when many senators became simple proxies for the business concerns that controlled the levers of politics in their particular states. In fact, many storied leaders in our nation's history were elected in circumstances where shady campaign financing played a much greater role than it does today. Then, as now, it often seemed to observers like the roots of political scandal always traced back to greed. It was the influence of money that besmirched the standing of Ulysses S. Grant's administration in the 1870s. As one historian, having uncovered the $50,000 contribution railroad financier Jay Cooke made to the Grant campaign in 1872, suggested, "never before was a candidate placed under such great obligation to men of wealth." A half-century later, it was Teapot Dome—the most pernicious political scandal in American politics before Watergate—that stained the historical reputation of the Harding Administration. A few decades later, Lyndon Johnson used his control over the political donations of Texas oilmen to manipulate the Senate during the 1950s. And in the 1968 and 1972 presidential elections the liberal philanthropist Stewart Mott gave the equivalent of more than one million dollars each to Democratic candidates Eugene McCarthy and George McGovern. Thirty years later, the purportedly shady financial dealings sullying political life in the 1990s led Congress to pass McCain-Feingold.

It's a conundrum: If some of the most productive periods in American political history have been rife with the influence of "money" in politics, how much of today's dysfunction can really be ascribed to the year-round building of campaign war chests? Many, including former and current members of Congress, believe that the answer is a lot. The public clearly agrees. A recent CNN poll revealed that two-thirds of Americans believe that elections are generally for sale, and that more than four in five believe elected officials are influenced most by the pressure they receive from campaign donors.

If there were one thing we could do to change the chemistry of our democracy, it would surely be to fundamentally change the way we finance elections. *But we can't.* We can't substantially change, alter, dilute, restrict or otherwise meaningfully drive private money out of public campaigns. It doesn't matter if we "should." (A minority argues that we shouldn't.) While the theoretical debate is actually quite fascinating, it doesn't really matter because we can't—at least not any time soon.

Why? An honest assessment of the current judicial landscape suggests that the Supreme Court will not curtail any individual or corporation's ability to make a political donation. And legislative efforts to nibble around the edges of the First Amendment haven't accomplished much. If anything, the waves of campaign finance reform we've already endured have simply pushed those with means to find other, less transparent ways to use their deep pockets to affect the outcome of elections. It was McCain-Feingold in combination with subsequent Supreme Court rulings that, by most accountings, spurred the creation first of 527s and then "Super PACs," the shadowy organizations that now influence elections *outside* the campaigns and candidates themselves. And that can hardly be held up as a measure of progress in the right direction.

Alcoholics Anonymous, an organization that helps people attain and maintain sobriety, has adopted a Reinhold Niebuhr quote into what they call the Serenity Prayer: "God grant me the serenity to accept the things I cannot change, courage to change the things I can and wisdom to know the difference." It is a tactical insight that we could use more of as we seek to strengthen American democracy. The headwinds we're so prone to blame for today's political dysfunction are as old as our Constitution, and in most cases there's very little we can do to tamp them down.

It is time to set down our obsession with influences largely beyond our control and embrace the glorious mess of American democracy.

It's not that things are just fine in Washington; as the litany of challenges described above makes clear, they're most certainly not. But it has also become apparent that the prevailing diagnoses—media, money, and 'mandering—aren't exclusively to blame either. But if the typical explanations don't suffice, where does culpability really lie? To answer that question, the first thing we need to do is establish some perspective. And to do that, let's temporarily set the world of politics aside.

Imagine, for a moment a house nestled into the Gulf Coast. Now imagine that the same house is being battered by a storm. At that moment, the question for those inside the house would not be how they might diminish the intensity of the storm. They might curse the storm, but their primary interest would be whether the building was erected to withstand the ominous winds swirling outside.

Now apply that analogy to what is happening to American democracy. Washington is the house, and "media, money and 'mandering" are the violent winds being whipped by the storm. There is, without a doubt, evidence that the winds have strengthened in recent years—that the pernicious influence of partisan journalism, campaign fundraising, and manipulative redistricting are battering our government like never before.

But, as the winds batter the house, there's very little to be gained by cursing the storm. The more productive strategy is to strengthen the structure. And that is the central insight: Rather than attempt to eliminate the crosswinds that have *always* challenged American democracy, we ought to focus in on the features of the nation's political life that have allowed Washington to stand fast against the tempests that have challenged our democracy over the last two-hundred-plus years. The question we need to be asking is: What has happened within the engineering of the American political system to compromise its ability to withstand the thrust and parry that has *always* been part of our democracy? And what can we do to strengthen it?

THE EROSION OF CULTURE

In the narrative of media, money, and 'mandering, the agents of exploitation are the so-called "special" interests. As the story goes, these scoundrels are marginalizing the "local" interests of regular people. By manipulating news stories, campaign fundraising loopholes, and jurisdictional boundaries, the privileged few have managed to separate regular Americans from their government. It is a compelling narrative, but it obscures the real problem.

Indeed the "special" interests we vilify and the "local" interests we praise aren't really as different as we often presume. Those sitting at the Constitutional Convention in Philadelphia rarely focused on the distinction between the demands of commercial activities and ordinary constituents. Rather, as *The Federalist Papers* made clear, those lobbying on behalf of constitutional ratification worried most about how those *combined* interests might be weighed against something harder to tie down: the *national* interest.

We would be wise to rediscover that lost distinction. In all of our cynicism about whether a congressman is throwing his constituents over in pursuit of a hefty campaign donation, we've lost sight of the crucial question: Are our politicians properly weighing what is good for their supporters (constituents and donors alike) with what would be best for the country as a whole? In addition, have changes to the norms of American political life made it that much more difficult for the nation's leaders to collaborate in the national interest?

Look at that question from the perspective of any given politician. Elected leaders have ample incentive to do what their constituents and supporters desire. That is how any good public servant solicits both votes and donations. But particularized demands can't be the only consideration. If there weren't some incentive to do what was *un*popular, American democracy would have fallen into dysfunction decades ago. The sense of community and common purpose among our leaders has held our nation together through many trials. It has also allowed our elected representatives to occasionally look beyond short-term local concerns to forge policy that reflects the best interest of the nation as a whole.

David Brooks argues in *The Social Animal: The Hidden Sources of Love, Character, and Achievement* that more than intellect, economics, or class, "human nature is really based on . . . social connections, seeing relationships." Those relationships, to continue the metaphor, have historically kept the nation structurally sound.

That principle is as true in Washington as it is in any suburban office park. In Congress, the well of the Senate and the cloakrooms off the House floor serve the same purpose as an office break room. While waiting to vote on an amendment, two members might strike up a conversation about a kid's accomplishment in middle school or the traffic getting to the airport. While waiting in line for a sandwich, maybe they'll talk a little trash in anticipation of the upcoming Monday Night Football matchup. It's in the routines of their daily lives that the nation's leaders nurture the familiarity that many among the Founding Generation believed so crucial to a working democracy.

The idea that interpersonal relationships form the basis of collaborative thinking reflects an established "office science" that has been embraced across the business world. While chief executive at Pixar, Steve Jobs sought to create a "headquarters building . . . that promoted 'encounters and unplanned collaborations'" among employees. Jobs believed that "if a building doesn't encourage that, you'll lose a lot of innovation and the magic that is sparked by serendipity." Other companies and business leaders have followed suit. Google's London headquarters, for example, has been "made to look like a townhouse," with furniture and communal spaces that have a "homey feel"—an answer to the famed designer Robert Propst's declaration in 1960 that: "Today's office is a wasteland. It saps vitality, blocks talent, frustrates accomplishment. It is the daily scene of unfulfilled intentions and failed effort."

Unfortunately, the element of familiarity has been sapped from the routines of political life. Many members of the same party—even those who sit on the same committees—don't even know one another's names. Newly elected congressman Jason Smith (R-MO) recounted a recent experience in the House of Representatives' barbershop. Several members were there getting haircuts. After someone left the chair, the remaining members asked if anyone knew the guy's name. Only one person did: the barber. Afterward, Representative Smith set out on a mission to meet with every member of Congress. I asked Tony Calabro, who was the Senate barber for thirty years, what he thought about Representative Smith's experience. Mr. Calabro, who retired in 2013, told me, "Things have changed. Folks used to tease each other and joke around with whoever was in my chair—member of Congress or not. Now, folks are more cold. They tend to each stick to their own chair, keep their head down, and not interact with each other."

That marks the central observation this book intends to unearth. In today's political culture, personal relationships, private handshakes, and principled compromise are discouraged. While special interests may be pervasive, our current gridlock isn't the result of some recent surge in self-interest. Rather, the culture of collaboration that once steeled American democracy to withstand narrow interests and the occasional pernicious actor has been worn away. While familiarity can, in some circumstance breed contempt, in a democracy it is the lifeblood of progress.

The good news is that our democracy is always changing. It can get worse or better, but the collective will of millions of people simply can't stand still. While no single measure will change the culture of DC, there is a virtuous cycle to tap into—one that would help to restore the collaborative spirit and augment the government's ability to solve problems. There is a hunch embedded in my optimism: In my experience, bridging disagreements and solving problems are tremendously rewarding. Merging disparate interests into a shared solution and seeing the world change because of your actions is simply exhilarating—in fact it's almost addictive. I recognize that this may sound to some like a big government agenda—but it's not. The aspiration in any realistic scenario is for Congress to work just a little bit better. The gridlock has been so complete for the last several years that the problems offer something for everyone. We need investment in infrastructure, early childhood education, and an upgrade of aging environmental statutes. But we also must reform entitlements, address the hollowing out of the military, and fix our anti-competitive tax code. If Congress could just deal with one or two real problems each year, America would once again be on stable footing. There is a way forward that embraces the future while restoring a few critical elements of the recent past.

CHAPTER 3

Mr. Smith Goes Overboard

HE'D BEEN SNOOKERED. HAVING JUST BEEN APPOINTED TO REPLACE A long-term incumbent, Senator Jefferson Smith was prepared to take just about any advice his state's senior senator, Joe Paine, had to offer. But Paine wasn't the white knight Smith assumed him to be; he was actually in the pocket of a corrupt political boss back home. And so, to serve his shadowy patron, the elder statesman hoodwinked Smith into introducing a bill designed to enrich a few backroom powerbrokers. It was a sneaky and dishonorable ploy to take advantage of a young man who was wet behind the ears. And when Smith got wind of the corrupt bargain, Paine worked to frame him, burnishing a bogus campaign to make it look like Smith had secretly been trying to enrich himself.

Heartbroken and double-crossed, the young victim took to the Senate floor equipped with the only tool available to a good man battling a corrupt system: He would filibuster—talking nonstop until he had convinced his colleagues of the truth. For the better part of twenty-four hours, while fighting exhaustion and delirium, he sustained a filibuster, pleading his case to his colleagues and to the reporters in the gallery. Newspapers around the country covered the drama in detail, giving Smith an opportunity to make his case to the general public. Eventually, in the face of his colleague's anguish, Paine was overcome with guilt. Disgusted by his own behavior, he admitted the whole conspiracy on the Senate floor. Senate procedure served as a savior; for the junior senator, the filibuster acted as a life preserver in a violent sea of money and corruption.

Frank Capra's 1939 film *Mr. Smith Goes to Washington* defines our most hopeful vision for what the filibuster might represent. Jimmy

Stewart's Jefferson Smith typified what most Americans want out of a senator: honesty and fearlessness working in defense of the average citizen. In the hands of that sort of politician, nonstop Senate diatribes seem like powerful tools to speak truth to power. Unfortunately, over the seven decades since Jimmy Stewart employed the Senate rules in the righteous pursuit of principle, the filibuster has swung the other way, becoming a symbol of petulant discord and political gridlock. The sparingly used practice of "obstructing or delaying of legislative action, especially by prolonged speechmaking" has been transformed into yet one more everyday obstacle to legislative progress. In the process, our once proud Senate is now seen by many as a place where good nominees are stymied and good policy goes to die.

Pundits and voters alike deplore the fact that the once consequential and demanding choice to halt the legislative process has become streamlined, convenient, and common. As former Senate majority leader Tom Daschle said in an event alongside his one-time Republican adversary, Trent Lott:

> We don't suffer anymore. There's nothing painful about a filibuster. We just push it aside. You don't have to hold the floor. And because we've made them so easy and so routine and so procedural, they happen now with a frequency unlike anything we've ever seen in history.

Despite these frustrations, the right of the minority to interrupt debate has been fiercely protected as a defining and even superior feature of the upper house—that is, until 2013. The recent and dramatic changes barring use of the filibuster in the Senate confirmation process is both a pragmatic response to gridlock and an unfortunate accommodation to dysfunction. One domino has fallen, leaving the Senate in a precarious position with much hanging in the balance. The institution will either further succumb to its own dysfunction, banning the filibuster entirely, or it will reclaim the capacity to work within a system designed to force collaboration. In making this decision, Congress must balance the near term desire for expediency against the one-hundred-year history of the filibuster in American politics.

Tradition Abused and Abandoned

The filibuster is nowhere to be found in the Constitution. It is simply a long-standing Senate rule. While it takes sixty votes to override a filibuster, it only takes fifty votes for the majority in the Senate to do away with the filibuster entirely. Though it is technically easier to eradicate all filibusters than to stop just one, the damage that would be done by such a sweeping change is obvious. Senator Trent Lott coined the term "nuclear option," to convey the severity of a unilateral change in the rules of the Senate.

The fact that Senate majorities have time and time again chosen to protect the rights of the opposition party to thwart their own agenda is a remarkable statement about the culture of the US Senate. While use of the filibuster in legislation is aggressively contested, the Senate confirmation process has given the battle center stage.

Over the last decade, exasperated Senate majority leaders have repeatedly threatened to restrict or eliminate the use of the filibuster to oppose presidential nominees. In May 2005, the Republican majority, then led by Senator Bill Frist, declared that it was at DEFCON 1. Incensed by Democratic opposition to a series of President Bush's judicial nominees, Leader Frist asserted that he would proceed with the nuclear option unless Democrats ended a filibuster of Priscilla Owen, who had been nominated for the Fifth Circuit Court of Appeals. At the last moment a bipartisan group of senators dubbed the Gang of Fourteen stepped in with a negotiated agreement that allowed Judge Owen and two other Bush nominees to be confirmed while maintaining the right of the minority to filibuster "under extraordinary circumstances." The crucial language in the Gang of Fourteen Agreement reads:

> *Signatories will exercise their responsibilities under the Advice and Consent Clause of the United States Constitution in good faith. Nominees should be filibustered only under extraordinary circumstances, and each signatory must use his or her own discretion and judgment in determining whether such circumstances exist.*

An uneasy peace was maintained for a few years, but as always happens in our democracy, the roles were soon reversed. In 2010, when

Republicans decided to filibuster Caitlin Halligan, President Obama's nominee to the DC Court of Appeals, Democrats were furious, and White House counsel Kathy Ruemmler opined that the move amounted to a "new era of obstructionism." Sadly, things deteriorated from there.

In the spring of 2013, a showdown over controversial nominees to the Consumer Financial Protection Bureau and National Labor Relations Board brought Congress back to the brink. A last minute deal, forged in an off-the-record, senators-only meeting, again saved the day. Senate Republicans agreed to let a couple of nominees through and Democrats agreed to give up on a few others. In describing the compromise, Senator Reid stated, "We have a new start for this body. I don't know how I could be happier."

As homespun humorist Garrison Keillor advises, "If you should feel really happy, be patient: this will pass." For Leader Reid and the rest of us, the exhilaration was indeed short lived. Four months later, in November 2013, the frustration over the filibustering of nominees boiled over and Senate Democrats unilaterally changed the rules to enable nominees to be seated with only fifty votes. John McCain, a charter member of the Gang of Fourteen and a leader of the spring 2013 compromise, told reporters quite simply, "This changes everything, this changes everything."

While the rule change for confirmation of nominees will have lasting ramifications, the change does nothing to affect the right of the minority party to filibuster legislation. In fact, the rules governing its use on substantive pieces of legislation haven't really changed in decades. There have been some modifications at the margin, but the fact that senators filibuster bills with greater abandon today has not, by any stretch, been driven by a change in Senate procedure. Rather, the explosion of gridlock on the floor reflects an evolution in the *culture* of the Senate itself, not its rules. It has been a transformation propelled by a disruption in the rhythms that once defined life in Washington, DC. Before accepting the conclusion that the best way to fix the filibuster is to throw it out, let's make sure we have a handle on what has actually driven the explosion in its use.

JEFFERSON'S MANUAL OF ETIQUETTE

While the Constitution doesn't explicitly lay out a mechanism for delaying tactics in the upper house of Congress, it wasn't lost on the Founders that a tyrannical majority might be tempted at some point to trample over the rights of more marginal interests. The complex sets of checks and balances established in 1789 were designed to prevent any one faction from riding roughshod over everyone else. The filibuster—at least in principle—is certainly in line with the Founding Generation's impulse to erect obstacles to authoritarian majority rule.

However, the Framers were skeptical of obstructionary legislative tactics. In *Federalist 22*, Alexander Hamilton argued that raising the bar for legislative approval too high might render the government dysfunctional, making the perfect the enemy of the good. Hamilton believed that "contemptible compromises of the public good" were in many cases preferable to occasions when "the measures of government must be injuriously suspended, or fatally defeated." Better to find some sort of mutual accommodation, in his view, than let some impasse within Congress drive the legislative process to a halt. The trick was to strike a balance between majority rule and minority rights. Hew too far one way or the other and things might begin to dissemble.

Hamilton's admonition that legislators not use the power of debate to stymie the will of Congress held through the first few decades of our constitutional system—but largely by tradition, not by fiat. There was no mechanism to end debate through the nineteenth century, meaning that members could talk indefinitely if they were opposed to a bill. Nevertheless, by and large, they didn't. Instead, they followed the precedent set by Thomas Jefferson's *Manual of Parliamentary Practice*, which stated, "no one is to speak impertinently, or beside the question, superfluously or tediously." However, the tradition of circumscribed debate could not last forever and a new regime emerged in the early part of the nineteenth century.

The first recorded filibusters occurred in the House of Representatives where the most contentious debates centered on the issue of slavery and civil rights. The 1854 Kansas-Nebraska Act, a bill that empowered Kansas and Nebraska to determine by popular vote whether to enter the Union as free or slave states, was one of the first debates to pierce the veil of Senate decorum. In total, there were fifty-six filibusters between 1861 and 1876—half of which tied up bills concerned with slavery and Reconstruction.

Then came the presidential election of 1876. When both Democrat Samuel Tilden and Republican Rutherford B. Hayes each laid claim to the electoral votes of South Carolina, Florida, and Louisiana, Congress agreed to create a bipartisan electoral commission to determine the election's outcome. When the commission concluded that Hayes had won, some House Democrats (mostly from the South) threatened to obstruct the vote counting by challenging Hayes's claims to have won several *other* states. A negotiation ensued, and in the end, the Democrats commissioned a ransom of sorts: In return for their promise not to challenge Hayes's victory, Congressional Republicans agreed to end Reconstruction, the punitive policy imposed by Washington in the wake of the Civil War. It taught legislators of all stripes a clear lesson: A minority capable of holding a majority hostage could win major concessions.

Members of Congress took that lesson to heart. Through the 1880s, there was a notable increase in the use of the filibuster, especially in the House, where Democrats in some cases even filibustered the legislative program of their *own* party.

Grover Cleveland's Democratic Party received the bulk of the blame for that period of congressional paralysis, and so in 1888, Benjamin Harrison and congressional Republicans swept in to take complete control of both ends of Pennsylvania Avenue. Almost immediately the newly elected speaker, Tom Reed, launched a reform campaign that came to be known as the "Reed Rules." The new regime, as Reed became famous for noting, ensured that in the House of Representatives, "the best system is to have one party govern and [have] the other party watch." By eliminating the filibuster in the House, Reed placed the House under the control of the Speaker—where it remains today.

WILLFUL MEN

It was a different story in the Senate. "The world's greatest deliberative body" hadn't been nearly as eager to abandon the tradition of unlimited debate, and the relative comity prevailed through about Reconstruction and lasted well into the 1900s. That's not to say that no one was frustrated by the molasses-like pace of senatorial deliberations. Betraying no small bit of irritation, President Woodrow Wilson complained in 1917 that a "little group of willful men, representing no opinion but their own" had made it exceedingly difficult for him to advance his agenda. Wilson's frustration was born in the fact that the use of the filibuster had tripled from an average of five during the congressional sessions preceding his election to nearly fifteen each Congress during his presidency.

For good measure, a rule was enacted (Rule 22) during Wilson's White House tenure to allow two-thirds of voting senators to end prolonged debates through a "cloture motion." But just because senators had given themselves the authority to cut off a colleague's filibuster didn't mean they'd use it. Even then, a certain sense of camaraderie connected senators of different parties and with different views—they actually worried about angering their colleagues with procedural gimmicks that would interrupt their desire to speak.

That sense of admonition began to change, however, during Franklin Roosevelt's administration. The nation was struggling with the Great Depression, and Roosevelt's proposals were frequently being rubber-stamped by members of Congress fearful that a failure to act hastily would deepen the crisis. But that didn't sway Louisiana Democrat Huey Long, an infamous populist who was determined to disrupt Roosevelt's legislative agenda. Of the forty filibusters that occurred during his short tenure in the Senate (he was assassinated in 1935), Long was responsible for half. And in breaking the taboo that had discouraged many senators from tying their colleagues up in procedural knots, Long became a folk hero to some and, by many estimates, the father of the modern filibuster.

But the Senate's full embrace of the filibuster didn't begin in earnest until 1937. Frustrated that the Supreme Court was overturning too much of the New Deal, Roosevelt proposed a bill to "pack" the court. The administration's plan would have allowed the president to appoint an additional justice to the court whenever an incumbent justice reached the age of seventy and did not retire—ostensibly to reduce the workload on the more senior justices already sitting on the bench.

Most presumed that the new justices would be more sympathetic to the New Deal, and would therefore be primed to outvote the caucus of justices who sat in opposition to Roosevelt's agenda. Concerned that passage of the legislation would hand the president too much power, a group of senators decided to filibuster. Much to Washington's surprise, after an epic battle on Capitol Hill, the filibuster held, handing Roosevelt the most significant legislative defeat of his four terms in office.

It's not entirely fair to say that the court-packing filibuster opened the floodgates. For the better part of the 1930s and 1940s, senators chose most frequently to use other means to oppose bills they didn't like, fearful that *losing* a filibuster would mark a significant public humiliation. But over time the "talking" filibuster became a quintessential Washington spectacle. The first major filibuster fight of the postwar era emerged when Republicans sought to eliminate the "poll tax," a primarily southern institution that was used to disenfranchise African Americans. (At the time, southern states were represented in Congress almost exclusively by segregationist Democrats.) Infuriated that anyone might seek to federalize what they saw as a state prerogative, southern Democrats mounted a filibuster of the "motion to proceed," the procedural vote that must succeed before the bill itself can be considered. At the time, there was no way to shut down a filibuster on a motion to proceed—if a single senator was willing to talk indefinitely, he could prevent the bill from ever being considered.

Fearing gridlock, in 1949 a broad array of Democrats and Republicans embraced a compromise that maintained the prerogative to filibuster while empowering the Senate to end any filibuster with sixty-seven votes. In 1959, the Senate addressed the problem of members skipping cloture votes and lowered the threshold for cloture to two-thirds of senators casting ballots. Though filibusters remained uncommon, the general sentiment was that if a colleague cared enough to hold the floor he should be allowed to do so. In 1953, after setting a new record speaking for twenty-two hours and twenty-six minutes in opposition to offshore oil development, Senator Wayne Morse (I-OR) stated, "There is nothing improper about [the filibuster], so long as it is done with good taste, with dignity, and with sincerity." In this spirit, even on issues as profound as the 1964 Civil Rights Act, many senators who supported the underlying legislation would not vote to override filibusters.

HARDENED BY BATTLE

The legislative tenor changed dramatically in the 1960s. If the 1950s were defined by a buttoned-down ethos, the hallmark of the 1960s was agitation. And that shift had a definite effect on Senate decorum. Mike Mansfield, who took up the reins of Senate leadership when Lyndon Johnson assumed the vice presidency in 1961, was not nearly so bashful about invoking cloture to cut off a colleague's attempt to delay consideration of a bill. in 1962, after a period of thirty-five years when not a single cloture motion was successfully invoked (meaning that filibusters had always prevailed or been withdrawn), a supermajority broke through the filibuster holding up a bill to establish the public-private partnership designed to operate communications satellites. The seal was broken.

The most serious, and infamous, test of Senate rules came in 1964, when the Democratic majority called a new Civil Rights Act up for debate on the floor. Southern Democrats were vociferously opposed, and most were prepared to utilize any legislative maneuver required to kill the bill, decorum be damned. The fifty-seven-day filibuster that ensued remains the longest in Senate history. Initially, supporters of the bill hoped the filibuster would eventually fizzle out—that the southerners, having made their point, would let the Senate work its will. But when the filibuster continued, sixty-seven senators, spanning both parties, voted for cloture, bringing the debate to an end, and moving the bill up for a final vote, where it prevailed. It was the first time in over forty years that the Senate had broken the filibuster of southern Democrats on civil rights legislation. And while their victory reflected a profound (and overdue) triumph for social justice, it also marked a critical juncture in the life of the Senate. From then on, the upper house of Congress would be more battle hardened, and less likely to heed the demands of any vocal minority.

Over the eleven years that followed, sixty-eight Senate bills were filibustered, and the Senate invoked cloture on twenty-eight occasions. In this more contentious legislative climate, frustration with the filibuster intensified. Mansfield, the longtime Senate majority leader, grew to resent the filibuster as nothing more than "parliamentary buffoonery or quackery." In 1975, the Senate responded to this exasperation by reducing the threshold for achieving cloture from two-thirds to three-fifths. Since then there has been a skirmish over filibustering bills a second time, and additional restrictions have been placed on the length of time filibusters can last. (The limit was set at one hundred hours in 1979 and reduced to thirty hours in 1986.) However, the basic rules governing the filibuster have remained largely the same since 1975. The same can not be said for its use. In the forty-four years between Woodrow Wilson and Dwight Eisenhower's terms in office, the Senate considered only twenty-three cloture votes to end filibusters. From 2007 to the middle of 2014, the majority was forced to seek cloture 414 times. Even more stark: In the six years that marked the end of George W. Bush's presidency and the first term of Barack Obama's, there were twelve times as many filibusters as there had been in the four decades between Wilson and Eisenhower. And that raises a more confounding question: If the Senate's decline into dysfunction wasn't the direct result of a change in the *rules*, why did more recent years see such an enormous increase in delaying tactics and obstruction?

FILLING THE TREE

In December 1980, the Democratic majority leader and master tactician Robert C. Byrd employed an unprecedented legislative procedure: He "filled the tree." Some background: On the Senate floor, only a certain number of amendments can be considered simultaneously, and those amendments can only be further amended so many times. If a majority leader decides at the outset to offer meaningless or perfunctory amendments that fill all those slots, the bill can't be amended by other senators at all. Once the "amendment tree" is filled, the underlying bill is impervious to any changes during the course of floor debate.

Republicans, aghast at what they deemed as outright subversion, retaliated on subsequent bills by filibustering the motion to proceed. And so the seeds were planted for a tactical arms race bent on mutual obstruction. If the Democrats weren't going to let the Republicans offer amendments on the floor, Republicans weren't going to let Democrats bring the bills up for debate. For decades, the battle between majority leaders and minority parties smoldered at a low-level burn. Byrd and his successor as Senate majority leader, BPC co-founder George Mitchell, each filled the tree three times between 1987 and 1989, and between 1989 and 1995.

Trent Lott did it eleven times between 1997 and 2001. Daschle did it once between 2001 and 2003. Senator Bill Frist filled it fifteen times between 2003 and 2007. But then, as with the filibuster, things went haywire. Majority leader Harry Reid filled the tree a full *seventy* times between 2007 and 2013, an exponential increase.

With the regular process of considering bills alternating between tree-filling and filibustering, the Senate was subsequently forced to rely more heavily on the one legislative procedure that trumps all others: unanimous consent. Rather than consider bills by the regular process of calling legislation to the floor, allowing members to suggest amendments, and then voting on final passage, majority leaders of both parties became compelled to negotiate legislative roadmaps specific to each individual bill. Under a unanimous consent agreement, *every* senator "consents" to a roadmap that specifies which amendments can be considered and which can't. And that has led to a further perversion: If ninety-nine senators agree on a way forward but a single one does not, the bill dies. And so, in lieu of a system that allows forty-one senators to stifle a bill, the world's greatest deliberative body came to rely more heavily on a system that allows a single senator the same power.

Still, during the quarter-century that followed Robert Byrd's fateful decision to fill that amendment tree, the Senate managed, for a long time, to find a way to make it work. Former Senate leader Trent Lott reminisced, "I filled the tree one time and Tom [Daschle] got mad as a wet hen. But we had a relationship and got back to work the next day." And so we need to look beyond Senate rules to find out what has happened, because neither the problem, nor its solution, will be found in the annals of congressional procedure.

IT'S PERSONAL

For centuries, the Senate ran on one thing above all else: personal relationships. The men and women who represented their states appreciated that their individual success was contingent upon collective action. Moreover, their lives were entangled through both official duty and personal interaction. While the code of conduct was unwritten, it was vigilantly maintained. Members understood the power each wielded to obstruct the process, and there was an abiding wariness of legislative gamesmanship. Shutting down a bill based on a tangential concern was almost unheard of, and any member who failed to show proper deference to a colleague would risk alienation from peers and leadership.

That spirit of decorum was evident when a newly elected Republican from New Mexico, Pete Domenici, decided to pick a fight with one of the Senate's most influential and powerful Democrats, Finance Committee chairman Russell Long of Louisiana. Domenici had it in mind to begin imposing usage fees on river barge operators. The locks and dams that made it possible to transport grain and other goods from the heart of the Midwest into the Gulf of Mexico on the Mississippi River were expensive to operate and maintain; but to that point, the cost had been borne exclusively by the taxpayers, rather than those making a living on the water.

That free ride wasn't by accident. Russell Long, protecting the Louisiana businesses dependent on commerce coming down the Mississippi, had protected barge operators from usage fees as chairman of the Finance Committee. And so, to get a new fee past Long, Domenici devised a legislative workaround: Figuring that the barge industry wouldn't stand in the way of a bill accomplishing one of their highest priorities, he determined his best shot was to introduce his proposal as an amendment to a bill designed to improve one of the most important junctures along the mighty Mississippi, Lock and Dam 26.

Domenici knew the legislative fight wouldn't be easy. To get past Long, he would need to show his mettle, being open, forthright, and honest about why he wanted to impose the new fee. He also knew that, to be an effective senator, he would have to develop a real rapport with his colleagues—even those, like Long, who took a different position on most issues. As he said later, reflecting on the fight over the user fees, "the most important influence on an undecided senator [was] usually the personal appeal of another senator." And so, after months of negotiation and debate, the House and Senate had each passed bills endorsing Domenici's user charge concept.

That is when the prevailing ethos of the Senate became apparent. Russell Long was opposed to Domenici's proposal—but he respected the way the junior senator had gone about championing his cause. The Finance Committee chairman had seen how Domenici utilized "adroit parliamentary maneuvering [and] intense person-to-person lobbying." And so, when facing the last legislative hurdle—the Senate's passage of the compromise bill senators had worked out with the House—Long gave Domenici his word that he'd protect the New Mexican's language despite his personal opposition. The longtime chairman told the freshman to go home to New Mexico and campaign for what was shaping up to be a tough re-election battle. Long would take care of Domenici's amendment while he was gone.

To Long's dismay, within hours of Domenici's return to New Mexico, Illinois's Adlai Stevenson III, another opponent of the user charge, introduced a measure to strip Domenici's language out of the bill. When word got back to Domenici, he rushed back to Washington, hoping to salvage the months of work he'd put into the legislative campaign. But when he arrived back on the floor, Long approached the junior senator and said: "'You been up all night? Just come in from New Mexico? Gee, I hope you didn't fly back here just because of this waterway business. There's no problem—I'm going to take care of that for you.'"

Long hadn't necessarily wanted Domenici to succeed; his constituents back home would likely have preferred that the bill go down. But the Finance Committee chairman was also aware that his word to a colleague was more important than short-term political victory. He used his institutional clout to thwart Stevenson's efforts and preserve Domenici's language. As Long would later explain: "The Senate [can] only operate . . . if senators [can] rely on each other's word.'"

NOBODY'S HAPPY

Senator Domenici's dealings with Russell Long seem so remote from the current climate in Washington that one might imagine they date from the 1800s, not the 1980s. Senator Pete, as he's known around the office, is the most senior of BPC's senior fellows, but he just retired from the Senate five years ago. It hasn't been that long since personal friendships and mutual respect enabled the Senate to solve problems large and small.

The breakdown in the Senate's culture and capacity was on stark display on November 21, 2013, when Senate Democrats invoked the "nuclear option," lowering the bar for confirming most presidential appointees from sixty votes to fifty votes.

Like in most big legislative battles, there were compelling arguments on both sides of the debate. First, consider the argument that Senate Democrats, led by Harry Reid, made at the time. As progressives pointed out, roughly half of all the filibusters of presidential nominees in our nation's entire history had occurred during the Obama Administration (eighty-two under Obama vs. eighty-six under the prior forty-three administrations). In response, the Republican leadership had argued that they had worked with Democrats to confirm 1,707 of Obama's nominees, while only rejecting four. Regardless of whose statistics were more compelling, the decision to invoke the "nuclear option" poses stark choices for the democracy.

One option is to essentially give up, accept that things are forever changed, and alter the rules to best accommodate the dysfunction. This is the preferred approach of those arguing to get rid of the filibuster entirely. Indeed, since the day majority leader Harry Reid invoked the rule change, a whole bevy of nominees have been ushered through to confirmation. It is therefore not surprising that many are calling to eliminate the filibuster altogether, allowing the majority in the Senate to pass any legislation at will. This would be a grave mistake. In the absence of any obligation to engage the other side, a unique bond of American democracy would unravel. According to former senator and BPC senior fellow Olympia Snowe (R-ME), "The key is not allowing the Senate to become a majority institution. If we go down that path we will lose the ability to build consensus and might never get it back."

In the alternative, the Senate could draw a firm line at nominees, clearly sustaining the right of the ability of any group of forty-one or more senators to hold up legislation until their concerns are satisfied. If possible, working within the current structure and rules would be clearly best for the long-term interests of the nation. The way to achieve this is a negotiated détente. The majority leader would promise not to "fill the amendment tree," allowing members of the minority an opportunity to debate and influence legislation. In return, the minority would commit to allow legislation to get to the floor and not use the filibuster to challenge the motion to proceed. The key would be to ensure that a majority of amendments offered were substantive and offered in good faith. If either side returned to the pattern of using amendments merely to score political points, the agreement would quickly unravel. The Senate rules confer little ability to compel constructive behavior. In the end, it all turns on trust, peer pressure, and faith in party leaders.

If Congress cannot achieve this basic agreement to have actual debate, it seems likely the further changes to the filibuster will be adopted. Fortunately there are options short of eradicating the filibuster altogether that would sustain the obligation of the two parties to interact. One reform, first introduced by Senator Jeff Merkley (D-OR) in 2011 and again in 2013, would compel senators intending to filibuster to hold the Senate floor with a "talking filibuster," eliminating their ability to bottle up the agenda from the comfort of their offices. Merkley's proposal has failed twice, but now that we are in a post-nuclear environment, it could be revisited as one means to resolve this debate. A second, more aggressive option would be to eliminate filibusters on the motion to proceed. Under this approach, no one can filibuster on the issue of whether or not to even bring a bill up for debate, though opponents could still use the filibuster to require sixty votes for final passage. Since he has been majority leader, Senator Reid has expressed support for this idea to the predictable ire of the minority leader. No matter how structured, further rule changes are certain to further inflame the minority.

Even worse, none of these variations address the underlying issue: the decline in senatorial comity and personal connections. We don't simply need members to stop filibustering; we need them to begin collaborating. Taking away an enemy's weapons rarely leads to lasting peace. While recapturing the culture of the Senate won't be easy, there is a reason for some optimism. Senators today may be even more frustrated than the general public. If reading about dysfunction is exasperating, imagine living it sixteen hours a day. After the scrutiny of campaigns, endless fundraising, long days, and arduous travel, US senators find themselves to be accidental tourists on a cruise to nowhere. They are bored and angry and something has to give. As BPC senior fellow and former Senate majority leader Trent Lott said in early 2014: "The level of frustration among members is as high as I've ever seen—nobody's happy."

If the bonds that once compelled senators *not* to filibuster have only withered recently, it is worth trying to rebuild the connections and processes that fostered deliberation. In the spring of 2014, two US senators, Lamar Alexander (R-TN) and Chuck Schumer (D-NY), set out on an experiment to resuscitate the Senate. Together, they convinced Senate leadership to identify several comparably noncontroversial pieces of legislation and test if the Senate is capable of conducting an open debate. In March 2014, Senator Reid handed control of the floor to senators Barbara Mikulski (D-MD) and Richard Burr (R-NC) to lead a debate on legislation to improve the quality of federally subsidized child care. The unusual process agreement allowed the bill's bipartisan sponsors to consider dozens of amendments by members of both parties. After a robust debate, the legislation passed by a vote of 96–2. Commenting on the process, Senator Schumer stated:

> *This is a small but significant step on the road to repairing a broken Senate. The fact that both sides worked together on an important bill and were able to fend off difficult amendments in order to pass it should pave the way for future bills to pass, and soothe some of the damaged feelings in the Senate.*

Veteran legislator Barbara Mikulski (D-MD) noted the importance of the exercise for the forty-five senators serving their first term. "Many members who've come here since 2006 and 2008 have no idea when we say what regular order is," she said. "To them, regular order was chaos, confrontation and cloture votes." For the nearly half the Senate that has only experienced the frustration of gridlock, the chance to join in a real debate, resolve differences, and forge policy just might prove exhilarating. We can only hope so. No matter how satisfying it might feel to eliminate the filibuster, we cannot fix gridlock by decree. As Senators Schumer and Alexander understand, the challenge is not to fix the Senate rules. The challenge is to fix the Senate.

CHAPTER 4

Cracking the Monocle

As the presidential campaign of 1996 wound down, Washington was as divided as many had ever seen it. President Clinton was on the verge of re-election, yet the Republicans who had taken over Congress in 1994 remained committed to their conservative agenda. Less than a year before, a lengthy government shutdown had ratcheted up cross-partisan tensions. And "the politics of personal destruction," as some called it, had emerged as a central feature of Washington life, sweeping those nominated to fill powerful positions into a storm of often malicious attacks.

The vitriol that seemed fairly new in the 1990s is now seen as an entrenched feature in our national politics. Once again the two sides seem inextricably at odds. Once again, their disagreements prompted a shutdown of the government roughly a year before an election. But there's a fundamental difference between today's perpetual conflict and the protracted disagreements of the 1990s. Behind the scenes, and even while publicly excoriating one another, Democrats and Republicans in the 1990s were collaborating on important policy solutions *despite* the rancor. Noting the distinction, a reporter for Bloomberg News recently wrote:

> Back then the dispute was over Medicare spending and took place in the context of broader bipartisan talks about how to balance the budget. Even as Clinton chided Congress daily, he was deeply engaged in negotiations with then-House Speaker Newt Gingrich and Senate Majority Leader Bob Dole, both Republicans. Today, Republicans are pushing to defund or delay the health-care law that is Obama's signature legislative achievement and holding up a standard extension

of government funding. And there are no substantive talks—not even
back-channel negotiations—going on between the White House and
Republicans.

The fact that we look back longingly to the happier, more productive years of the Clinton-Gingrich battles, Whitewater investigation, and
Lewinsky scandal says a lot about our current situation. But it wasn't long
ago when conflict and collaboration coexisted as the yin and yang of our
democracy. Understanding how our government functioned through the
rough and tumble Clinton years is key to getting the system working once
again.

THE END OF TIME

In 1996 Bob Bennett, a junior member of the Senate known for quietly
working the levers of power, began to grow concerned that the United
States wasn't adequately prepared for the massive computer glitch poised
to strike at midnight on January 1, 2000 (Y2K). The fact that most software programs had been designed to accommodate only the last two digits
of any given year meant that many information systems would presume
the new date to be January 1, 1900. And the effects had the potential to
be catastrophic: electrical grids might quit; banking systems might fail;
defense installations might go offline. To Bennett's distress, few bureaucracies—both inside the government and in the private sector—seemed
poised to face down the challenge.

Unfortunately, at least for those worried about the potential crisis,
Y2K wasn't a terribly sexy political issue. The apocalyptic consequences of
a global computer meltdown might have been compelling to the techie
crowd, but despite riffs on late night TV, ordinary voters weren't paying
too much attention. The controversy didn't speak to a core social issue, like
abortion or gay marriage. And it didn't have the sort of moral undertone
that drove debates over issues like campaign finance or ethics reform.

At the same time, Bennett knew that a failure to act would almost
guarantee a crisis. Surveying the government's preparedness agency by
agency, he uncovered vast disparities: the SEC, for example, had extensive
contingency plans for a data meltdown; but other agencies had barely

registered the risk. And so he approached the Senate Republican leadership, and suggested that he lead an effort to spur more decisive action. Because the problem threatened to run through the whole gamut of American life, affecting elements under the jurisdiction of nearly every Senate committee, Bennett argued it would be better to have a discrete set of senators look at the problem as a whole. Republican majority leader Trent Lott agreed to give Bennett the authority to set up a special committee with Senator Chris Dodd (D-CT), whom the Democratic leader, Tom Daschle, designated as co-chair.

For those of us trying to understand political collaboration, here's where it gets interesting. Bennett, a conservative from fire-engine red Utah, and Dodd, a liberal from deep blue Connecticut, were on the opposite sides of most contentious issues of the day. Moreover, in town hall meetings and television interviews, they were less apt to be asked about the impending software Armageddon as they were likely to be pressed on the salacious details about President Clinton and Monica Lewinsky. But those headwinds didn't steer them off course.

During the years when so much of the public's focus was on a scandal that would eventually lead to the president's impeachment, Bennett, Dodd, and several colleagues held thirty-five hearings and issued a series of reports spurring preventive action on Y2K. The day before the House of Representatives impeached President Clinton, Bennett and Dodd's Y2K committee held a hearing to examine the crisis's impact on the country's water supply. And one week after the Senate acquitted Clinton, the committee headed to Oregon for a field hearing to examine whether Oregon was prepared for the "millennium bug." Moreover, while working collaboratively with the Clinton Administration, they eventually issued a string of recommendations that encouraged all institutions to prepare themselves and develop contingency plans in the event of a broader meltdown.

Americans spent an estimated $100 billion to head off the Y2K problem, spurred in large part by the prodding of the federal government. Democrats and Republicans managed to get the federal bureaucracy working on a solution to the problem while jolting private industry to act as well. Most important, there were no fireworks at the hearings—there were no threats to filibuster a bill on the floor, to embarrass an incompetent bureaucrat, to manufacture a politically potent side issue that would encourage additional political contributions. According to the 9/11 Report, the Y2K prevention efforts represented "the one period in which the government as a whole seemed to be acting in concert."

Bennett and Dodd never got a lot of media coverage for their efforts—at least by the standards of Whitewater or Travelgate. But they did get *results*, despite the slings and arrows that defined the political atmosphere of the day. This was the Senate operating in a way that was so substantive and technocratic that the effort didn't warrant the attention of political operatives.

Today, many of us remember Y2K as the over-hyped problem that never was. We laugh about how silly it seemed. (Why hadn't the computer programmers thought about the implications when they'd originally designed their software?) Even on December 31, 1999, we waited with bemused anxiety, hoping that nothing too serious would go awry when the clock hit midnight. But the fact that nothing happened—that no weapons systems malfunctioned, that no region of the country faced an extended blackout, that no financial institution melted down or lost its customers' private account data—is testament to a quiet competence in the nation's capital.

The Y2K Committee's successful collaboration amid intense external partisanship seems like something from another world. However, this is not some paean to ancient history. It was barely fifteen years ago. Sure, we weren't peering ceaselessly at handheld devices, we hadn't suffered the terrible shock of 9/11, nor had we crowned our first American Idol, but neither technical nor cultural shifts can explain the stark decline in legislative function. And it has to make us wonder why, in one highly polarized era, Washington was able to function, while it has not more recently?

The answer is firmly ensconced in a shift that has been entirely overshadowed by our preoccupation with "media, money, 'mandering" and the filibuster. The rhythms that once defined the lives of the nation's powerbrokers have changed over the last decade. And the effects of this change are at the root of the country's widespread frustration.

GUESS WHO'S COMING TO DINNER

Senator John McCain, reflecting on the bipartisan relationships that developed in 1950s Washington, recently painted a picture of what it was like:

> *In the evenings, literally every evening, [Lyndon Johnson, Hubert Humphrey, Everett Dirksen and other prominent Republicans and Democrats] would convene in a room in the Russell Senate Office Building . . . and they would have drinks. And sometimes they would drink to . . . excess. But they would use that time not just to socialize but to really get work done.*

The White House also assumed and promoted a culture of familiarity with leaders of both parties. Every Tuesday morning during his two terms, President Eisenhower would invite several members of both houses of the congressional leadership to the White House to discuss the week's agenda. For much of the nation's history, those relationships protected the realm of legislating from the pernicious demands of campaign politics. Indeed, until not so long ago, it was a tradition that members of the congressional leadership would refrain from campaigning against one another. Democratic Speaker of the House Sam Rayburn had such a close relationship with Republican minority leader Joe Martin of Massachusetts that once, when asked if he would campaign against his counterpart across the aisle, Rayburn replied: "Hell, if I lived up there, I'd vote for him."

Moreover, regional interests often trumped partisan demands. When discussing one of his father's re-election campaigns, former senator Evan Bayh recalled that Republican leader Everett Dirksen of Illinois "approached [Indiana Democrat Birch Bayh] on the Senate floor, put his arm around my dad's shoulder, and asked what he could do to help." Dirksen's offer would have no doubt irked his Republican colleagues who who were hard at work to recapture the majority. But it's still a far cry from the situation today, where a leader would be thought to have committed political malpractice were he or she to do anything so collegial.

And it wasn't just that there were more moderates in Congress. Even the most committed conservatives and progressives were more inclined to cooperate across the aisle. As Rich Arenberg discovered: "Even those among the staunchest conservatives would work with Democrats to address the nation's problems. Senator Barry Goldwater (R-AZ), for example, once told Senator Carl Hayden's (D-AZ) biographer, 'I have more bipartisan political genes than you think . . . I don't want Republicans to know this . . . I always raised money for Carl Hayden's reelection to the Senate because it was so damned important.'" Goldwater was referred to as "Mr. Conservative" throughout his Senate career. Even the bitter conflict over the Vietnam War did not upend the collegiality within the Congress. When he first moved to Washington in 1968, future Senate majority leader Trent Lott found that members of both parties tended to spend Thursday evenings together playing cards, drinking bourbon, and smoking cigars. As late as the 1980s, as many as sixty senators would eat lunch in the "members only" dining room in the Capitol building. And until Bob Dole ended the practice, the majority leader's office in the Capitol—just steps from the Senate Chamber itself—was kept stocked with a full bar. The result was that, even while senators would stand on the floor to excoriate one another's ideas, many tended to step out and enjoy each other's company late into the night.

Senator Dole recently reflected on the complexity and depth of these relationships at an event honoring his longtime colleague George McGovern. "I used to argue [with McGovern] about Vietnam all day," Dole said, "and then in the evening we would talk about food for poor people. . . ." While their conflicts were intense, these heart-felt disagreements did not calcify relationships or preclude collaboration in other areas,

It's not just that members of Congress became acquainted with one another *inside* the Capitol. From the beginning of the republic—through most of the twentieth century, in fact—Washington was beset by social traditions and institutions. To read a biography of John Hay, the accomplished American diplomat who rose from being one of President Lincoln's private secretaries to become Theodore Roosevelt's secretary of state, there was a "season" of social events that national leaders were expected to attend. And the traditions of the day made it inevitable that those from different corners of Washington society would get to know one another.

But the tradition of sociability wasn't limited to the "season." For generations, there were dining rooms, bars, and restaurants where those charged with leading the nation got to know one another. The Monocle, a restaurant opened during the Eisenhower Administration just a block from Senate office buildings, was a regular gathering place for politicians from both sides of the aisle. The menu offered hearty but dignified dishes and some of the nation's eminent political figures—including John F. Kennedy and Richard Nixon—became regulars. Walter Mondale, after retiring from public life, once described the restaurant as a place "where laws are debated, where policies are set, where the course of world history is changed."

It wasn't just the routines of everyday life that compelled members of Congress to forge connections across the aisle. It was the way they structured their family lives. For generations, members were encouraged by leadership to move their families to Washington once they were elected, hoping that they'd get to know one another, and develop a real rapport. Robert Caro's multivolume biography of Lyndon Johnson details just how he exploited his wife's hospitality—demanding, at times, that Lady Bird prepare a meal for a group of congressmen at a moment's notice—in an effort to ingratiate himself with his colleagues.

THE ART OF THE DEAL

Our experience at the Bipartisan Policy Center bears out the importance of personal interaction outside of the negotiating room. Our mission is to bring people with various and often conflicting interests together to forge collaborative solutions. In almost every project, from housing to energy to health care, the "deal" that begins to emerge among the various interests hits a wall before it can be fully consummated. A subgroup inevitably decides late in the game to draw a new line and the rest of the group becomes incensed. It's a "late hit," bordering on "bad faith," many complain. But in every single case, a compromise has eventually been found.

The equation for resolution almost never rests on some novel policy twist or newly uncovered fact, but rather on the bonds that have formed among those who are negotiating to find a resolution. Whether it is a condominium board, a university, or a national legislature, human relationships form the core of our institutions. Inevitably, the obstacle is cleared by a few people from opposing camps who really like each other. They have discovered common interests at group dinners, worked together on prior aspects of the evolving agreement, and seem to take some delight in having befriended someone of alien views in this highly partisan city.

The path forward often represents something entirely different from what *both* sides of the dispute had initially proposed—a third alternative, of sorts. When two people of starkly different views articulate a shared vision, it is captivating. In most every case, the broader deadlock is broken. The bond formed between one-time combatants allays the spirit of antagonism, recommitting the group to the notion that there is a solution out there and they're going to find it.

The repetition of this experience is not a mere coincidence. In every tough negotiation, each side is committed to getting the best possible deal and worried about giving away too much. Finding your opposite's "bottom line" is fundamental, and unearthing it is rarely a gentle process. In general, a bottom line is never truly drawn until it has been crossed. And when it is, the success or failure of the negotiation depends on the personal relationships involved.

On Capitol Hill, like at the BPC, policy breakthroughs often begin at the edges. Moderates are always crucial to sealing an agreement and getting it over the line—but because they are seen as "too quick to cut a deal," they have to endure the mistrust of more aggressive partisans. In the BPC energy project, for example, agreements forged by coal interests and environmentalists generally carry more weight than proposals by the natural gas industry, which is seen as a "moderate" fuel (it still comes out of the ground, but burns cleaner than other fuels). The same holds true in our Housing Commission where critical movement on reforming Fannie Mae and Freddie Mac was spurred by an agreement between homebuilders and poverty advocates.

Over the course of the last several years, the routines that bonded politicians have begun to wither. The change hasn't been sudden, and it hasn't been the result of any single breakdown. But, taken as a whole, the shift has been profound. Like an invasive species, seeds of alienation have overwhelmed the delicate balance between short- and long-term interests that the Founding Generation sought to nurture.

The presumption today is that Washington insiders love their perches. We assume that it is a great plum to arrive in the nation's capital, in the shadow of Jefferson and Lincoln, and to work among the grand marble buildings that are a testament to power and prestige. Watch an old classic movie about Washington—*Advise and Consent*, for example—and you get the sense that members are reveling in the "scene." And for many generations they did.

Today, by contrast, members of Congress are generally loath to be wrapped up in the pomp and circumstance of official life. It is telling that the one thing Democrats, Republicans, incumbents, and challengers all have in common is a stump speech that disparages the institution they are desperately seeking to be part of. Indeed, if a member of Congress admitted to liking the nation's capital, it wouldn't take half a day for his or her opponents to be airing a negative ad replaying the footage.

The near-universal disdain for DC is partly due to a generational change. Members of the cohort who endured the Great Depression and fought in the Second World War tended to revere the national government; by contrast, the wounds of Vietnam and Watergate made the Baby Boomers far more suspicious of the corridors of power. Incumbency and experience—traits once viewed as a great advantage in the course of a campaign—have come to be seen as something more of a liability. A 1955 Gallup poll found that only 38 percent of Americans favored term limits, By 2011, according to a 2011 Rasmussen Reports poll, that figure had grown to 71 percent. The popularity of the sentiment, "Throw the bums out," is a testament to our changing view of public service.

The nation's increasing distaste for Washington was used as a political weapon in 1994 by a little-known Republican congressman from Pennsylvania, Rick Santorum. Initially, few expected Santorum to beat the incumbent, Senator Harris Wofford, who claimed the pedigree of having served as an aide to President Kennedy. But an attack ad Santorum produced that featured Wofford's spacious home in the Washington suburbs turned the tide. The implication was that the Democrat was so firmly ensconced in the Washington scene that he had lost touch with the people he represented. And that sent a clear message to the rest of Congress's incumbents: beware of moving your family to Washington.

Newt Gingrich, who assumed the House Speakership on the wings of that same election, took the lesson to heart. While previous Speakers, namely Democratic legend Tip O'Neill, had encouraged new members of Congress to make their lives in the nation's capital, Gingrich proffered exactly the opposite advice: spend as little time in Washington as possible and as much as you can with your constituents back home.

SLEEPING ON THE COUCH

The explosive growth of air travel over the last several decades—and the commensurate drop in fares—made that new impulse more attainable. In conjunction with the Congress's desire to get out of DC were new opportunities to do exactly that. During the 1960s, members were only allowed three paid trips home each year, a limit later raised to forty and eventually lifted altogether. Given the prevalence of more affordable plane tickets, it became that much more feasible to make quick getaways home for the weekend or, in some cases, just for the evening. Not surprisingly, the structure and cadence of congressional life have been transformed to accommodate a commuter-Congress.

The congressional schedule has always bent to suit the desires of those in power. As former senator Olympia Snowe recently explained, when senators were allowed to collect honoraria for speeches (a perk since rescinded by ethics guidelines), the congressional schedule was adjusted so that they had ample time to fan out across the country to earn some extra money. But in the mid-1990s, the schedule was changed even more drastically. In a desire to allow members to spend more time in their districts, the first votes of each week weren't held until the evening (allowing members to travel on Monday afternoon for Monday evening votes, for example).

Suddenly, members could keep their lives centered at home without missing votes in Washington. With families at home in their districts, members chose more menial existences during the short weeks they were in the Capitol. Following the 2010 election, *Newsweek* recently reached 46 of the 107 freshman members of Congress, and only one—newly elected Senator Mike Lee (R-UT)—said he was planning to move to Washington with spouse and children in tow.

Until recently, members who did not want to move their families to DC generally rented or shared an apartment—often with other members. Congressman George Miller (D-CA) rents rooms to senators Chuck Schumer (D-NY) and Dick Durbin (D-IL) in a small house within walking distance of the Capitol. Leon Panetta (D-CA) lived there in the 1990s and Representative Bill Delahunt (D-MA) slept in the living room for a while. The arrangement inspired Garry Trudeau to create the TV show "Alpha House," which premiered in 2013.

The "frat house" aura of the Schumer/Durbin/Miller residence sometimes reveals more than some may want to know about their national leaders. For example, Congressman Miller (aka the Landlord) likes to keep a public tally of how many days since Chuck Schumer last made his bed—over seven thousand and counting. However, too much proximity is far better than the new trend of members choosing to "sleep over" in their offices. Rather than spend the money required to rent an apartment in Washington—and often in an abject demonstration of their commitment not to be swept into the national political scene—elected representatives choose to sleep in their offices, and shower in the House gym. The idea of "sleeping over" isn't new. Previous generations of members had considered doing the same, if only because they thought it to be a dramatic demonstration of their frugality in the face of big government profligacy. But in a sign of just how dramatically the ethos of Washington changed over the course of a few years, quite opposite Gingrich's encouragement, Tip O'Neill had been so infuriated by a young Dick Armey's attempt to sleep in his office that he ordered him out. While earlier eras of legislators had been invested in Washington life, today members flee the Capitol like rats off a sinking ship.

NINETY-SEVEN DAYS

The overall effect of the changes made to accommodate this new ethos has been drastic—even if the gradual evolution has failed to make headlines.

A political class that was once a community of its own—made mutually familiar by hours of working side-by-side *and* living side-by-side—has become a collection of strangers. Between 1961 and 1985, Congress was in session for an average of 160 days a year—a fairly full schedule, when you consider holiday recesses, work in district offices, and campaigning for re-election. However, time in session has been on a steady decline over the past thirty years. Between 2000 and 2006, the average number of days in session fell to 125. In 2013, the House spent a mere 118 days in session and in 2014 the House is expected to conduct legislative business on only ninety-seven days. While the decrease is stark on its face, these numbers mask the full reality of Congress's diminished presence in DC. Votes on the first day of the week are often scheduled for the end of the day—so members haven't spent the day together in any true sense of the term. If votes were scheduled to begin at 9:00 a.m. on Monday and end at 5:00 p.m. on Friday, members would likely be compelled to spend the full week in the Capitol. But if an entire week's votes can be scheduled between, say, 6:30 on Tuesday night and noon on Thursday—which might nominally be considered a three-day workweek—then members actually spend little more than a day and a half in DC. Moreover, certain days spent "in session" don't include a vote—and so many members don't show up at all.

A century of voting data tells the story. The percentage of midweek votes has steadily increased, from about 50 percent in the 60th Congress (1907–1909) to about 80 percent in the 100th Congress (1987–1989). Observers might react to the trend away from Washington in a whole variety of ways. Some might think it marks a step in the right direction: Time away from the Capitol is sometimes spent interacting with constituents. The notion of a part-time, citizen legislature, rooted in the customs and interests of their communities, still has resonance. We remain tethered to the idea that our leaders should be patriots who set down their plows to serve the public interest, returning to their fields when their public duty is complete.* Being a professional is generally admired in athletes, pilots, and all manner of employees. However, being referred

---

* Legend has it that Cincinnatus was a Roman citizen who dropped his plow to lead the Roman army against invaders and then, when he could have named himself emperor, chose instead to go back to plowing his small farm.

to as a professional politician is an insult often reserved for attack ads. In the public imagination, policymakers would get more done if they weren't tainted by their environment and, instead, maintained the same sensibilities that got them elected to office in the first place. The growing disdain for the profession of governing appears to be at the root of our problems.

It is a challenging balance for members of Congress to strike. Surely, some politicians get enamored with the DC lifestyle and lose touch with the people they represent. But keeping these people away from their colleagues is not an effective solution. By eroding the time allotted for our nation's leaders to meet one another, engage in frank exchanges of ideas, and develop fuller understandings of varying perspectives, we've diminished our ability to harness the power of the nation's ideological diversity.

We've quietly, but inarguably, tipped the scales of American democracy away from broad collaboration and toward narrow interests. And so, to the degree that Washington used to be a town defined by an extended sense of community, it has become something of a convention hotel filled with passing strangers.

PHONING IT IN

The results are unmistakable. Compare, for example, Washington's recent efforts to address the heightening challenge of cybersecurity with its historically successful campaign to combat Y2K. Today, America's critical infrastructure (electrical grids, water supplies, financial networks, transportation systems, etc.) is interwoven with digital networks vulnerable to being hacked by foreign powers—or even tech-savvy terrorists. It seems almost inevitable that the nation will suffer a serious attack through our fiber-optic networks. In April 2013, Janet Napolitano gave her final speech as secretary of the Department of Homeland Security. In her farewell remarks, she defined the threat in no uncertain terms stating, "Our country will, at some point, face a major cyber-event that will have a serious effect on our lives, our economy, and the everyday functioning of our society." As with Y2K in the mid-1990s, we are once again woefully unprepared.

In 2012, Washington tried to tackle the challenge in the spirit of the Bennett-Dodd effort more than a decade earlier. At both moments, the looming threat was real and dire, but the public's interest fairly tepid.

Driven by private sector concerns, Congress seemed poised for action, but then everything fell to pieces. Joe Lieberman, an Independent Democrat from Connecticut, and Susan Collins, a Republican from Maine, had spent months negotiating what they believed was a fairly noncontroversial approach to the underlying problem. But a few days before the bill was brought to the Senate floor—and despite expressed support from a majority of senators and vocal backing from military and defense experts—it was made subject to an unexpected filibuster. Acrimony between the Democratic and Republican leadership (centered in part on entirely unrelated issues) subsumed the debate. And so in the end, the bill was put on ice—unable to clear even the procedural hurdles required to prompt an up-or-down vote. There are certain elements that make Y2K and cybersecurity an imperfect comparison. But the similarities are hard to miss. Both situations posed a substantial threat to all Americans regardless of party, region, or class. In each case, a solution was negotiated that sought to protect public and private infrastructure without imposing onerous government mandates. The specific solutions were opaque, not particularly ideological, and free of anything that could be described as an emotional hot button or wedge issue. But the changing tenor of Washington has, through the intervening period, made opportunities for real bipartisanship less common and freighted with political risk.

Changes in the rhythms of political life have upended the culture of collaboration. The Framers were intent on making Washington a cauldron of competing impulses, forced to interact in service of the common interest. From ratification of the Constitution through the Great Depression, Cold War, and politics of personal destruction, Washington managed to persevere despite the contempt that is often borne by high stakes, core differences, and close quarters. Absent familiarity, today's legitimate differences have rendered the system largely unworkable.

FISHING AND FOOTBALL

There are exceptions. The president and members of Congress still meet on occasion, and sometimes they get to know one another. But the interactions are generally superficial, and the bonds that compelled previous generations to collaborate have withered.

In his first news conference of 2013, President Obama acknowledged that reality when asked about whether he had socialized enough with Republicans, and particularly with House Speaker John Boehner. "When we went out and played golf, we had a great time, but that didn't get a deal done in 2011," the president said, referring to the budget impasse of that year. He added later:

When I'm over here at the congressional picnic and folks are coming up and taking pictures with their family . . . we have a wonderful time, but it doesn't prevent them from going onto the floor of the House and . . . blasting me for being a big-spending socialist.

Before the nuclear option was invoked to eliminate the filibuster in late 2013, efforts to avert it also drew on the power of collegiality. A moment of seemingly meaningful connection occurred in July of that year, when the entire Senate came together and met for three hours in the old Senate Chamber with no TV cameras. If one listened to the members' reactions, it was as if they had discovered the alien idea of conversation for the first time. Senator John Boozman (R-AR) described the meeting as involving "no rancor at all."

Senator Angus King (I-ME) reflected that the meeting featured senators making "compelling arguments" while also listening to and learning from their colleagues—an embodiment of how the Senate "ought to work." Senator Jeff Merkley (D-OR) noted that the closed door, intimate setting of the Old Senate Chamber allowed members to enjoy what Merkley deemed to be certain essential qualities a legislature must possess—"listen[ing] to each other, hav[ing] confidence in our own views, but also be[ing] willing to explore, listen to and ponder the points being made by our colleagues." The next day senators struck a deal, paving the way for the confirmation of several Obama appointees.

After that, there was talk of making talking a regular activity. Following the meeting, Senator Kelly Ayotte (R-NH) immediately said "we should do it more often." Senators Martin Heinrich (D-NM) and Dean Heller (R-NV) wrote a letter to the Senate leadership requesting additional bipartisan meetings. Senator Reid even suggested he might reach out to BPC leaders George Mitchell and Trent Lott to ask them to attend a bipartisan meeting of senators.

Nevertheless, once the pixie dust settled, none of these professions of future engagement took hold. After winning re-election, President Obama made a point to spend more time meeting privately with members of Congress. It's a part of the job, but strategic outreach cannot replace the drive for real friendship. President Obama riffed on the aloofness critique at the 2013 White House Correspondents' Dinner:

Some folks still don't think I spend enough time with Congress. "Why don't you get a drink with Mitch McConnell?" they ask. Really? Why don't you get a drink with Mitch McConnell?

President Obama's reserve is quite the opposite of the prior Democrat to occupy the White House. Trent Lott tells the story of being fast asleep one night at around 2:00 a.m. when the phone rang:

I answered and heard the White House Operator say, "please hold for the President?" I of course took the call and for the next several minutes Bill Clinton talked a blue streak. He explained that he needed my help. It was a very important issue and he expected my support. I told him that I would be happy to work with him. I hung up the phone and my wife asked "what did the President want?" I told her that I didn't really know but I thought it might have something to do with Latin America.

Senator Lott isn't certain, but he thinks he probably supported the president.

The same lesson was revealed during one of the few triumphal moments for Congress during an otherwise bleak 2013. To avoid yet another appalling government shutdown, Congress needed to reach a last minute budget agreement. Determined to get a deal, congressional leadership assigned the Republican chair of the House Budget Committee, Representative Paul Ryan (R-WI) and the Democratic chair of its Senate counterpart, Senator Patty Murray (D-WA) to lead the negotiation. The decision was by no means out of the blue: Ryan and Murray are extremely competent legislators and they have considerable credibility with those on the ideological edges of their respective parties. Still, when they reached an agreement, it was immediately attacked by those on the left and the right.*

Why were Ryan and Murray able to succeed where others had failed? Both credited the importance of their having forged a personal relationship. They claimed to have bonded over fishing and football. Murray expressed sympathy for Ryan as his Packers went into a tailspin after an injury put star quarterback Aaron Rodgers on the bench. Ryan expressed appreciation that Murray did not gloat as her Seahawks stormed to the top of their division. Murray's enthusiasm for salmon fishing and Ryan's affection for walleye also became a source of friendly competition and personal connection.

As Senator Murray stated, "one of the things we had to learn to do is to listen to each other and to respect each other and to trust each other. . . . Either one of us could've taken out and blown up and killed the other person politically. We agreed from the start we wouldn't do that. Very important to where we are today." Ryan seconded her view saying, "We spent a lot of time just getting to know each other, talking, understanding each other's principles, and we basically learned that if we require the other to violate a core principle, we're going to get nowhere and we'll just keep gridlock."

In the current environment, the Ryan-Murray story seems exceptional. But for decades, hard fought negotiation and principled collaboration was simply the way that Congress worked. That is not an insight that applies exclusively to the world of politics—and it is not some new revelation. The science of exploiting collaboration has long been a staple of the business world, and it makes sense to look at successful companies for guidance. Not surprisingly, the patterns that *used* to define life in Washington are mirrored in the best business practices in the private sector.

---

* To offend conservatives, the deal relaxed the sequester, increased spending, created new "fees," and did nothing to reform entitlements. Those on the left complained that the agreement cut federal pensions and failed to extend unemployment insurance, while providing resources to maintain doctor's fees under Medicare.

CASUAL INTIMACY

When Bell Labs executive Mervin Kelly was tasked with overseeing the creation of a new headquarters for AT&T's research arm in the 1930s, he had the opportunity to choose between several conceptual options. During the years when Ma Bell still had its monopoly, Bell Labs was awash in money. The firm's laboratories were at the vanguard of efforts to modernize and improve the nation's telecommunications systems, among other technologies. And Kelly, who worked his entire life at the company, rising eventually to become chairman of the board, was heavily involved in designing the firm's new campus in Murray Hill, New Jersey.

The obvious plan for those looking to enhance efficiency was to give each of the wide-ranging fields of study within Bell Labs their own space. They'd put the scientists focused on transistors in one building, and those working to improve wire technology in another. That way, conventional wisdom suggested, those working on the disparate projects would be free from the idle chatter of unaffiliated researchers. Better to reduce the burden of centralization; let people have their own entrance into their own lab, and give them a parking spot nearby.

But Kelly rejected that entire theory. Innovation, he believed, depended largely on whether an organization could combine a critical mass of talented scientists, inserting them into a constant flux of conversation. People working on different projects, he believed, should interact as much as possible—while grabbing lunch, walking down the hall, or taking a cigarette break outside. Sequestering experts into discrete groups might leave them with fewer distractions, he acknowledged. But that sort of approach came at a serious cost: It would cut them off from the free flow of ideas that spurred big new breakthroughs.

The campus design he eventually championed placed researchers at labs scattered along packed corridors. Moreover, he insisted that the researchers from headquarters spend time in satellite facilities set up at AT&T's manufacturing plants so that the company's engineers could share their thoughts with the scientists designing the next generation of technology.

For most of the nation's history, Washington has looked and operated, however inadvertently, like Kelly's labs. Most obviously, the long corridors in the catacombs of the US Capitol drove policymakers together in chance meetings. But more broadly, the patterns of life that dictated that policymakers spend real time together made Washington ripe for just the kind of dynamism the world's most powerful nation demanded. Conservative Republicans and liberal Democrats often took the brief walk from the Capitol back to their offices together. They ate together at the restaurants that litter the neighborhood surrounding the Capitol and picnicked together after watching their children compete in Little League.

For nearly a century, a favorite gathering place for senators was the barbershop. First opened in 1909, the shop—now called "Senate Hair Care Services"—is still located in the exposed brick basement of the Russell Senate Office Building. According to Tony Calabro, who worked in the shop from 1983 to 2013, the place was like any barbershop. Senators and staff sat around, told jokes, shared stories, and talked about the issues of the day. But the intimacy and friendship of the Senate's small-town barbershop started to fade over the past several years, according to Mr. Calabro:

> Back in the 1980s and 1990s, we used to throw a Christmas party in the shop. Each of us on the hair care staff would bring homemade food and we would serve drinks. The senators would come as well as folks from the Sergeant-at-Arms offices. This tradition died out—for no particular cause that I'm aware of. But the party was moved to a conference room outside of the shop, attendance died down, and fewer people seemed to know each other.

The personal contact and cadence that once enabled policy innovation and collaboration in Washington have been disrupted. Members of Congress don't chat as they walk to their offices anymore—they race to fundraising call centers around town. They rarely lounge around the cloakrooms between roll calls because votes are "stacked" so that several bills can be discharged in a shorter period. When votes are completed for the week, members hightail it to the airport and train station to see the families they missed over the course of the legislative week. The average legislator's life has much more in common with traveling salesmen and telemarketers than statesmen or even CEOs.

There are many obvious ways that our leaders could spend more time governing. Congress could return to a five-day workweek. They could spend one week a month in their districts and the schedule could be relaxed during campaign season. As further incentive to spend time at work, members could be limited to one reimbursable trip home per month. When they are in DC, the full Senate and full House could meet at least once a month with no staff and no cameras to talk about whatever they want. The president could host congressional leaders at the White House and attend some of the off-the-record congressional sessions. More fanciful ideas also abound. A favorite of mine is building a sort of "campus" of subsidized housing for members of Congress. Implausible as this might seem, the current situation of members bunking on their office couches and showering at the gym demands creative thinking.

These are all good ideas, but they address the symptom and not the cause of the challenge. The alienation we find in Congress has not occurred due to poor scheduling or a lack of affordable housing. Do we really need political pundits going on TV with the insight that our leaders would get more done if they spoke with one another? For these worthy ideas to succeed, we need to look deeper at the causes of estrangement and develop a strategy that encourages our leaders to want to spend more time together.

CHAPTER 5

The Dark Side of Sunlight

FOR DECADES, WHAT PEOPLE EUPHEMISTICALLY CALLED THE "TROUBLES" had been one of Europe's most intractable problems. The conflict that pitted Catholics against Protestants in Northern Ireland had traumatized innocent civilians in Ulster for years, and defied multiple efforts to broker a peace. But that began to change during the early 1990s when the Clinton Administration took a more active interest in bringing the long-boiling and often deadly dispute to a resolution. In 1995, the president appointed former Senate majority leader (and later BPC founder) George Mitchell as his special advisor in Northern Ireland. The following year, the British and Irish governments asked Senator Mitchell to serve as the independent chairman of the peace talks in Northern Ireland—a role Mitchell would later describe as "the most difficult task I have ever undertaken, far more demanding than the six years I served as majority leader of the United States Senate."

At first, the senator's charge seemed nearly impossible. The factions were divided by decades of bloodshed and mistrust, and it took months of prodding and positioning simply to get them to the negotiating table. Moreover, the issues between them were complicated to resolve. What sort of political structure would give Catholics confidence that they wouldn't be subject to discrimination in a region dominated by Protestants? What would be done to assuage Protestant fears that the violence might start up again at a moment's notice? After a lengthy and challenging process, a final accord was signed on April 10, 1998. Named The Good Friday Agreement, it established a roadmap for peace.

But the Troubles didn't end there. Little more than a year later, on July 16, 1999, just as Queen Elizabeth was knighting Mitchell for his role in ushering through the accords, news broke that the ceasefire was falling apart. At issue was whether the combatants would "decommission" their weapons before or after the new government in Northern Ireland was set up. As Mitchell said at the time, "It is a sad irony that we received these honors just as the peace process is suffering . . . setbacks."

It wasn't that the lead negotiators were having second thoughts—they had all staked their reputations and influence on the accord's success. But pressure had mounted from those *outside* the process to make things more favorable for each faction's interests. In the autumn of 1999, negotiators met at Stormont, a facility just east of Belfast that housed many of Northern Ireland's main government buildings. But Stormont also housed something else: throngs of press. Years later, Mitchell reflected in an interview, "You remember how it was—everybody walking into that building had to run the gauntlet of the press in or out." And the constant barrage of media camped out at the negotiating site served as more than a roadblock to entering the building; it made it impossible to avoid harmful leaks that undermined the ability of adversarial negotiating parties to build trust.

The negotiators couldn't publicly disavow their brethren and they couldn't trust that concessions made to secure a lasting peace would not be used against them by critics within their own faction. They needed a place to rebuild their mutual trust—away from the press, and protected from any leaks. And so they again turned to Mitchell. This time, the request was simply to find a location where the sides could engage absent the outside pressures that were threatening the accord.

For nearly a week, unbeknownst to the outside world, Senator Mitchell hunkered down with leaders on both sides behind closed doors at the US ambassador's residence in London. During that period, everything was done in private. There were no press conferences, and no post-negotiation interviews. Those attending didn't have to worry that exploring new ideas would make them look weak to their constituents. And it worked. Over the course of their time in London, they made enough progress, especially at rebuilding trust, that when they returned to Belfast they were able to get the process back on track. This was possible not because the two sides developed a clever new solution. What got the negotiations back on track was simply the ability to rebuild confidence outside the prying eyes of the media and the public at large. Trust restored, a lasting peace was secured.

What Doors Are For

The story of Senator Mitchell's resuscitation of the peace process in Northern Ireland holds an enormously valuable lesson that goes far beyond its particulars. Even as Edward Snowden's 2013 release of secret national security information has alarmed many committed to keeping the country safe, the sense that transparency begets honesty has become a tenet of American political life. The two concepts have become so interchangeable that if you ask a person on the street what the opposite of "transparency" is, he or she might well answer "secrecy" or even "corruption." The chance that the answer would be "privacy" seems slim. After all, the tag line of the organization Transparency International is: "The global coalition against corruption." We've become so convinced that honest government must be done in public that it is hard to imagine what good might come of *anything* done behind closed doors.

It is not difficult to understand why that sentiment has emerged: Political misconduct is often incubated in dark rooms and hidden places. But much as openness and transparency now appear to be unmitigated goods, history suggests that there may also well be a dark side to sunlight. American history is rife with examples of *privacy*—transparency's true opposite—serving a crucial service to our democracy. As the Good Friday Accords showed, those open to collaboration needed room to maneuver absent the scrutiny of their critics and supporters. While many aspects of policy development depend on real-time public engagement, certain elements of the deliberative process can only be done behind closed doors.

The best example of privacy's crucial role in American democracy can be found at the beginning, in the years that followed our founding. The Constitutional Convention, in fact, was closed to the public-at-large.*

---

* Though we know very little about what was actually said in the convention, we still hold up the Constitution as a bastion of liberty. There are only a couple of sources, most famous of which are Madison's notes, which give us a window into what the Framers were thinking.

In determining the rules for the Constitutional Convention, the founders decided "to forbid 'licentious publications of their proceeding'"—and for good reason. (Essentially, all the sessions were closed to the public, and none of the participants was allowed to discuss the deliberations in the press.) Had the public been privy to the delegates' negotiations, it is almost impossible to imagine how they might have emerged with the thoughtful, balanced, and effective document we now hold up as the cornerstone of American government.

Think of the whole host of compromises forged during the course of that long, drawn-out deliberation. How would the various states be represented in the new Congress? Would the delegations be equally divided, or would the states be given delegations designed to approximate their populations? The deal that eventually dispatched that question, labeled "The Great Compromise," satisfied both sides by providing for *two* legislative bodies, a Senate in which states would be equally represented, and a House of Representatives, for which states would have delegations proportional to their size. With that arrangement, the small states felt protected against being swallowed in the legislative process, but their larger neighbors felt that their size counted for something a little extra.

Today, as much as we're frequently frustrated with the gridlock on Capitol Hill, we honor The Great Compromise, understanding it as a pragmatic solution to what might otherwise have been an intractable quagmire. And we can only imagine what would have happened had the deliberations been public: Convention delegates from smaller states like Delaware might well have felt pressure from those at home—particularly those disinclined to support *any* new constitutional framework—to reject any arrangement that failed to provide utterly equal representation. Maybe Delaware's delegates, seeking to prove their bona fides to the radicals back home, would have signed a pledge making an equal distribution of members a *pre*-condition for negotiations. Maybe the delegates from the larger states would have taken the opposite view, threatening to remove any of their own members who failed to honor the core value of proportional representation.

The same sort of dilemma might have applied on a whole range of other issues, from how the Executive Branch would be organized to the status of slavery. A convention open to the public would have most likely fallen into acrimony, as the various sides delivered fiery speeches for those who would read about them in the newspapers back home. Absent the privacy afforded the delegates in Philadelphia, the Constitutional Convention might have been gridlocked before any document emerged for ratification. It is a poignant irony that a government, *of* the people, *for* the people, and *by* the people could only be developed *without* the people. The document extolled, promoted, and carried in myriad politicians' pockets and purses was written in a backroom by political insiders.

But that is hardly the end of the story. Throughout American history, whenever we've been faced with a deeply entrenched internal divide, the solution has nearly always been forged within a certain zone of confidentiality. One need only watch Steven Spielberg's film *Lincoln*, which traces the harrowing path that led to passage of the Thirteenth Amendment (banning slavery), to realize that the president's heroic stand could never have succeeded in a glass house.

Spielberg's epic depicts a private conversation, in what looks like the basement of the White House, between President Lincoln and Congressman Thaddeus Stevens, leader of a more radical cohort of Republicans in Congress. Stevens lays out for Lincoln his intention to jam a vindictive plan for Reconstruction down the throats of the states that had seceded from the Union. Lincoln retorts that Stevens's radical agenda, which aimed to wipe out racial inequality in one fell swoop, was less likely to do any real good for the nation's former slaves. Real progress, the president argued, could only be made through small steps, like an amendment that provided citizenship (though not all its privileges) to former slaves.

Not to spoil the film, or the basics of US history, but Stevens acquiesced and the Thirteenth Amendment became the law of the land. Though many historians take issue with the film, Lincoln and Stevens's frank exchange of positions, whether accurate or apocryphal, depicts how crucial business has generally been conducted in Washington. Outside the view of reporters, and even of aides, politicians in positions of influence were able to negotiate over items of real disagreement.

And this is not a Ye Olde vestige of simpler times. As recently as the mid-1990s, the Senate's majority and minority leaders (Tom Daschle and Trent Lott, BPC's co-founders) each had a phone on their desk that connected directly to the other. Some worried at the time that this direct interaction might compromise their partisan interests. (Their respective staffs had the additional anxiety that the leaders might actually make decisions by themselves.) But the regular interaction did not diminish their commitment to principle or their determination to win; it just meant that they sought, whenever possible, not to injure one another.

According to Senator Lott, when, on any given issue, he had the votes to win, he would tell Senator Daschle where things stood. But he was always willing "to do something to make the loss a little easier for Tom." That is a far cry from the dynamic connecting today's Senate leadership. Senators Harry Reid and Mitch McConnell, who recently touted an agreement to meet once every two weeks, seem more interested in scoring political points off each other than softening any blows.

SHOUTING AT AN EMPTY ROOM

In the abstract, people accept that the art of politics is about balancing the demands of competing interests and constituencies. However, in practice, the act of harmonizing different positions is often viewed in the public with considerable disdain. For many, the handshake behind closed doors signals the ultimate treachery: It is the moment when someone who promised to be *your* advocate abandons integrity in favor of expediency. Fearing the proverbial "sell out," many Americans have long pushed to shine a light into the darkened corners of the political world. A healthy suspicion of government is as old as the Republic itself. However, the "high crimes" perpetrated by the Nixon Administration created new urgency to expose and monitor our elected officials.

The Watergate scandal, combined with the public's outrage over the Vietnam War, convinced most Americans that our government was severely off track and unworthy of public trust. Once John Dean asserted that a "cancer" was growing inside the Nixon White House, it was easy to assume that anything hidden from the public eye was nefarious. And it wasn't just the bugging scandal or the "dirty tricks." Nixon's secret bombing of Cambodia and surprise expansion of the war gave credence to the supposition that the nation's leaders were wildly out of step with popular opinion.

But the country's stepped-up desire to know what was happening behind closed doors marked only half the equation. Over the course of the following decades, a series of technological advances dramatically increased the public's capacity to keep an eye on Washington. Four decades after Nixon left the White House in disgrace, every legislative hearing, floor speech, and position paper offered during the course of any given public debate are accessible in real time. And one need look no further than C-SPAN to see how powerfully the landscape has changed.

The House and Senate floors have always been public places. The galleries situated above each chamber have long provided the public with entrée into what was happening on Capitol Hill. But C-SPAN, which began broadcasting the proceedings of the House floor in 1979 and expanded to the Senate in 1986, has wrought at least two profound effects. The first, and more obvious, is that nearly anyone can now watch the public's business being done—or not done—live. Government has joined the ranks of reality television, albeit one that few Americans watch. It has become part of what is "on"—it is now available, open, and accessible.

The second change has been even more profound. Until congressional debate began to be broadcast around the country, floor speeches had been part of a conversation mostly among colleagues. That's not to suggest that those delivering remarks didn't hope to have their pithy quotes reported back to the public at large. But it did mean that the wells of the House and Senate were places where interested colleagues actually discussed legislation with one another.

The moment those speeches began to be broadcast on C-SPAN, Congress began speaking to a very different audience. In addition to the general interest of a relatively small number of engaged citizens, legislators could now direct their remarks to narrower bands of interests and supporters. Instead of exploring the nuance of complex legislative questions, speeches became advertisements aimed at very specific audiences: lawyers focused on medical malpractice reform; hedge funds intent on maintaining particular tax provisions; environmentalists opposing nuclear power. Members of the House today line up in the morning to give "one-minute" speeches that are designed exclusively to be sent out as YouTube clips to interested admirers.

Washington has become subject to what psychologists call the "observer" effect, whereby subjects who know they are being watched alter their behavior. Many predicted this result long before C-SPAN became a Washington institution. In the Senate, Howard Baker, the longtime majority leader, faced broad opposition to allowing cameras in the Senate chamber. His colleagues feared that senators would begin to talk to cameras instead of each other. Predictably, members of Congress now pay little to no attention to their colleagues' statements. C-SPAN hasn't simply exposed dialogue that was once partially shrouded; it has entirely changed the substance of the conversation itself.

Nothing illuminates that change more abjectly than the stunt that vaulted Newt Gingrich into the national spotlight during the 1980s. Taking advantage of the fact that C-SPAN was, at the time, restricted to showing only the podium, also known as the "well" of the House floor (and not the surrounding seats), the brash, young congressman from Georgia began delivering incendiary speeches late into the evening, accusing Democrats of being "blind to communism," among other things. It looked to the average viewer—most of whom were political junkies or insomniacs—as if Gingrich were accusing Democrats of transgressions to their faces, and that they were too cowed to defend themselves. But the truth was that the chambers were largely empty; most everyone had gone home for the night. Gingrich became a star by yelling at an empty room.

The Speaker of the House at the time, Democrat Tip O'Neill, was so incensed when he found out that he took to the floor, wagged his finger at Gingrich and said: "You deliberately stood in that well before an empty House, and challenged these people, and challenged their patriotism, and it is the lowest thing that I've ever seen in my thirty-two years in Congress." But the die had been cast. Floor debate had transitioned from being a tool of internal deliberation to a platform for political posturing.

It is not hard to imagine what happened: The substantive conversations that were once held in the House and Senate chambers were moved to the cloakrooms, or at least to private deliberations held away from C-SPAN's cameras. At one point the franker debates were still held in committee hearings—though eventually even many of those were put on C-SPAN as well. The real negotiations began to be held in leadership offices. Rather than expand access to decision-making to a wider range of viewers, C-SPAN has in fact done the opposite: It has inadvertently pushed real deliberation *further* into the shadows by centralizing power among a smaller group of leaders.

No member of Congress these days would try to kick C-SPAN off of Capitol Hill. Beyond the fact that any effort to re-cloak the Congress would look like an attempt to separate Americans from their government, most members like the fact that they can talk to their constituents directly through the cameras recording House and Senate proceedings. That ship has sailed. But there are ways to walk back the coverage, even marginally. And there's precedent for doing so.

One setting that has transitioned from private to public and back again is the weekly (or biweekly) party caucus meeting. Often, some of the most intense political battles occur not in two opposite extremes engaging but rather *within* the political parties. For a short period in the mid-1970s, the Democratic Caucus—a group deeply divided between southern conservatives and northern liberals—decided to open their caucus meetings to the public. Some hoped that airing these meetings would make them more consequential, drawing power away from powerful southern committee chairmen and conferring greater authority on the caucus majority and party leadership. But the experiment failed in large part because members quickly tired of the grandstanding that took place at these "open" meetings and simply stopped attending. The cameras were kicked out and caucus meetings have since remained private affairs.

OVEREXPOSED

The corrosive effect of publicity on candor and deliberation doesn't just apply to Congress. Across the federal government, there are myriad government activities that even the most ardent transparency advocates agree are entitled to some privacy. Just because you're a member of the civil service doesn't mean, for example, that every draft memo you write should be posted on a government website. Few would suggest that the pursuit of transparency should extend to recording and posting the text of the US president's phone calls—though German chancellor Angela Merkel might. We wouldn't think it appropriate to bug the offices of cabinet officials or agency heads. Neither would we demand that all senior staff meetings be posted on YouTube.

That said, there are things that nearly all of us do think should be public: We expect the decisions that come out of those meetings to be subject to public scrutiny. In some cases, we expect to know who participated in major decisions. We want to know that no one is profiting privately from decisions made purportedly in the public interest. There is a crucial balance to be struck—and while certain stages in the deliberative process require privacy, others have to be kept open. Expectations about where to strike this balance have changed dramatically over the last several decades.

A critical arbiter of the lines between public and private communication are two laws that were established and strengthened during the 1960s and 1970s: the Freedom of Information Act (FOIA)*, and the Government in the Sunshine Act. It is hard to dispute the altruistic motives behind the movement to increase transparency in government—a guarantee that, in many cases, both laws have managed to provide. And it is a blessing that American government, unlike repressive regimes around the world, is committed to the spirit of public accountability. For official meetings, FOIA sets a high bar, requiring, with limited exceptions, that "every portion of every meeting of an agency shall be open to public observation."

But the changes haven't only given the public access to more information; they've actually changed the way the men and women staffing the government perform their jobs. In cases where the most efficient way of sharing an idea might make them subject to public scrutiny (e-mail to a dozen of their colleagues), they will often find less efficient ways to

---

* As much as we see it as a commonsense law today, President Lyndon Johnson strongly resisted signing the 1966 Freedom of Information Act (FOIA). As Johnson's White House press secretary Bill Moyers said years later, "LBJ had to be dragged kicking and screaming to the signing ceremony. He hated the very idea of the Freedom of Information Act; hated the thought of journalists rummaging in government closets; hated them challenging the official view of reality. He dug in his heels and even threatened to pocket veto the bill after it reached the White House." Things were even tougher when the 1974 FOIA amendments were sent to President Gerald Ford for his signature. Ford was counseled by White House chief of staff Donald Rumsfeld and his deputy Dick Cheney to veto the amendments. Others in the administration, including the head of the Justice Department's Office of Legal Counsel, Antonin Scalia, were also organizing opposition. In the end, Ford did veto the legislation, but Congress easily overrode his decision.

deliberate (tracking their colleagues down individually for conversations in the hall). Worse yet, government officials from scientists and engineers to lawyers and political appointees have grown afraid to express doubts, or raise challenging questions for fear that they'll be made public and used to undermine agency action—embarrassing them along the way. In 1996, NewsHour's Jim Lehrer asked then first lady Hillary Clinton whether she kept a diary, or at least took good notes. "Heavens, no!" she laughed. "It would get subpoenaed. I can't write anything down."

This concern is not reserved to the Clintons nor to the president's inner circle. As one longtime civil servant explained to me, the clear understanding among staffers at executive agencies is, "don't write it down unless you want Congress to see it." When briefing a cabinet secretary, agency staff will often go "paper free"—not to save the trees. It is simply too high of a risk that memos weighing the pros and cons of different decisions might wind up in public. Instead, a general agenda is often prepared and lead staff provide a verbal briefing. The process is profoundly inefficient; it is rarely possible to assemble all the experts in one place to brief the boss. Moreover, there's often no effective internal record to organize issues for further reflection. According to former Clinton speechwriter Jeff Shesol, "The climate of fear in the Clinton White House exerted, without doubt, a dampening effect on the Administration's internal dialogue."

Diligent public servants doing their best to grapple with complex problems never know what among their thoughts and written utterances will be made public. And like the cameras now pointed at the floors of the House and the Senate, that has fundamentally altered the substance of government documents themselves.

WE'RE LISTENING

But it's not just that government officials have become fearful of writing down what they really think. As our hunger and penchant for transparency has grown, the ways in which information is passed between colleagues has also evolved. As we've moved from analog to digital, and from inter-office envelope to instant message, more of the ideas and opinions considered among members of the government have become subject to capture. Face-to-face meetings and conference calls have been replaced with quick e-mails. Regional administrators spread across different time zones can now commiserate through their smartphones. There can be little doubt that the advances of the last several decades have offered the promise of greater efficiency. What is less obvious is the effect that change has had in balancing the demand for transparency with the need for deliberation.

The prime benefit is obvious: More can be done at much less cost. How much can taxpayers save if those regional administrators don't all have to travel to Washington to meet on a subject that might otherwise be debated online? How much efficiency is born of the fact that they don't have to schedule a conference call that can delay a final determination on an issue by a matter of weeks or months?

Moreover, the *new* way of deliberating offers the promise of even greater transparency. The substance of debates handled in the old, inefficient way would have remained largely outside the scope of any transparency expectation. Few would expect that a transcript be made available for a spoken interaction—be it a meeting or phone call. But if the deliberation is done on a computer screen, our expectations are different: E-mails exchanged by members of the government are considered to be written records that should be subject to public disclosure. Somehow, if it is written down and sent across fiber-optic cable, many seem to think it should be subject to no greater privacy protection than an official government report. Anyone who has mistakenly distributed a private e-mail understands the panic in this proposition.

That shift in perspective has been made evident in litigation, like in the Competitive Enterprise Institute's (CEI) efforts to gain access to text messages sent by the Environmental Protection Agency administrator Gina McCarthy. According to the organization's website:

> *CEI first asked for her texts on 18 specified days when she was known to have testified before Congress and been seen sending texts. After EPA acknowledged no such records existed, CEI obtained information relating to McCarthy's PDA bill that showed she sent 5,392 text messages over a three-year period.*

CEI has since filed suit in the US District Court for the District of Columbia asking the court to "enjoin and prevent the destruction of certain EPA text message transcripts, by EPA pursuant to a policy and practice that violates the Freedom of Information Act and the Federal Records Act." It feels as though we're careening toward a place where *everything* is fair game, without even considering the necessity or the consequences. Paul Wester, the chief records officer for the National Archives recently told the *Washington Post*:

> *The notion is all e-mails should be captured. Certain people in an organization are called "capstone" officials: Their e-mails are permanent. One of the things we're looking at is having a schedule that identifies certain senior positions within the agency and the e-mail accounts for them, the assistants to them; those would be presumed to be permanent, captured and transferred to the archives.*

Having every e-mail written from your office stored for posterity in the National Archives will certainly have a chilling effect on electronic communication. But Wester's comment hints at a much broader shift in expectation. If e-mails and text messages sent on government-purchased smartphones are now public domain, telephone conversations and voice-mails—all of which can be digitized—cannot be far behind.

In his recent novel *The Circle*, Dave Eggers explores a future dominated by complete transparency. In the author's dystopic portrayal, a company called The Circle (an amalgam of Google, Facebook, PayPal, and other Internet behemoths) demands transparency in all things—both within the company and, as their power grows, in society at large. Two of its many slogans are, "secrets are lies," and "privacy is theft." While anyone over thirty will see this future as the horrifying obliteration of personal freedom, it is sadly not that far from the obligations that many would impose upon our federal officials.

Regardless of whether you believe we are careening toward the complete obliteration of privacy in all things, our unencumbered embrace of transparency is certainly not making government any more efficient. Ideas that might be vetted and disposed of in a quick series of e-mails now must wait for a meeting to be scheduled, be resolved without broad input, or simply not be raised at all. But it's not just that the government is taking longer to make decisions.

The far greater problem is that our leaders are being deprived of the information needed to make good decisions. The disincentive for staff to raise challenging issues, flag weaknesses in analysis, or do *anything* contrary to the perceived interests of senior political leadership runs contrary to the public interest. It is no mystery why a system so rife with transparency so frequently falls short of our expectations. A private sector company run this way would go belly up within a year.

DRIVEN UNDERGROUND

But the government hasn't been entirely flat-footed in the face of this evolving dynamic. Indeed, as the number of FOIA requests has skyrocketed, the Executive Branch has been redesigned to essentially work *around* the challenge of transparency. The principal safe-harbor that members of any administration have from prying eyes is "executive privilege," namely the power the Supreme Court has proffered to the White House to resist subpoenas and other demands for information. If, for example, Congress were to ask for the minutes of a meeting held between the president and his chief of staff, the White House could claim that the notes were protected, and a court would likely back the president up.

But there's a wrinkle: Executive privilege is the prerogative of a limited number of senior White House staff, and so it's not available to the members of the president's cabinet or to senior officials in Executive Branch agencies. The predictable result has been to insulate the White House and diminish the role of expert agency staff in favor of a small cluster of White House "czars" who are not subject to Senate confirmation and who function largely outside the scope of congressional oversight. At the outset of the Obama Administration, health care and climate change were two domestic policy priorities. And in both cases, rather than leave the debate to the expert agencies with Senate-confirmed leaders and legions of civil servants capable of bringing vast experience and expertise to the discussion, the administration opted to hire a White House policy czar to lead each respective legislative campaign. It is becoming increasingly common for the White House to disenfranchise the more expert advisors outside the building for fear that their honest assessments and private advice cannot be protected from public scrutiny. Here again we see the double edge of transparency's sword. While some government actions are brought to the surface, others are driven farther underground. In the latter case, the unique attribute of the decisionmakers is not their expertise but their ability to secure privacy.

Take, for example, the President's Council on Environmental Quality (CEQ), created in 1970 to coordinate decision-making on environmental issues within a more political lens than is appropriate for the seventeen thousand people who work at the Environmental Protection Agency. CEQ is a relatively nimble bureaucracy that has ranged from thirteen to seventy staffers over the past few administrations. But the council's influence today has been diminished because President Obama chose to create a three-person office within the White House to perform the same role. Why replace several dozen staffers with a mere three? One reason, a White House staffer privately told me, is that CEQ staffers aren't protected by executive privilege. I'm not suggesting that White House staff are doing anything inappropriate behind the shield of privilege. However, it does reveal that three people having an honest conversation is viewed as producing a better decision than the collective wisdom of seventy people who cannot express themselves freely.

While members of Congress are indignant whenever an administration from the other party takes steps to protect the privacy of its decision-making, Congress doesn't embrace the unadulterated value of transparency when considering its own deliberative needs. A recent example of that hypocrisy was revealed when certain members of the legislative branch began to explore changes to the nation's tax code—a body of legislation that has not been seriously amended since 1986. In the spring of 2013, senators Max Baucus (D-MT) and Orrin Hatch (R-UT), who led the Senate Finance Committee, sought to conduct a wide-ranging review of ideas to improve the complex US tax system. They proposed starting from a "blank slate" and asked their colleagues for suggestions. They were not seeking detailed proposals or any commitments of support—just ideas to begin a deliberative process.

They received no responses. Not a one. No member of Congress wanted to be on record calling for either the elimination or continuation of a tax provision favored or reviled by anyone. So to prompt more meaningful input, the senators wrote a memo to their colleagues on July 19, promising that any records of lawmaker suggestions would be locked in a safe near Capitol Hill. Baucus and Hatch promised that any ideas written and transmitted to them would be transferred to the National Archives and stored in a special vault, separate from the committee's other records, and sealed until December 31, 2064. Though widely ridiculed for its absurdity, the plan worked and the committee received over one thousand pages of proposals.

PROCESS OVERLOAD
Often, when confronted with a particularly vexing challenge or actual disaster, Congress and the White House outsource their work. Rather than allow a committee or a bureaucratic department to handle a particular investigation, the nation's leaders assign a federally chartered panel of experts the task of studying the problem. Roughly one thousand of these committees are currently in operation. Most are quite technical and not particularly controversial, but several have addressed major national crises. The Rogers Commission, for example, was assigned the task of looking into the 1986 Space Shuttle *Challenger* disaster. More recently, there have been two high-profile commissions: The Financial Crisis Inquiry Commission was created to examine the domestic and global causes of the 2008 financial crisis, and The National Commission on the Deepwater Horizon Oil Spill and Offshore Drilling was created to make recommendations after one of the worst environmental disasters in US history.

Commissioners are selected to represent a wide range of different perspectives to ensure that the solutions they recommend are the product of vigorous debate. Former regulators, academics, nonprofit advocates, CEOs, and politicians might be placed together on the same panel. Consumer advocates and industry insiders who would normally be adversaries might be asked to collaborate on a new regulatory regime. And after careful fact-finding and deliberation, the hope is that representatives with wildly different preconceived impressions will be able to come to some sort of comprehensive conclusion. *E pluribus unum.* From many, one.

In the early 1970s, Congress established the basic oversight structure for these committees via adoption of the "Federal Advisory Committee Act" (FACA). Over the last several decades, an accretion of requirements designed to increase public engagement has become an obstacle to effective deliberation. A federal official who spent thirteen years leading a variety of advisory committees noted the process tradeoffs:

> *For timely issues it is very difficult for the FACA to offer effective guidance. You need to post when you will meet, prepare minutes from the last meeting, and create and circulate a meeting agenda before you can even get in the room. As a result, we generally don't look to FACA for advice on really pressing problems.*

At first glance, most of the rules seem reasonable. Meetings of the full committee must now be noted in the Federal Register at least fifteen days ahead of schedule. In practice, this requirement prevents a group meeting with less than a month's advance planning. While a hindrance to spontaneity, it is appropriate to require reasonable public notice for these formal sessions. Often expert testimony is presented and there are opportunities for public statements and general input. In addition, each commission's investigative material must be made available for public review.

However, a series of additional requirements seem designed to directly confound the very deliberative purpose of these diverse advisory bodies. Committee members are often prevented from interacting with experts outside of the restricted committee process. In one committee, a leader of a large technical organization was told not to consult with her expert staff as that would be an unfair advantage of her group over others—as if a level playing field, and not the best solution, was the point.

Even interactions among commission members are highly constrained. For example, it is unlawful for more than three members of a committee to have a conversation outside of a formal public meeting.

Committees often have a dozen or more members and it would seem obvious that a group of five to six members might desire to have a series of conference calls to think through some tough issues.

To get around this obstacle, committees often divide up into mini-groups of two to three members and try to conduct "shuttle diplomacy." Different federal agencies interpret the rules differently and sometimes even two members are discouraged from engaging outside of the formal recorded sessions. In addition to being highly inefficient, the goal of broad-based exploration is lost. Worse yet, there are practically no opportunities for these committees to honestly hash through their differences. All deliberations by full committees must occur in public. In cases where there is inadequate meeting space or members are remote, a phone line is required so that interested parties can listen in. Committees are allowed to have private "planning meetings," to think through logistical issues like where and when to hold meetings, but there is a federal "minder" at all such sessions to ensure that the conversations do not become substantive. These rules are not just an inconvenience. Alumnae of the process complain that the red tape makes it much harder to fulfill their assignments and often shrinks the scope of their exploration.

In the recent National Commission on the Deepwater Horizon Oil Spill and Offshore Drilling, for example, most of the attention was appropriately devoted to understanding the proximate cause of the accident so that the commission could make recommendations to avoid a recurrence. But the Spill Commission co-chairs subsequently realized that their work could be even more useful if they explored the relevance of their recommendations to other challenging offshore environments—in particular, the questions surrounding new offshore production in shallow waters off Alaska. Ultimately, they chose not to. According to commission staff, the inability to have frank and private discussions on these extremely sensitive issues was a factor in preventing them from even trying.

According to a senior advisor to the Spill Commission:

> *The FACA rules demanded such constant public disclosure of full Commission deliberations that they inhibited rather than fostered frank discussion, turning the full Commission meetings into a type of kabuki*

theater exercise. Honest discussion of the political ramifications of rec-
ommendations—that is, how they would be greeted in the real world,
for example by Congress—was impossible. My personal view is that
this restricted greater policy impact by the Commission despite incred-
ibly hard work and dedication by all involved.

Like with the White House's use of executive privilege, FACA committees have tried to find workarounds. While no one wanted to get too specific,
several participants in FACA processes acknowledged that it simply would
not be possible to deliver a solid product without skirting the rules.

Many states employ equally aggressive "open-government" requirements to similar effect. In the state of Washington, the desire for government transparency has collided with the equally progressive aspiration
to end gerrymandering. Throughout 2011, former senator Slade Gorton
(R-WA) was one of four leaders appointed to lead a redistricting commission to draw new election lines based on the 2010 census data. Senator
Gorton believes that Washington state's process is the best in the country,
in large part because the legislature appoints an even number of commission members—two Democrats and two Republicans—which obligates
real interaction and a true consensus.

According to Senator Gorton, the biggest challenge in the entire process was the application of Washington open meeting law. Under state
law, the public had to be included in any discussion among a quorum
(i.e., three or more) of commission members. "It was simply impossible
to even begin to explore trade-offs or design a strategy with all the interests listening in," Gorton explained. "After a couple of sessions that were
reduced to posturing, we did the only thing we could and split the Commission in two. This allowed us to grapple with the most challenging
issues through informal discussions." From there, the deliberative work
was largely conducted in private and the commission achieved an effective consensus within the time allotted.

If the American public is going to get what it expects out of its blue
ribbon commissions, it needs them to be able to operate with independence and internal trust. The balance between transparency and deliberation has come undone, and we need to find a new equilibrium.

GLASS HOUSES

Anyone who is part of the decision-making process is acutely aware that openness, for all its virtues, also has its vices. But, for most everyone in public life, there's very little upside to pointing the problem out. No one pushed back when, in the aftermath of President Obama's election, a group of advocates labeling itself the "Right to Know Community" published a long set of recommendations on openness that took little account of the effect their proposals might have on deliberation. The day after his inauguration in January 2009, the President issued a memorandum that began with the following statement:

> *My Administration is committed to creating an unprecedented level of openness in Government . . . Government should be transparent. Transparency promotes accountability and provides information for citizens about what their Government is doing.*

The same rhetoric had flavored the Obama campaign's core critique of the Bush Administration in the run-up to the Iraq War. The upstart candidate embraced the populist narrative that "special interests" were crowding out the voices of regular people. In politics, it's a truism that before you get to do the job, you have to get the job and it's never a bad campaign strategy to say, "I want you involved." The 2008 Obama campaign soared on the wings of small donors and newly engaged voters.

It's not just Democrats who are drawn to the easy populism of open government. Several conservative groups joined the "Right to Know Community" in calling upon the incoming Obama Administration to champion sunlight without limits. Less than two years after the Obama Administration pledged its commitment to transparency, House Republican leader John Boehner included the following in his pre-election "Pledge to America":

> *Americans have lost trust with their government . . . Backroom deals, phantom amendments, and bills that go unread before being forced through Congress have become business as usual. Never before has the need for a new approach to governing been more apparent . . . We cannot continue to operate like this.*

Unfortunately, while the rhetoric of transparency appeals to everyone, when push comes to shove, pride in open government often gives way to humiliation. The administration's drive for ever-increasingtransparency hit a rhetorical pothole when Edward Snowden began disseminating state secrets while camped out in Moscow. It's obvious that certain information needs to be kept under wraps in the realm of national security—even if it is reasonable to want certain elements to be public. Shouldn't a similar balance be struck in other spheres of public life?

As it turns out, even those who tout the "right to know" at the outset of their terms in office tend, over time, to seek a better balance between openness and collaboration. Congressional Republicans certainly didn't lay bare the internal deliberations that eventually brought the 2013 government shutdown to an end. If they had, the voices of wisdom who stopped the madness might have stayed silent or been shouted down in a frenzy to impress the Republican base.

At the same time, President Obama has retreated from the pledge to keep his administration entirely open. When a contractor working on HealthCare.gov was subpoenaed for information by the House Oversight Committee, the Obama Administration tried to prevent them from producing what the committee had asked to see. Even fellow Democrats were troubled by a lack of transparency when the administration was telling the public that Syria's Assad regime had used chemical weapons while refusing to reveal its evidence. Republicans have frequently sought to contrast the administration's rhetoric and actions. As Iowa senator Charles Grassley once complained: "There's a complete disconnect between the President's grand pronouncements about transparency and the actions of his political appointees."

Openness is an important value that should be pursued and celebrated. But transparency must be balanced against candor and efficiency. There's a dark side to sunlight, as articulated famously by former vice president Dick Cheney, who argued: "What I object to . . . is mak[ing] it impossible for me or future vice presidents to ever have a conversation in confidence with anybody without having, ultimately, to tell a member of Congress what we talked about and what was said." You don't have to embrace the intensity of Cheney's view of executive privilege to concede that he has a point.

DELIBERATIVE BODIES

Fortunately, there are institutions in Washington that effectively balance public accountability with private deliberations, and they can point a better way forward.

Take, for example, the House Permanent Select Committee on Intelligence, known colloquially as the HPSCI. Congressional committees, which were once beacons of deliberation, are today shadows of their former glory. Their hearings have become too vitriolic and partisan, with members trying to impress those sitting in the galleries and watching on television. Rather than providing a forum for thoughtful debate and discussion, legislative panels have become arenas for showmanship and sparring.

The HPSCI, however, has sidestepped the plight of most other committees. For reasons of national security, many of its hearings and deliberations are held behind closed doors. There are no cameras for members to play to and no journalists to impress. Some of their legislative findings are kept under wraps—but most are made public. Absent the pressure to score political points they need, members are given the latitude to develop much more deep-seated relationships with their colleagues. The result is a level of collegiality and collaboration too frequently absent in other important committees. According to Michael Allen, former HPSCI staff director, "When members are in the cocoon of the intelligence committee, they are able to dedicate undivided attention to their constitutional oversight duty. The atmosphere frequently promotes careful deliberation and study from which extraordinary cooperation can develop."

The same basic dynamic is true at the Supreme Court. The justices have vehemently resisted requests to have court proceedings broadcast on television, and there is no serious consideration of publishing draft opinions, internal memos, or transcripts of their internal meetings. People may not like the decisions made by the Supreme Court. But the questions the justices pose to counsel are meant to sway their dark-robed colleagues, not the public at large. If they were instead more prone to influence public opinion, the reflective dynamic that is supposed to characterize the court would surely decline.

The Federal Reserve's Open Market Committee, the powerful board that makes most of the nation's important monetary policy decisions, marks yet another example of the same phenomenon. To balance transparency and deliberation, minutes are kept of its meetings, and they are released to the public—but not until weeks *after* the committee has made its decisions. By design, the delayed release provides those who sit on the committee with the opportunity to have a full and fair hearing of any given policy proposal. None of the members have to worry that their comments might affect the financial markets, for good or ill. If cameras were allowed in the room, this carefully designed system would be upended. Members would calibrate all their comments based on the public or the market's reaction, and, most likely, their deliberations would grind to a halt because of the scrutiny.

The Fed, the Supreme Court, and the House Permanent Select Committee on Intelligence all have their quirks, shortcomings, and critics. But on balance, they are high-functioning government institutions.

REDUCING THE GLARE

Why can't we apply a similar balance of measured privacy and ultimate accountability to the less functional parts of the government? How do we intentionally create protected places that allow, foster, and encourage real deliberation? How, in the end do we protect policymakers from the glare of too much sunlight?

Despite the fact that unmitigated openness is harming productive deliberation, few politicians want to go on record waging a campaign against transparency. Fortunately, the things we need to do to recalibrate the essential balance are incremental. At the core, we need to re-legitimize the idea that there are stages in the public policy process where the imperative for deliberation trumps the imperative for access. Federal officials need to have confidence that they can raise challenging questions and doubts at the early stages of a policy discussion without being humiliated down the road—or diminishing their own latitude in addressing the underlying challenge. Blue-ribbon commissions must be enabled to confer offline—even as we continue to require that the rationale for their decisions be made public. The conversations that the participants themselves have in small groups—over lunch maybe, or on an ad hoc conference call—should be private.

Second, we should urge each house of Congress to meet with some regularity behind closed doors, in a bipartisan manner, with the cameras turned off. What if, for three hours each week, the floor of the House and Senate were closed off to the public? No votes would be taken. No decisions would be made. But members would at least have time to talk to one another—rather than addressing everything to the television audience.

It's not an idea without precedent. During President Clinton's impeachment trial, the arguments made to the senatorial jury—all of which were broadcast live on television—were followed by private discussions. The cameras were turned off, and members of the Senate spoke privately in the Senate chamber. According to Senate Democratic leader Tom Daschle, the conversations were profoundly meaningful—and almost entirely at odds in tenor from the vitriol that emerged inevitably whenever the cameras were turned on. Given the space to voice their honest opinions, people "poured their hearts out . . . they really talked in a very candid way." Moreover, senators learned profound lessons from that experience. "As much as it is important to have transparency and media scrutiny," Daschle later said, "there are times when not having media, so people can open up, be more expressive and more honest with each other, really can make a difference."

Finally, it is time to reconsider which sorts of internal communication should be subject to outside inquiry—whether from Congress or the broader public. But to do that, we need a better sense of how the existing regulations are being used. It's not John and Jill Q. Public who are seeking frequent access to the notes and memos circulating within the Consumer Product Safety Commission, the Department of Transportation, or Environmental Protection Agency. It is big organizations like the Sierra Club, the National Trucking Association, and the National Retail Federation who are employing FOIA and other laws intended to open the government up. The irony is that we've come full circle: Efforts to open up government to the public have, by and large, expanded the tool kit and influence of highly organized and well-funded "special" interests.

In practice, tenets of a movement designed to diffuse power have, instead, further consolidated it.

That is not to suggest that organizations with lobbyists aren't the legitimate representative of substantial and broad-based interests; they play a critical role in the democracy. But the supposition that transparency uniquely empowers regular folks is quaint fantasy. By and large, those combing the public records and filing information requests are not your neighbors. Generally, they are junior associates at big law firms searching for some detail that can be used to challenge a federal decision that is at odds with their client's interests.

——◦——

The popular distrust of government officials has taken a toll on a political system that requires the collaboration of divergent interests. It is time to dispel the simplistic notion that transparency in government is an unmitigated good and recognize the role of privacy in nurturing honesty, creativity, and collaboration. The United States is and will always be a participatory democracy. Our goal must be to draw an effective line between active engagement and voyeurism. It's good to watch. We just need to allow our public servants the respect to remain clothed while at work.

No reasonable private-sector company would allow itself to operate under the naked and constrained conditions that paralyze government agencies. To turn a profit or to execute an effective strategic plan, businesses need to be nimble and adaptive; messages need to be timely and frank; ideas need to be inventive and collaborative. And if those roaming the halls of federal bureaucracies are spending considerable time worrying that what they put on paper, or on e-mail, will be interpreted by any variety of readers down the line, they are liable to be less responsive to the demands of their office. The Administrative Conference of the United States, looking specifically at the Sunshine Act, agreed, recently concluding that:

A longstanding criticism of the Act has been that, despite its laudable goals, its actual effect is to discourage collaborative deliberations at multi-member agencies, because agency members are reluctant to discuss tentative views in public. Rather than deliberate in public, agencies resort to escape devices, such as holding discussions among groups of fewer than a quorum of the agency's membership (which are not covered by the Act), communicating through staff, exchanging written messages, or deciding matters by "notation voting" (i.e., circulating a proposal and having members vote in writing).

In American democracy, privacy and transparency are partners, not enemies. As we strive to eliminate corruption and increase public engagement, we also have to protect opportunities for creativity and collaboration. The disdain for government combined with the explosion of information technology has conspired to sabotage deliberation in the blind pursuit of disclosure. Meanwhile, our government is frozen in the camera's lights, but at least everyone can watch the show.

CHAPTER 6

True Laboratories of Democracy

It is one of the happy incidents of the federal system that a single cou-
rageous state may, if its citizens choose, serve as a laboratory; and try
novel social and economic experiments without risk to the rest of the
country.

—JUSTICE LOUIS BRANDEIS, SUPREME COURT

Justice Louis Brandeis penned this famous quote at a moment when, mired in the depths of the Great Depression (and frustrated with the Hoover Administration's apparent indifference), Americans were desperate for creative solutions. The better part of a century later, Brandeis's notion that state policies should inform and often lead the national debate remains a foundational tenet of our democracy. And because the Supreme Court icon's turn of phrase conjures up such an appealing image of government—policymakers working like scientists in pursuit of an intellectual breakthrough—it has become one of the most oft-quoted phrases in the public policy lexicon.

Who is not convinced that if politicians attacked social problems with the same fervor and honesty that Einstein used to explore physics, or that baseball GM Billy Beane employed to remake the Oakland A's in the *Moneyball* model, they'd be less prone to screw things up? It's what most Americans want from our leaders—even in today's divided politics. The authority vested in our state governments has created fifty proving grounds where new ideas are developed, refined, and implemented. The federal welfare reforms adopted during President Clinton's second term were an outgrowth of a series of state experiments led by Wisconsin.

Numerous federal environmental standards were first implemented in California, and today an array of state-led health care innovations promises to reduce the spiraling Medicare and Medicaid costs that are driving our national debt. In fact, it is difficult to identify a significant domestic policy that was not first explored and implemented by a state.

At the same time, Brandeis's analogy doesn't make a perfect comparison. While state capitals today are functioning a whole lot better than DC, it's also the case that few state agencies resemble the beehive-like atmosphere of a serious research lab. Anyone who has waited in line for two hours at the DMV only to be told that they have filled out paperwork for the incorrect class of boat trailer knows that local bureaucracies can be just as unwieldy as their analogs in Washington. And it is not as if state capitals are immune from the frustration Americans have with Congress; many of the same conflicts that disrupt collaboration in DC are pervasive across the country.

Fortunately, when the states fall short, there is a federal institution that has, at times, demonstrated the best features of a true laboratory: the legislative committee. Generally, it is assumed that big legislative bodies divvy themselves into discrete panels because no single member can be expected to become an expert on everything. It was James Madison who had foreseen the rise of real expertise in Congress when he wrote in *Federalist No. 53*:

> *A few of the members, as happens in all such assemblies, will possess superior talents; will, by frequent re-elections, become members of long standing; will be thoroughly masters of the public business, and perhaps not unwilling to avail themselves of those advantages.*

But the success of legislative committees is not simply due to members' expertise. They have become a staple of good government because, like laboratories, smaller groups are more conducive to incubating intense, thoughtful collaboration. In seeking to explain Apple's incredible success, author Ken Segall noted, "The small-group principle is deeply woven into the religion of Simplicity. It's key to Apple's ongoing success and key to any organization that wants to nurture quality thinking."

The insight that real work requires intense collaboration and intimate settings is not new to Congress. Several decades before becoming president, a young Professor Woodrow Wilson wrote, "Congress in session is Congress on public exhibition whilst Congress in its committee rooms is Congress at work."

The wisdom of small-group collaboration is widely embraced in contemporary organizational theory. As explained in a Bain and Company report, the key to ensuring that any organization remains dynamic is found in "linking" different elements of an organization so that its constituent parts are sharing ideas and collaborating in harmony. That is the role committees have sometimes played in Washington, each imbued with a sense of camaraderie—even among those on opposing ends of the political spectrum.

For the same reasons that businesses have departments and militaries form platoons, congressional panels are designed to enable the creative and robust ideas that result from the focused blending of varied expertise. The committee system is a competitive enterprise. Each panel is established to compete on behalf of a constituency for limited federal resources, limited legislative time, and limited public attention. At many times in our history, these bonds have made committee affiliation as important as party affiliation.

Americans embrace bipartisanship because they correctly believe that legislation that appeals to politicians on both sides of the aisle will amount to better and more resilient public policy. In their ideal form, congressional committees offer forums where that sort of policy innovation can thrive. If states are the institutions best equipped to experiment with novel policy ideas, committees are the places in our federal system where those ideas are most likely to bubble up. And to that end, congressional panels are a crucial mechanism for harnessing the resilience of American diversity.

WHO'S THE BOSS?

The struggle for power between party leaders and committee chairs has been a defining feature of our legislative process for over a century. Before 1911, the House was largely dominated by the Speaker's gavel, in part because the Speaker wielded direct control over who would serve on each panel. The term "Czar Speaker" emerged because Thomas Reed and Joseph Cannon, who each served in the top job near the turn of the twentieth century, were practically unchallenged in their perches. But members eventually rose up to challenge the leadership's strong hand. Motivated to rein in abuses of power, rank-and-file members embraced reforms designed to give the committees additional autonomy. Historian Joseph Cooper noted this shift when he wrote:

> *[As a result of these reforms,] House committees and committee chairs became more independent and powerful than they had been even in the decades that preceded czar rule. Chairmanship positions were transformed into personal property rights because seniority in the years after 1911 became inviolate in order to avoid exacerbating internal party divisions. In addition, chairmen inherited the plenary power over committee agendas, proceedings, and organization they had enjoyed in past years when they had, not unreasonably, been assumed to be responsible agents of the House and majority party.*

Once empowered, the movement toward greater committee independence grew steadily through the following decades, provoked in part by the growth in federal programs that Congress was obligated to oversee. As Washington's mandate grew through the course of FDR's New Deal, congressional leadership simply couldn't keep up and committees became the venue for the majority of congressional oversight. The existing committee structure quickly proved to be inadequate to the task so Senator Robert La Follette Jr. (R-WI) and Representative Mike Monroney (D-KS) set out to fundamentally restructure the committee process.

At the time, conventional wisdom suggested that there were at least three things wrong with Congress. First, there were too many committees: Legislative panels had proliferated to the point of absurdity. Second, committee authority was poorly defined: Bills introduced in each house of Congress weren't always understood to be in the exclusive jurisdiction of any one committee; Executive Branch agencies were rarely accountable to any one panel; and the committees themselves rarely had enough staff.

Finally, the committees had grown to be too large and unwieldy: With too many members on any given panel, it was impossible to build any sort of collaborative environment. The explosion of committees was undermining each panel's ability to do the public's business. And so LaFollette and Monroney created a Joint Committee on the Organization of Congress, to which they were subsequently appointed co-chairs.

After months of work and negotiation, many of the Joint Committee's recommendations were woven into the Legislative Reorganization Act of 1946. It was not ideal, but they were able to streamline the system and clarify each committee's scope of authority. The four-dozen panels then serving in the House were reduced to nineteen; the number of Senate committees was more than halved; individual committees were given exclusive jurisdiction over discrete issues; and a limit was set on the number of panels any individual member could join.

Truman's signature of the 1946 Legislative Reorganization Act opened one of the most productive eras in American political history. Over the following three decades, committees became productive engines of public policy, broadly independent of each chamber's floor leadership. In turn, many of the legislative panels developed cultures of their own and formed a camaraderie that, in many cases, was as close as the ties members had to their party or state delegation.

———

Those who sat together on the dais invariably spent time together, traveled in groups, and relaxed in the committee anterooms. Committee members embraced and guarded their unique responsibility for a slice of public policy. Never was that more clear than in the early Cold War period. As the scholar Julian Zelizer explained:

> [During the 1950s and 1960s,] people who would serve for a decade or more in the same position and develop very thick personal networks and institutional knowledge over the course of their period. . . . By the time [Lyndon] Johnson was President most of the committee leaders, most of the leadership, had already fought over issues such as civil rights and Medicare. They knew how they ticked, they knew a lot about

their opponents and their allies. And the informal ties that bound this
family of legislators . . . often facilitated negotiations within the House
and within the Senate.

That is not to suggest that committees were solely responsible for the productive bipartisanship that prevailed through so much of the postwar period. As many conservatives have noted, Democrats enjoyed near complete control over both houses of Congress for all but a handful of years between 1946 and 1994. In their eyes, this period was less about bipartisan collaboration and more about Republicans' acquiescence. Robert Kuttner, founder of the liberal magazine, *The American Prospect*, has acknowledged that in the 1960s, Democrats often defined the agenda and Republicans just "offered a pale, me-too imitation." And it was no small fact that conservative Democrats and Rockefeller Republicans, two groups that claimed large memberships throughout the early postwar years, agreed on much more across the aisle than the more polarized partisans who dominate their respective caucuses today.

Still, this period of committee dominance coincided with a remarkable record of legislative accomplishment. Between 1947 and 1980, the number of laws passed by any given two-year Congress never fell below five hundred, rising to over one thousand between 1955 and 1956. Admittedly, not all of those laws were of real legislative import—some among the litany were pieces of commemorative legislation (many like "National Dairy Goat Milk Awareness Month," and "National Clown Week" were banned after Republicans took control of the House in 1995). However, during this thirty-three-year span, Congress enabled both national prosperity and social mobility. The government deregulated vast industries while strengthening the safety net and confronted racial and ethnic injustice while staring down the Soviet Union. Without exception, these legislative achievements were stoked in the furnace of congressional committees.

RUNNING OUT THE BULLS

The most recent Congress (112th) passed only 283 laws, including numerous post office dedications, legislative extensions, and technical

corrections. But they achieved little of significance, and hardly any substantive legislation moved through the regular committee process. Though
committees continue to hold hearings and occasionally debate legislation,
their engines no longer purr, and in many cases the air has leaked out of
the tires. To understand how the once potent committee process deteriorated, we have to return to the golden years.

Not long after the Legislative Reorganization Act of 1946 was signed
into law, members *without* committee authority under the new regime
began to chafe. Most frustrating for the rank and file, chairmen's terms
were almost unlimited and an obstinate chairman could hold up legislation indefinitely and for almost any reason. If, for example, the chairman
of the Judiciary Committee didn't like a bill on criminal law that was supported by the broad majority of his peers, he could simply choose not to
schedule it for consideration, leaving very little anyone could do to press
the case.

In broad strokes, that is why civil rights legislation was so difficult to
enact during the 1950s and 1960s. Democrats enjoyed a near monopoly
on political power below the Mason-Dixon Line. Impervious to defeat,
many southern Democrats rose through the ranks to acquire powerful
committee posts. From these unshakable perches, a small number of
southern Democrats were obstructing the civil rights agenda. Once again,
rank-and-file members rose up in frustration, but this time the target
of reform was not the leadership—it was the committee chairmen. In
1959, the Democratic Study Group (DSG) began working with reform-
minded Republicans to modify the House rules. In 1965, after an intense
period of wrangling with the Old Bulls (as the southern chairmen came
to be called), the reformers managed to push through a "committee bill
of rights." This reform package returned some power back to the rest of
the committee by restricting a chairman's ability to tie up legislation or
protect a bill from any amendments on the floor. Slowly, but surely, the
reformers were gaining steam.

Then history intervened and the reform movement took off like a
runaway train.

On June 17, 1972, five burglars were caught inside Democratic National
Headquarters at the Watergate building in downtown Washington. The

resulting constitutional crisis provoked by President Nixon's effort to withhold information would dramatically alter the relationship between Congress and the White House. It also propelled major changes in the legislative branch. The 1974 elections brought a huge class of young Democrats to Congress. The group, known colloquially as the "Watergate Babies," was determined to send a message to the old guard. They were indignant and what they did to shake things up was fairly crafty.

The authority to appoint Democratic members to committee slots had been wielded by members of Congress's influential tax-writing panel, the Ways and Means Committee. This practice prevented the Speaker (who was thought to be more directly answerable to rank-and-file members) from shaping the committee rosters. The reformers saw that process as an opening for change: They pushed through a rule that shifted appointment authority to a new Democratic Steering Committee, chaired by the Speaker. Then the reformers took a few scalps for good measure, deposing three longtime chairmen from the South—two Texans and a Louisianan.

By the mid-1970s, there was no mistaking which way the House was heading. The new Speakers weren't nearly as powerful as their predecessors had been at the turn of the century. But there was a growing consensus that the best way to prevent future abuses of power was to shift even more control from the select to the whole, from committees to the floor.

THE HAMMER GRABS THE GAVEL

By most respects, the reformers of the 1960s and 1970s were very successful in pulling power away from entrenched committee chairs. But, those expecting that power would flow back to the floors of the Senate and the House were in for a surprise. It is almost impossible for any group of dozens, much less *hundreds* of members, to work in real harmony. The chaos of any big group forces participants to fall into greater lockstep with their leaders. *More voices consolidate the power of a single voice.* And so, the House Speaker and the Senate majority leader, rather than the rank and file, ended up with the bulk of the Old Bulls' power.

Central power provided its share of advantages. It is now much easier to hold an individual member (namely the Speaker or the majority leader) responsible for how each house of Congress performs. However, the new model, whereby party leadership runs the show, tends to prioritize national politics over the interests of each committee. When greater power was vested in the chairmen and their gavels, committee agendas were generally dominated by the substantive and often regional interests of their distinct constituencies: Members of the Agriculture Committee, for example, tended to promote the interests of farmers, regardless of their party affiliation. They were legislators first, party members second.

By attempting to return power to the floor, the progressive-minded reforms championed by Democrats through the 1970s inadvertently put politics back at center stage. Floor leaders were (and are) focused on growing the size of their respective caucuses, not the vested interests of any given constituency. And so, over time, the sort of committee camaraderie that had defined so much of the early postwar period began to fade.

Some of the shift began when Democratic House Speaker Jim Wright took greater control of the legislative agenda during the mid-1980s. But the full weight of the transformation wasn't apparent until Speaker Gingrich took the helm in 1994. After leading the charge to install the first Republican majority since 1948, Gingrich expanded the authority of his office by naming his choices for committee chairmen before his fellow Republicans had even met. A few years later, the Republican House majority leader Tom DeLay—true to his nickname "The Hammer"—made clear that committee chairmen either followed leadership's agenda or risked losing their gavels. And so, by the 2000s, even the pretense of committee autonomy had been removed.

House leadership also moved to restrict members' ability to amend legislation during the voting process. In the early 1980s, only a fifth of House bills were protected from amendments using what is known as a "closed rule." But under Speaker Wright, the number of closed rules tripled such that two-thirds of all legislation was cooked by leadership and sent to the floor for an up-or-down vote. Since then, under the leadership of both parties rank-and-file legislators have had little real opportunity to shape legislation either in committee or on the floor.

THE SPORK EFFECT

While the role of committees has been largely defined by the competition for power between congressional leaders and committee chairmen, the structure of the committee system has also cycled between brief periods of clarity and longer stretches of chaos. In the mid-1940s, reformers like LaFollette and Monroney successfully argued that a key to legislative productivity was to limit the number and size of committees. To increase engagement, expertise, and shared mission, they had set hard limits on the numbers of slots per committee and sought to focus committee jurisdictions. But in the years that followed, committee rosters and missions began to creep. The world was changing rapidly and there were several hundred members of Congress who wanted to control some piece of it. The number of committee seats in the House of Representatives doubled from roughly five hundred in 1947 to nearly one thousand in the 1980s. Roughly the same thing happened in the Senate. The number of subcommittees also began to grow almost immediately after the 1946 reforms. In the Senate and the House the number of subcommittees doubled between 1947 and 1973. In Congress today, most House committees have a minimum of five subcommittees and many have more. For example, Appropriations has twelve separate subcommittees and Armed Services has seven. And like the move to return more power to the rank and file, the proliferation of panels serving beneath the committees cut at the power wielded by the committees themselves. It was rarely clear whether the job of working through a policy challenge should fall to the committee or its subordinate. And the effect, according to Princeton professor Julian Zelizer, was to bolster "legislative fragmentation," thereby increasing the "uncertainty of policy outcomes."

Finally, there were the battles between the committees themselves. The jurisdictional outline crafted in 1946 had been aligned to fit with the government bureaucracies of the day. But, of course, the federal bureaucracy refused to stand still. Issues once comfortably resting within the jurisdiction of a single committee often expanded into the purview of others. Executive Branch agencies once subject to a single committee's oversight morphed into bureaucracies whose responsibilities spilled out into several jurisdictions. Predictably, the result was confusion and conflict, resolved sometimes by mutual agreement, but more often by the issuance of "joint" jurisdiction. The blurring of authority created competition over popular issues (generally defined by publicity and fundraising potential)—with often disabling results. For example, FBI director Robert S. Mueller III noted that while the cyber threat could soon eclipse the terrorist threat, the seven congressional committees claiming jurisdiction over the issue couldn't even agree which federal agency should be responsible for addressing it. The broadening of agendas also reduces expertise creating a "spork effect," in which committees sought to serve multiple functions but none very well.

These problems came into sharp focus during the financial collapse of 2008, when Congress was resolved to address the roots of the worsening recession. Hard as it is to believe, oversight over derivatives, which many blamed for the near ruin of our financial system, didn't fall exclusively under the jurisdiction of the Senate Finance or Banking Committees. Because derivatives had long been used to help farmers hedge against commodity price fluctuations, they remained largely under the control of the Agriculture Committee, of all places. Imagine: The Senate was debating one of the most important and complex provisions of a bill meant to stave off another financial collapse, and responsibility was imbued in a committee whose principal expertise is farming.

The same problem was made evident, more infamously, in the wake of 9/11. After Congress reorganized the nation's national security apparatus, moving a whole swath of agencies under the control of the newly created Department of Homeland Security, the 9/11 Commission noted that the new cabinet-level bureaucracy was subject to the oversight of dozens of congressional panels. In turn, the commissioners declared in 2004 that "Congressional oversight for intelligence—and counterterrorism—is now dysfunctional . . . Congress should create a single principal point of oversight and review for homeland security."

But Congress never managed to reorganize itself in any real way and so, in the decade since, things have only gotten worse: As of 2012, the department whose job it is to protect our homeland was responsible to a daunting 108 panels. As the former chairmen of the 9/11 Commission and current leaders of BPC's Homeland Security Project, former governor

Tom Kean and former congressman Lee Hamilton wrote recently in the *New York Times*:

> In the 112th Congress, which ended in January [2013], Homeland Security personnel took part in 289 formal House and Senate hearings, involving 28 committees, caucuses and commissions. In 2009 alone, Homeland Security personnel spent the equivalent of 66 work-years responding to questions from Congress, at an estimated cost to taxpayers of $10 million.

It is not melodramatic to conclude that overlapping committee jurisdictions is undermining the efficiency of our national security apparatus, delaying adoption of critical new protections, and endangering American lives.

Congress has essentially come full circle. From a period of nearly unmitigated floor power in the early 1900s, to a period of overwhelming committee autonomy during the 1950s and 1960s, the legislative branch is now controlled by a select few. "Mission creep" has become "mission leap," undermining the efficiency of both congressional oversight and the development of legislation. Having ridden the extremes of Czar Speakers and Bull Chairmen to their logical and destructive conclusions, could there be a new era that borrows some of the best elements of each approach?

CLOSED MEETING/OPEN BAR

Committee membership is not nearly as important today as it once was in defining a politician's identity and reputation. Beyond a few powerful committee chairs, few people even know which committees their representatives serve on. All too frequently, slots are now used to enhance fundraising prowess, allowing junior members with little influence on the legislative agenda to secure support from moneyed interests. Noticeably absent is any sense that newly assigned committee members are welcomed into any sort of fraternity.

Both these factors were evident in 2009, when Congressman Paul Kanjorski (D-PA) called me at the BPC. Kanjorski was then the chairman of the House Subcommittee on Capital Markets, Insurance, and

Government-Sponsored Enterprises. The financial crisis was in full bloom and Kanjorski needed help. A colorful but plain spoken man, Kanjorski noted that many members on his forty-nine-member subcommittee were in their first or second terms, had been placed there to help them fundraise, and would not know what a derivative was if it bit them on their posterior. The chairman wanted to find an effective way to educate his members—but he was also eager to build some sense of camaraderie among the unwieldy group given responsibility for rescuing key elements of our financial system from near meltdown. After enlisting the support of the ranking Republican on the committee, New Jersey's Scott Garrett, Kanjorski asked if the BPC would host a series of "off the record" dinners in which members of their committee could hear from leading figures in the field. Over the course of the next five months, we convened six dinners at the Washington Court Hotel—a congenial setting most noteworthy for its proximity to the House office buildings. Each was attended by a politically balanced group of about thirty members of the committee; nearly every one of the roughly four dozen members attended at least one of the sessions.

Members of the congressmen's senior staff were also invited, but relegated to a separate table. No press of any kind was allowed to attend. Speakers included Treasury secretary Tim Geithner, former Federal Reserve chairmen Paul Volcker and Alan Greenspan, former Federal Reserve vice chair Alan Blinder, SEC chairwoman Mary Schapiro, former acting chairman of the Commodities Futures Trading Commission Sharon Brown-Hruska, JP Morgan CEO Jamie Dimon, and Jim Simons, founder of Renaissance Technologies hedge fund and one of the originators of mathematically driven "quant" investing.

Though the committee members had not changed, the atmosphere in the room was profoundly different from the acrimony that often dominated committee hearings. Instead of the staged seating and formality of committee hearings, Democrats and Republicans were mixed around the tables. There were no opening statements and none of the posturing that dominates formal hearing procedures. Members came to ask real questions, learn from experts, and hear what their colleagues had to say. Before and after each session, there was an open bar, and after each formal program concluded, a good number of members and staff stayed on to continue the discussion and get to know one another. In a press statement describing the discussion process, Chairman Kanjorski wrote: "It is with the help of our speakers at these events that this subcommittee can learn to openly discuss, and then hopefully act in a bipartisan way to come to some sort of consensus on many of the important financial issues affecting our country."

While Kanjorski and Garrett were able to develop bipartisan legislation on a complex set of topics, the bridges built were not strong enough to prevent polarization from overtaking the political response to the financial crisis. The ultimate law, commonly referred to as "Dodd-Frank," was passed on a party-line vote in the House. Nevertheless, the BPC's efforts with Kanjorski, Garrett, and their colleagues demonstrated the enthusiasm that members have for engaging in meaningful deliberation when given the opportunity. Think what Congress might do if that were the norm, and not the rare exception or experiment.

FORUMS OF FUTILITY

Unfortunately, even when committees do collaborate and produce bipartisan legislation, the floor leaders have no compunction about ignoring even those bills that are successfully voted out of committee. The field of energy policy, where I have focused over the past twenty years, offers several examples of the inefficiency of the committee structure and the heavy-handedness of congressional leadership. It provides a particularly interesting case study as the Senate Energy Committee remained productive until just a few years ago. In 2005 and 2007, the Senate Energy Committee successfully crafted major pieces of legislation that passed the full Senate with broad bipartisan support and were signed by the president. Unfortunately, since 2008 the committee has become far more polarized, particularly on issues like climate change.*

In the Senate, the challenge of regulating carbon (the element most responsible for climate change) is divided in a manner that would make

---

* The successes enjoyed in 2005 and 2007 followed on a failed Republican effort in 2003 to pass a bill without any support from across the aisle. As then–Energy Committee chairman Pete Domenici's staff now acknowledges, the chairman's commitment to working with the committee's ranking member, Jeff Bingaman (their roles were switched in 2007) was driven by a recognition that bipartisan efforts tended to be more successful.

even Rube Goldberg wince. The oversight of fossil fuels *before* they are burned is generally understood to be within the purview of the Senate Energy Committee, while legislation designed to handle the carbon that results from the burning of fossil fuels is the domain of the Environment and Public Works Committee.* To the atmosphere, this was a distinction without a difference; but to the senators, committee staff, and interest groups, the lines of distinction define, still to this day, the strategic terrain of energy and climate legislation.

In 2005, the National Commission on Energy Policy (NCEP) that I directed was working with a politically diverse group of energy company executives, environmental advocates, and scientists to propose a new mandatory (but comparably modest) national cap on greenhouse gas emissions. At the time, the Senate Energy Committee was led by Democrat Jeff Bingaman and Republican Pete Domenici—two legislators from New Mexico known for their ability to make a deal. The Environment and Public Works Committee was led by senators Barbara Boxer (D-CA) and Jim Inhofe (R-OK), who were, to put it mildly, diametrically opposed on most issues of concern.

Common sense dictated that it would be more productive for us to draft a proposal that would fall within the jurisdiction of the Energy Committee, lest it be caught up in the dysfunctional warfare between Senators Inhofe and Boxer. We had to craft a policy that placed the regulatory obligation on the carbon content of the fuel *before* it was combusted, as opposed to placing the restriction on big smokestacks or vehicle tailpipes. In addition to considering what policy would be most effective, we were constrained to craft the approach that would land us in a productive forum. Not surprisingly, congressional leaders often point to the ills of "forum-shopping" as a basis for ignoring the committees altogether—a baby with the bathwater proposition if there ever was one.

A similar circumstance prevails on the other side of the Capitol. In 2007, House Speaker Nancy Pelosi (D-CA) was intent on imposing a cap on carbon emissions. Speaker Pelosi had been through many battles with Energy and Commerce Committee chairman John Dingell, a Michigan

---

* Four other Senate Committees—Foreign Relations, Commerce, Transportation, and Finance—each assert primary jurisdiction over a substantial aspect of of the climate change debate.

Democrat whose views of good policy often varied significantly from her own. To bypass Dingell's authority, Pelosi established a temporary committee, chaired by a more progressive member, to handle the issue beyond Dingell's reach.* When that committee failed, Pelosi supported her ideological ally Henry Waxman in his successful effort to depose Dingell of his committee perch.

While Pelosi's tactics succeeded in pushing her preferred bill through the House (on a party line vote), the legislation never had a chance in the Senate. In the House, a quarter of all the supportive votes came from New York and California. In the Senate, the best these two states could marshal was 4 percent. Moreover, the economy was in free-fall, the White House was focused on health care, and there simply wasn't the confidence, courage, or political capital to do something so big and divisive.

However, there had been another option. Over the preceding months, the Senate Energy Committee had been hard at work on a bill of its own. Led at the time by Chairman Bingaman and ranking member Lisa Murkowski (R-AK), the committee had negotiated a bill that had support from both sides of the aisle. It did not contain an overall national limit on greenhouse gas emissions—but it did contain an array of hard fought measures that would have advanced the climate and clean energy agenda, including a nationwide mandate that 15 percent of all electricity be generated by renewable resources. The committee legislation had been developed over the course of thirty-nine staff briefings, twenty formal committee hearings, and eleven open business meetings. But because a group of senators *outside* the committee was trying to put together a more aggressive alternative to the legislation, the Democratic leadership let the committee's bill twist in the wind.

It is a sad and unfortunately common story. When the outside-committee effort finally stalled, it was too late for the committee's original proposal to be considered on the Senate floor. As Senator Byron Dorgan (D-ND), lamented, "the result was a huge disappointment to those of us who believed the energy bill we passed out of the committee on a bipartisan vote would have been a big step in the direction of producing more

---

* Eventually, Dingell convinced the Speaker not to give the special committee any actual legislative authority, further dooming the effort.

energy, using less energy and emphasizing the clean, renewable energy sources that would reduce the threat of global warming." After all the effort that went into the committee process, the whole effort died on the vine, sacrificing an opportunity that was years in the making and unlikely to come back anytime soon.

It is no wonder that members are frustrated. While committees played such a big role in the productivity of the postwar years, things have swung sharply the other way. Legislative panels today simply can't get much done. Having been sapped of their authority by leadership, members are rarely compelled to invest the time or focus required to forge real solutions.

Gang Warfare

Largely because Congress has become so unproductive, a new phenomenon has emerged over the last decade in the Senate: the proliferation of "gangs." Democrats and Republicans are choosing more frequently to collaborate outside of committees to craft the compromises that committees once authored. In each case, members working largely against both the leadership and the committee chairs seek to forge agreements that will propel leadership to act. It is instructive that these associations of legislators are not called "groups," "clubs," or "teams" but feel compelled to form a gang to protect themselves—principally from their own party leaders and aggravated committee chairs. I suppose we should take heart that they are not referred to as "mobs."

The prevalence of "gangs" has exploded most notably in the Senate. The Gang of Fourteen (seven Democrats and seven Republicans) helped to avert a crisis in 2005 over judicial nominations during the Bush Administration (a compromise that was obviated by the Democrats' invocation of the nuclear option in 2013). The "Gang of Six" (three and three) tried to avert the fiscal cliff near the end of President Obama's first term.

While senatorial "gangs" have been highly effective at framing and advocating for broad agreements more often than not, the legislative gang creates more political heat than actual legislative light. For all that they're celebrated, rogue bipartisan groupings rarely succeed, if only because they're seen as competitors by committee chairs and congressional leaders.

While the Gang of Fourteen managed to prevent the Senate majority leader from invoking the so-called "nuclear option" at the time, the proposals adopted by the Gang of Six were lost in the shuffle and a variety of recent extramural efforts to work out a budget deal never got off the runway.

The proliferation of these impromptu collaborations is a symptom of well-meaning reforms that have upended the committee process. However, the gang phenomenon also represents real hope in demonstrating the clear and often courageous desire of many legislators to collaborate. Congressional leadership must find a way to capture this productive energy and channel it back into the formal committee system.

A MODEST PROPOSAL

In an ideal world, Congress would undertake a major reorganization like that undertaken in 1946 and 1970. A lot has changed since 1970—the Internet, the fall of the Soviet Empire and the rise of Mainland China, the tragedy of 9/11. It is far past time to adapt our congressional committees to the realities of the twenty-first century. Short of wholesale restructuring—which is unlikely—there is an option that combines the prerogative of leadership with the inspiration of the gangs and the authority of the committees: At the outset of each session of Congress, the leaders of the House and Senate—the Speaker and minority leader from the House, and the Senate majority and minority leaders—could meet to select a couple of issues that they would designate for a "special" congressional focus over the ensuing two years. Like a sequestered jury, the four figures would meet behind closed doors every other December or January in the pursuit of a deal that respected the interests and political imperatives for all four caucuses.

They wouldn't specifically resolve *how* the "special" issues would be addressed—indeed, they wouldn't even develop an outline for substantive legislation. They would simply draft a rule, to be presented to both chambers, which would provide special two-year jurisdictional exemptions for the topics selected, mandating that each topic be resolved by a discrete ad hoc committee whose mandate would expire upon the next election. Each of these special ad hoc committees would glean an exclusive mandate over their issue, the latitude to hire an expert staff, and the guarantee that their report would be given timely consideration on the House and Senate floors.

Once the four leaders announced their joint proposal, both houses of Congress would meet in closed session to debate its merits. No staff would be invited, and the leadership-sponsored proposals would be considered *en banc*, meaning that each chamber would have to accept or reject all of the ad hoc committees together—an all-or-nothing proposition with no substitutions or dining off the menu. Once the closed-door debate was concluded, a privileged vote (no amendments permitted) would be taken on each floor. A simple majority would be required in both chambers. If enacted, the leaders would then nominate chairs and members to be ratified, by the standard rules, by each caucus.

We might expect that the president would get involved at some point, suggesting that a certain White House priority be made the subject of one of the ad hoc committees. Maybe the leadership would announce their intentions after consulting with the White House right before the State of the Union Address, and closed House and Senate meetings would commence the following day. What is almost guaranteed in this proposal is that the combination of subjects of ad hoc committee jurisdiction would be politically palatable to both parties because either side could spike a deal that seemed unfair. The Democratic leaders might not accept an ad hoc committee to focus on Medicare reform if the Republicans refused a focus on infrastructure investment, and vice versa. And if the leaders were unable to come to an agreement, the proposal would simply die.

There would certainly be challenges to creating a system of ad hoc committees. After all, the super-committee designed to craft a comprehensive solution to the nation's budget problems in 2011 failed to come to any agreement. There would be fights about how to pick members, and the ability of standing committees to develop rapport across the aisle would be more hit-or-miss with assignments of a shortened duration. But, in the long run, those challenges could likely be overcome. While it is natural for incumbents to be suspicious of reform, congressional leadership should see some value in co-opting the gang mentality and putting it to work toward actual legislation.

Unlike the super-committee, which was tasked with reforming the entire federal budget over the course of three months with almost no staff support or clear rules of engagement, these ad hoc committees would not be sent up roaring rivers with no paddles. Instead, they would work on more focused questions for a full two years with the support of expert staff drawn from other committees and members' personal staff. Moreover, the goal would be to find complex issues that transcend single committee jurisdiction and require a priority focus—like cybersecurity or disaster relief—as opposed to the super-committee, which was established in large part as political cover for the latest congressional budget failure.

Finally, the very act of seeking to establish legislative priorities at the outset of each congressional session could have a number of appealing benefits. Obviously, the ability of Congress to successfully establish a few bipartisan priorities would make progress much more likely. But even in years when there were no major agreements, the ideas themselves and the conversations had between members would surely be of some value. Even the question, "I wonder if Congress is going to work on anything together this year?" would be a welcome intrusion into the cacophony of base-pleasing mayhem that dominates the current twenty-four-hour news cycle. While these debates might only occasionally result in focused and successful legislative efforts, at least Congress would be arguing about something that mattered.

CALENDAR WEDNESDAYS

Congress would also do well to tip the balance of power back to where it was during the years when it was more productive. While being cognizant of the problems that emerged to spur the reforms of the 1960s and 1970s, we should re-empower the standing committees and the powerful members who chair them.

However, any fundamental effort to breathe new life into these weakened panels needs to be grounded in two realizations. First, politicians will only devote their time and energy to institutions that reward their investment. Second, the quality of committee collaboration is directly related to familiarity members have with one another. So making committees work again, and molding the rhythms of legislative life so members spend more time together, would go a long way toward resuscitating the dysfunctional status quo.

There's reason to believe that the committees can be re-enlivened. Even with all the changes that have befallen the committee system over the last several decades, chairmanships remain the plum at the end of any long-term congressional career. Whoever holds the gavel sets the agenda, and members still spend decades running for re-election in the hopes of eventually rising to the top spot on a given panel.

One way to make committee service more alluring would be to tie a member's effectiveness to the odds that he or she would get a gavel. Today, chairmanships are generally awarded to those with some combination of seniority and fundraising prowess. While winning elections and raising money are important signals of political skill, they should not be confused with actual public service. There's little recognition for those who develop innovative policy solutions, create a collaborative mood that respects members' different values, or thoughtfully engage experts. Members are frequently loath to attend a committee session absent some auxiliary benefit, like the opportunity to champion a local cause. As a result, many hearings convey an enthusiasm reminiscent of summer school or traffic court.

Hearings have become theatrical events staged for the cameras, rather than meaty discussions of national priorities. Former member of Congress Phil Sharp (D-IN) describes hearings as events in which Congress gathers leading experts and then lectures them for two hours with opening statements and leading questions written by staff to reinforce their bosses' existing positions. The experts are not there to share what they know but to refract and reflect the politicians themselves. This sad state of affairs highlights an opportunity: If the leadership of *both* parties agreed to make committee attendance an element in assignments and selecting the next chairmen, members might well be more inclined to stick around. And they might get to know one another in the process.

The committees would also be energized if we invigorated their weakened chairs. No one wants a return of the imperious Old Bulls, but it was absolute power that made them dangerous, not power itself. A good step would be to empower committee chairs to do things while not enabling them to simply bottle things up.

For example, bills passed out of committee by large enough majorities should be placed *automatically* on a calendar that propels them to floor consideration without delay. There already exists a mechanism in the House called "Calendar Wednesday" that allows chairmen to force bills to the floor without the leadership's acquiescence. But the power dynamics are such today that any committee chair threatening to pull a stunt like that risks retaliation from the Speaker. Moving bills with strong committee backing to the floor would strengthen the committee chairs and increase the engagement of committee members who have grown weary of a process that has little chance of shaping outcomes. None of these reforms would pass without controversy; they all threaten the status quo, and each would be met with resistance from members worried that the changes would imperil their own authority. But there's an important and powerful feature working in the other direction: boredom.

Senator Chuck Schumer (D-NY) and Lamar Alexander (R-TN) have been working to resurrect a more open and dynamic legislative process. Schumer describes their joint motivation. "I've only been here 14 years," Schumer says, "and Alexander's been there about 11, but we were there, both of us were there, and remember when the Senate used to legislate and thoroughly enjoyed it and wish it would return."

Politicians who put in the time, energy, and sacrifice to win elections want the opportunity to affect policy when they get to Capitol Hill; by today's standards, they haven't got it *and they know it*. Returning the committees to a position of real influence might just instigate a virtuous cycle: members would want to attend committee meetings because they would know that time on the dais was well spent; the committees themselves would become more cohesive and productive; and the leadership would benefit from the fact that the committees were producing more pragmatic and substantive legislation.

THE SENATE'S MUSCLE MEMORY

In early 2013, Congress took up an issue long mired in contention: immigration reform. The debate had been subject to fits and starts for the better part of a decade—most notably when a promising proposal from President Bush was narrowly upended in 2007. But following the 2012 presidential campaign, the reform movement was given new life. A "gang" of eight senators crafted a compromise proposal. It was introduced in the Senate, and then referred to the Judiciary Committee. The unusual influence of this gang was enabled by the fact that many of the participants were also members of the Judiciary Committee, which has clear jurisdiction over immigration reform. After a series of Judiciary Committee hearings, the bill was scheduled for proper consideration.

The immigration markup that followed in May 2013 was a throwback to a bygone era. Over the course of several days and nights, scores of amendments were offered, considered, adopted, or dismissed. It was a vision of what Washington looks like in the mind's eye: a spontaneous, substantive, thoughtful display of legislating. Senators debated and sparred over the bill's key provisions; alliances were forged and strained. And after three hundred amendments were introduced and considered by the Judiciary Committee—over a third of which were adopted—the bill was reported to the Senate floor on a bipartisan vote of 14–4.

It was, for many observers, an indication that the Senate still had some muscle memory from the old days. The hours-long sessions had many of the committee's aides more excited about working on Capitol Hill than they had ever been before. Even for many opposed to the underlying bill, it was a refreshing display of Congress at work. From that momentary glimmer, two things were clear.

First, the well of bipartisanship in Washington is not entirely dry. Given the right circumstances, ideologically divergent senators from the two parties are perfectly capable of working together. Moreover, it seems as if both senators and staff genuinely enjoyed the art of legislating. It is some comfort that the negative campaigning, constant fundraising, and petty behavior that defines current politics can still be described as the regrettable evils of a system capable of real progress.

Second, the immigration markup revealed that the secret to re-enlivening congressional committees is to re-imbue them with real responsibility. The hours that members of the Senate Judiciary Committee spent sitting around wooden tables debating the details of various amendments were hours they couldn't spend dialing for dollars—something that is an essential but burdensome aspect in everyday congressional life. But the senators were willing to pay the opportunity cost because the issues being debated really mattered. The bill they passed onto the floor would almost surely be debated by the full Senate. And whatever bill the House and Senate might agree on would be significantly affected by the final draft that came out of committee.

Some may wonder whether changing the rhythms of committee life could really breathe new life into Congress. It is a fair question, if only because we're so accustomed to the vitriol that dominates cable television. But our experience at the Bipartisan Policy Center has pierced the presumption of dysfunction. On issue upon issue, we've built projects designed to replicate the committee process of old: Stakeholders with various viewpoints—each carrying a combination of political commitments, economic interests, and policy expertise—are brought together on a task force and challenged to produce detailed consensus recommendations.

In many cases, those sitting on the task force are at ideological odds. But like in the committees of old, after developing a certain rapport and engaging in some focused and extensive dialogue, they've nearly always managed to come to an agreement. In the rare cases where time constraints or other obstacles prevent our participants from forging real bonds, the willingness to stray from party or interest-group orthodoxy is notably diminished.

Of course, the BPC isn't Congress, and those who serve on our projects don't have to worry about the wrath of angry primary voters back home. The BPC often chooses to hold project meetings behind closed doors, cognizant of the fact that anything that is put on stage becomes a play. Our experience argues strongly that the current congressional polarization is a function of individual nature and institutional nurture. By and large, successful politicians are people pleasers. They have finely tuned radar to external environments. Often, the system in place has much greater effect on the success of negotiations than the issue at stake or the individuals leading the discussion.

By allowing Congress's committees to decay, we've eliminated or shrunk the spaces where legislators can deliberate; even worse, we have diminished the expectation that they *even should*. We have also concentrated power in the leadership, who have disproportionate incentives to amplify party orthodoxy and drive wedge issues.

Put simply, we have replaced a highly productive structure driven by a combination of political, regional, and substantive incentives with a poor structure driven principally by political incentives. Add a few flawed individuals and faulty rules to the mix and the result is pervasive gridlock.

CHAPTER 7

Breakfast at Signatures

THE FIRST LAW OF HOLES

There are few contemporary political figures more universally reviled than Jack Abramoff. Since the Watergate era, no single player has more completely epitomized the spirit of political corruption. From his booth at Signatures, the expensive restaurant he owned on Pennsylvania Avenue, Abramoff subverted the public interest with an uncommon proficiency. After a decade of repugnant schemes including a disgraceful effort to defraud Native American tribes, Abramoff's house of corruption came crashing down. In 2006, he pled guilty to fraud, tax evasion, and conspiracy to bribe public officials.

Released from prison in 2010, Abramoff is now touring the country as a vocal critic of his own past deeds. But crookedness casts a long shadow in American politics. While Jack has moved on, the system he violated is still suffering in his wake. Abramoff's deceit affirmed the public's worst fears about Washington. For Congress as an institution, the scandal was bad; for the country as a whole, the over-corrections it triggered have been even worse.

Before and after Abramoff's fall, advocates for good government have made real progress changing the way American politics works. Over the last several decades, Washington has imposed significant limits on campaign fundraising, substantially strengthened ethics laws, made sure no one has any fun on congressional fact-finding trips, and eliminated earmarks—the popular local projects once used to soften the political pain of hard votes.

Yet if, in the spirit of the late Mayor Ed Koch, Washington was to ask the country "how are we doing?" the objective answer would be "terribly." Despite the string of "good government" victories, the director of CNN's polling unit recently stated that "men, women, rich, poor, young, old, all think [2014's] Congress has been the worst they can remember." While it would be exaggerated to argue that recent reforms are responsible for the current state of affairs, it is pretty hard to claim that these restrictions have increased congressional productivity or enhanced public confidence.

The public naturally assumes that any effort to make Congress more ethical would only be for the good. But what we find when looking at the reforms of the last several years is that they're as much a source of our frustration as the cure. Abramoff-style corruption, while egregious, simply isn't that common. As a rule, it is ineffective to control rule-breakers by adopting more rules. All the proliferation of restrictions does is affect the vast majority of Congress already playing by the rules. If we want to get Washington working again, we need to embrace a different strategy. The truth is that the impulse to monitor and restrict Congress is actually driving us deeper into a ditch. So it's time that we embrace what might be deemed the First Law of Holes—stop digging.

THE DEVILS WE KNOW

Among all the complaints leveled at American democracy today, none is more pervasive than the harm wrought by money that fuels political campaigns. As many have complained, not only do our elections often take place on uneven playing fields, the constant imperative to raise money is controlling how our elected officials invest their time, influencing how they govern, and beholding them to people beyond their constituents. Those effects are unquestionably problematic. But what is lost in our outrage is the recognition that the existing rules are an anachronism adopted in 2002 to constrain a system that the Supreme Court, with its more recent decisions—Citizens United in 2010 and McCutcheon in 2014— has since turned on its head.

For many good government activists, that is a bitter pill to swallow. Most progressives simply do not understand or accept the Supreme Court's rulings, which have been premised on the notion that campaign giving is a protected form of free speech. Of course progressives are not the only ones who take issue with recent Supreme Court decisions. But we call it the Supreme Court for a reason: Once the nine justices issue a ruling, that's pretty much it—at least for a while. So the reformers upset with the current state of affairs have to choose from among three possible resolutions.

The first possibility is to revise the Constitution. The call for a constitutional amendment to differentiate campaign contributions from protected speech has become quite popular among those frustrated by money's continued influence on politics. But those in favor of a constitutional amendment need to realize that convincing two-thirds of both houses of Congress and three-fourths of state legislatures to agree on a specific modification to the constitution is a daunting, likely impossible task.* Some go even further, suggesting a new Constitutional Convention. While equally unlikely, a Constitutional Convention is also an extremely high-risk endeavor. When you open up the Constitution, the entire document is up for grabs—not just the parts disfavored by campaign finance reformers.

The second option is to wait for a new slate of justices. While the court often takes pain to honor precedent, the current court's thinking clearly evolved when conservative justices Roberts and Alito joined the bench. As the thinking goes, if Justices Scalia and Kennedy, each of whom is in his late seventies, were replaced with a justice nominated by a Democrat, money and speech might one day be parted. Unfortunately for those biding time, the current doctrine is a result of a series of decisions rendered over several years. If the court does shift to the left over the next decade, it is still unlikely that significant change would occur rapidly.

There's a third option, however, and while it is more limited in its aims, it has two things in its favor: It is both legal and achievable. Option three is premised on the grudging acknowledgment that a torrent of money will continue to course through our political system for the foreseeable

---

* To modify the Constitution, two-thirds of both houses of Congress or two-thirds of a national convention called by Congress at the request of two-thirds of the state legislatures must ratify an amendment. Then, the amendment will be sent to the states, where three-fourths of state legislatures or ratifying conventions in three-fourths of the states must ratify it.

future. Again, we must accept what we cannot change. Rather than try to curtail money's existence, we could try to channel campaign spending to more responsible and accountable institutions. If we can't rid American politics of money, we can stop encouraging nondisclosed, "dark money" spending by anonymous or intentionally obfuscated groups. In the land of caustic attack ads, the anonymous donor is king. Under current law, the institutions most likely to incubate thoughtful campaigns are the devils we know: the Democratic and Republican parties.

For some, that may sound like terrible advice. Few Americans are fans of the entrenched political parties—as evidenced by the fact that more and more voters are registering as independents. In recent decades, the national parties have undermined their own reputations by taking on the role of campaign attack-dogs. In what were essentially good cop–bad cop arrangements, candidates would spend their campaign money promoting themselves while their party committees did the dirty work of undermining their opponents. The Federal Election Campaign Act of 1974 tacitly supported this approach: While Congress imposed a $1,000 cap on how much an individual donor could contribute to an individual campaign per election, it placed only a $20,000 cap on how much an individual could give to a party.

Compared to the vitriol now spewed regularly in American elections, the negative campaigning the DNC and RNC sponsored during the 1980s would seem to have come from attack-puppies. Nonetheless, by the 1990s advocates for good government had seen enough. Working with a group of allies like senators John McCain (R-AZ) and Russ Feingold (D-WI), the reform community spearheaded a movement to eliminate soft money altogether.

TEARING OFF THE ROOF
The Bipartisan Campaign Reform Act (BCRA), or "McCain-Feingold," as it is commonly referred to, was enacted in 2002. For those intent on cleaning up Washington, BCRA was supposed to change everything. Starting on January 1, 2003, the parties were prohibited for the most part from raising and spending soft money. Even better, with certain exceptions, the law banned political advertisements that referred to a federal

candidate within two months of any general election. But things didn't go as planned. Whether it is a measure of a diverse society built around active political speech, an expression of the importance of politics in our lives and commerce, or a Supreme Court with strong views about the First Amendment, the new law failed to reduce campaign cash. Quite the opposite, "soft money" was simply shifted away from national party organizations—where, we should note, it had been easily identifiable—and poured into an array of obscure third-party operations.

Initially, "527" organizations (named after the section of the Internal Revenue Code that exempts certain political organizations from paying taxes) became the preferred recipients of the checks once given to the DNC or the RNC. The 527s weren't allowed to use the magic words "vote for" in their political advertising, but they could otherwise comment on a candidate's view of a particular issue. The most notorious 527 was Swift Boaters for Truth, an organization which, along with other groups, effectively blurred these lines to undermine John Kerry's presidential ambitions in 2004.

A few years later, the fashionable place for those same dollars switched to the organizations now known as "Super PACs," which unlike 527s, *can* engage directly in encouraging votes for or against specific candidates. Super PACs, while still being precluded from coordinating with any given campaign, don't have to walk the line that limited 527s. As a result, while the parties themselves have been subject to significant constraints, the total amount of money invested in politics has grown by leaps and bounds. The financial figures detail what happened next. According to data from OpenSecrets.org, total expenditures on federal campaigns in 2000, prior to passage of BCRA, were slightly over $3 billion. In the 2004 cycle, under the constraints of the new statute, spending topped $4 billion. In 2008, campaign cash topped $5 billion and then in the last presidential cycle, profound dismay was expressed that more than $6 billion was spent on federal campaigns. To give some perspective on this spending: This outlay is slightly larger than the GDP of Bermuda and slightly smaller than the entire economy of Haiti.

The stark increase in funding is clear demonstration that the BCRA has not succeeded. But the total dollars are not the most important measure of the impacts of the new law. Even more significant is the dramatic change in who is spending the money. While money has poured into independent political committees, state parties with their funding restrictions, transparency, and accountability have suffered since the enactment of the BCRA. According to a fifty-state analysis of in-state elections, state Democratic and Republican parties raised an average of $5.4 million in 2000. By 2008, that number had dropped to $4.1 million. By 2012, state party average resources had shrunk by nearly half to $2.8 million. The former chairman of the Republican National Committee, Jim Nicholson, argues that the parties have lost the ability to manage the process leading to "more chaos and disequilibrium in the campaigns."

Moreover, it has become challenging to even figure out where the campaign money is going. In a January 2013 press conference, the Federal Election Commission (FEC) announced that their initial estimate that the 2012 figure had been roughly $6 billion was wrong; the real figure was actually closer to $7 billion. When noting the challenges tracking this explosion in campaign money, FEC chairwoman Ellen Weintraub commented, "It's obviously only an estimate. It's really hard to come up with 'the number.'" That is the most revealing and troubling aspect of the last decade of campaign finance reform: Through a well-intentioned effort to constrain the system, we completely lost control.

Why has the amount of money spent on campaigns roughly doubled since adoption of McCain-Feingold? Any reformer will tell you it began with the Supreme Court's decision in *Citizens United vs. FEC*. In 2008, the conservative organization Citizens United sought to air a ninety-minute program titled *Hillary the Movie* during the Democratic primaries. The FEC deemed the highly critical account to be a political advertisement (for her opponents) and required it be paid for with "hard money." Citizens United promptly went to court. The result was, in the eyes of most advocates for good government, an abomination. In January 2010, the Supreme Court rendered an expansive ruling not only striking down the advertising limits in McCain-Feingold, but simultaneously allowing corporations to make unlimited donations to third-party political groups.

Justice Kennedy, writing for the majority, reiterated the view that campaign spending is protected speech by stating: "If the First Amendment has any force, it prohibits Congress from fining or jailing citizens, or associations of citizens, for simply engaging in political speech." Limits on independent expenditures were dealt another blow in March 2010 when a federal Court of Appeals made it clear that individuals, like corporations, could also make unlimited contributions to independent political groups that refrain from actively coordinating with the candidates they seek to support.

When McCain-Feingold closed a door, 527 organizations opened a window, and then the Supreme Court ripped off the roof. The wild west of money in politics had begun—but with one crucial exception. While other political efforts had been freed from regulation, the DNC and RNC were still barred under McCain-Feingold from receiving soft money donations. The result has been to shift power from the somewhat accountable political parties to the least responsible corners of election advocacy. And that has had a profound effect in determining who actually jumps into any given race: Weakened parties now have less ability to influence the types of candidates who seek office. As one reporter explained, due to McCain-Feingold, "Republicans will be far more interested in finding candidates who can fundraise or self-fundraise for their campaigns, rather than focusing on finding candidates who would make good legislators and agree broadly with the Republican Party's objectives."

We often forget about the law of unintended consequences. In Providence, Rhode Island, where I went to college, there was a stretch of highway where several dangerous accidents had occurred. The state erected a phalanx of bright lights on a bridge that would flash SLOW DOWN when triggered. The average speed increased because people wanted to see the pretty lights go off. In our zeal to free politics from money, we placed big bright lights on top of the political parties. Unfortunately, we didn't drive the money out of politics; we just sped it up and drove it under the bridge.

"We Love USA" Sponsored This Hateful Ad

Money by itself isn't necessarily bad for campaigns. In the final equation, we should want big political questions to be decided by an engaged electorate—and as is plainly apparent, it takes money to get salient messages out to the public. But the way that things have evolved—the diffusions of cash and authority—has contributed mightily to a more troubling trend: a dramatic increase in attack ads. If it felt like ads tearing at President Obama and Governor Romney were everywhere in 2012, it's because they were. Researchers at Wesleyan University tallied over one million campaign advertisements in the 2012 presidential campaign, seven hundred thousand of which were negative.

But while the number and tenor of these ads may not surprise the average television viewer, the breakdown of who was sponsoring them might. The spots sponsored by the candidates themselves were divided fairly evenly, 50/50, between positive and negative. By contrast, interest group ads were nearly 90 percent negative. Maybe most astounding, those ads sponsored by the national parties, namely the DNC and RNC, were over 90 percent positive. The overwhelmingly positive character of party ads is to some extent a reflection of the fact that there were no negative ideas left. But it also reveals important differences in incentives.

National parties care about their reputations. They are easily identifiable and publicly accountable. The parties have high-profile leaders and they run some risk of mutually assured destruction (or at least retaliation) if they step too far across the line. If DNC chairwoman Debbie Wasserman Schultz signed off on a campaign ad indicating that Mitt Romney's actions at Bain Capital resulted in a woman's death, she would have been called on the carpet and Democratic officials would have been challenged to denounce the ad. But when that very same ad is run by a Democratic Super PAC which, by law, cannot coordinate with the party or campaign—the opprobrium is lessened.

How would RNC chairman Reince Priebus have fared on national television if the RNC had run an ad stating that as a state senator, President Obama had "voted to deny constitutional protections to babies born alive from an abortion." The Susan B. Anthony List, a conservative Super PAC/501(c)4 named after a social reformer and leader of the women's suffrage movement, had no such reservations about broadcasting that message. And while you may never have heard of them, the Susan B. Anthony List has spent more money than the National Organization for Women in every election cycle since 1996.

That is the problem. Like many independent political committees, the Susan B. Anthony List is designed to obscure its political ideology. And obfuscation knows no party. Consider this quiz: Which two of the following actual Super PACs support Democratic candidates: (1) Citizens for a Working America, (2) Local Voices, (3) Texans for America's Future, or (4) We Love USA?* In most settings, the anonymous license to smear someone's reputation is called bullying. In politics, we call it the unintended consequences of the Bipartisan Campaign Reform Act.

DISCOURAGING DARK MONEY

The lack of accountability has predictably drawn the ire of reformers. It is not lost on them that the very law which was designed to clean up the nation's elections has teed up opportunities for a new generation of Abramoffs to play much more powerful roles in shaping election outcomes. Suddenly shady characters have been given the wherewithal to wield more power by directing money to backroom "independent" campaigns. As Abramoff himself admitted, "We were always able to get every dollar we needed to get into races and into the system through party organizations, through soft money, through 527s, through 501(c)(4)s."

Abramoff reminds us of an unfortunate truth: Since George Washington ran essentially unopposed in 1789 to the most recent contest between President Obama and Governor Romney, money has always had a role in determining who holds power in America. But the constancy of money in American politics is only part of the story. It is where and *how* the money is raised and *used* that matters the most. According to Ken Martin, chairman of the Minnesota Democratic-Farmer-Labor Party:

> If you're a donor and you can write a million-dollar check to an outside group with little or no disclosure and focus it on very specific activity and have no [regulatory] urgency or burdens in terms of disclosure hanging over your head, why wouldn't you go that way and give a contribution?

---

* The answer is #2 and #3.

The relative anonymity of Super PACs—and the opportunity to employ more searing tactics—is not lost on those creating the ads. Glenn Totten, a Democratic media consultant notes, "The work can be easier, demanding far less haggling with an apprehensive candidate or a spouse. What a candidate puts on the air directly reflects on them personally. That is not the case for a Super PAC." Super PACs have almost no alternative but to go negative. After all, how can you speak for a candidate who you're not allowed to speak to?

The negativity flowing from Super PAC advertising keeps the arms race going: It often requires increased spending from even the candidates they seek to support. Former senator Bob Bennett (R-UT) describes the frustration of running for office with uncoordinated, and often destructive, supporters:

> *Now you get these terrible ads claiming to support you and you either have to spend your own money repudiating people who think they support you, or keep your mouth shut and look like a bitter partisan. One of the reasons candidates feel the need to raise so much money these days is to not be drowned out by their so-called supporters.*

Until recently, there were few reasons to believe that the growth of "dark money" would be curtailed at any time in the near or distant future; it seemed inevitable that independent political committees would continue to get more powerful and aggressive with each successive election. The highest court in the land has upheld the constitutionality of unlimited soft money contributions and McCain-Feingold has restricted the ability to give these resources to political parties. The tragic result has been to drive seemingly unlimited resources to the least accountable and most destructive agents in our political system.

But then, in April 2014, the Supreme Court issued another landmark campaign finance ruling that holds the potential to slow down the Super PAC juggernaut. The majority's decision in *McCutcheon vs. FEC* overturned many of the restrictions on how much an individual can give to a political party during a campaign cycle. While the $5,200 limit on the amount that an individual can donate to any single candidate was left intact (for now), the court struck down the limit an individual can give to all federal candidates—$48,600, and the limit on all gifts to political party committees—$74,600. While not eliminating the advantages enjoyed by Super PACs, big donors once again have the option to write big checks directly to the parties. Instead of the $123,200 during any given campaign, individuals can now donate several million dollars each election to support Republican or Democratic candidates.

The money is going to flow somewhere. The system is best served if campaign resources are drawn back toward more accountable organizations with obligations to report their sources of funding and with greater capacity to engage on substantive issues. Commenting on McCutcheon, David DesJardins, a top Democratic donor, stated, "Undoubtedly, I will give more to individual candidates, and less through 'super PACs' or other organizations." Even if more money ultimately flows into politics, the public will benefit from the diminished power of "dark money." "The Republican National Committee sponsored this message," is much preferable to the cryptic, "We Love the USA sponsored this hateful ad."

To effectively shift power away from the Super PACs and back to the parties, the FEC should build on the *McCutcheon* decision and allow political parties more freedom to spend resources in coordination with individual campaigns. The current formula sets a limit on coordinated spending in each state based on the number of congressional districts and voters. For example, the DNC and RNC are presently allowed to coordinate $1.4 million worth of spending with a Senate candidate in Florida, but only $93,000 with his or her counterpart running in Alaska.

Sophisticated donors would pull away from Super PACs and the like if they saw their money being strategically deployed in service of their candidates. Together, these measures would re-balance the playing field, improving the tenor of campaigns and the quality of candidates.

COURAGE OF CONVICTIONS

There's one other important step to rein in shadowy campaign spending: real-time disclosure of political giving. Having spent several pages describing the harms that too much transparency has had on government, this position may sound hypocritical. But as Ralph Waldo Emerson famously opined, "A foolish consistency is the hobgoblin of little minds." Off-the-record political negotiations and off-book political contributions are simply not the same.

Government's decision-making capacity would benefit from more candid and unscripted deliberation. In political giving, however, there's no reason to believe that anonymous donations advance public policy or individual freedom. On this point, the Supreme Court agrees. Having equated political giving with speech, the court seems prepared to make certain that everyone knows who is lending his or her voice. In *Citizens United*, the majority opinion stated that "transparency enables the electorate to make informed decisions and give proper weight to different speakers and messages." Even rock-ribbed conservative Justice Scalia has embraced this view. In a case decided six months after *Citizens United*, Scalia wrote, "Requiring people to stand up in public for their political acts fosters civic courage, without which democracy is doomed."

And there's movement afoot. Some states like Virginia have opted to allow unlimited giving while requiring immediate disclosure. Only foreign nationals and foreign businesses are prohibited from donating to a political campaign in Virginia. However, a candidate must disclose the name, occupation, mailing address, and employer of any donor that gives more than $100 in a single election cycle.

At the federal level, the Securities and Exchange Commission may soon require corporations to reveal their political spending to shareholders. In addition, there are two bills moving through Congress, the DISCLOSE Act in the House and the Follow the Money Act in the Senate, which would require independent political groups to publicly disclose all donors within days of receiving their gifts. This legislation, if enacted, would provide interested voters with valuable context, enhance public confidence in the fairness of elections, and begin to level the playing field between the independent groups that can presently obscure their funding from the political parties that cannot.

Most important, strengthening the parties and increasing transparency would mark a blow against polarization. Super PACs are vehicles used to drive distinct and often extreme ideologies. Their increased influence has discouraged some more collaborative candidates from entering the political arena. Worse still, the threat of a Super PAC–financed challenger has spurred many legislators to maintain an ideological purity that is more strategic than sincere.

The attempt to keep money out of politics by restricting political parties has proven as effective as the attempt to control our borders by building higher walls. In both cases, real reform requires a deeper understanding of human nature and the surrounding ecosystem of our laws and values. Our efforts to improve campaign finance will be far more effective if we relinquish the fantasy that we can stop political giving and instead get behind a system that can effectively track it. By shifting the focus from regulating the parties toward system-wide transparency, we can establish a framework that is legal, practical, and effective in removing the advantages currently enjoyed by the most partisan and least responsible actors in our electoral system.

ALL VAGARY OF SCANDAL

Of course, money's influence isn't limited to the sphere of political campaigns. From Mark Twain's assertion that "there is no distinctly native American criminal class except Congress," to Kevin Spacey's depiction of the corrupt (and effective) Congressman Frank Underwood in *House of Cards*, political corruption has, for good reason, long been a topic of national interest and concern. In the fifth century BC, the Athenian politician and general Themistocles—from the true birthplace of democracy—said that it has no value to be a leader if you cannot enrich your friends.

Over the centuries, a number of American political leaders have embraced this idea with unfortunate vigor. Our history is riddled with damaging examples of corruption, graft, bribery, nepotism, embezzlement, and all vagary of scandal. In 1777, the ink was still wet on the Declaration of Independence when American politician and diplomat Silas Deane was accused of mismanagement and treason while serving as ambassador to France. In what is known as the Galphin Affair, President Zachary Taylor's attorney general and secretary of the Treasury conspired to utilize a loophole that helped George Crawford, Taylor's secretary of war, amass a large sum of public funds. Indeed, corruption was likely even more rampant during the Gilded Age when cronies inside President

Ulysses S. Grant's administration used a variety of shady methods to enrich themselves and their friends.

Those stories may come from a different age. But the modern era, beginning with the postwar years, has also been suffused with corruption. Many Americans were scandalized to learn that President Eisenhower's chief of staff, Sherman Adams, had accepted gifts from a businessman looking for special favors from the government. Adams eventually resigned. In response, Congress enacted an official "Code of Ethics for Government Service," which applied to all federal employees. That first set of principles might not seem particularly rigorous by today's standards. But it marked an important shift at the dawn of the Cold War: Those in the employ of the government were, in the wake of Adams's malfeasance, explicitly expected to meet certain ethical standards.

Not surprisingly, the new code didn't eradicate corruption. Just a few years later, an aide to then-senator Lyndon Johnson named Bobby Baker was caught in a bribery scandal, an episode followed soon thereafter by accusations that Congressman Adam Clayton Powell (D-NY) was using taxpayer dollars to fund his extravagant lifestyle. In response, both the Senate and House established Ethics Committees designed to police their members—though neither was empowered with any disciplinary authority. The new regime sought to ensure members weren't compromised—but they weren't aiming to eliminate every possible appearance of a conflict of interest. For example, members were permitted to accept payments from outside organization for speeches—but not at an unreasonable rate. The direction offered here is about as useful as Justice Potter Stewart's "I know it when I see it" definition of obscenity.

In the aftermath of Watergate, a commission recommended much stricter guidelines. Deeply disturbed by Nixon's transgressions and fearful of angry voters, the House and Senate each approved a series of regulations that mandated the public release of financial disclosures, prohibited outside earned income beyond 15 percent of a member's salary, and limited the size of honoraria (to $750 or less) and gifts (to $100 from those doing business with the government). Passage of what came to be known as the 1977 Ethics Codes marked the crest of the first wave of modern ethics reform.

Once again, however, ethics reforms didn't do the trick. The 1980s were suffused with new examples of shockingly dishonest behavior done in pursuit of self-enrichment. In the Abscam Scandal—the basis for the 2013 film *American Hustle*—several House members were caught taking bribes from agents posing as Middle Eastern sheikhs. Separately, five members of the Senate were cited for having tried to influence financial regulators on behalf of a donor, Charles Keating. Then, in the early 1990s, after nearly two dozen House members were caught bouncing checks from their House bank accounts, House Ways and Means Committee chairman Dan Rostenkowski (D-IL) was caught embezzling money from the Post Office. In turn, efforts began anew to squeeze the graft out of government.

The second wave of reforms began in the late 1980s, when Congress banned members from receiving any honoraria whatsoever, and put an upper limit on personal gifts at $300. To address growing public concern about congressional travel, limits were set on the number of days that any private entity could sponsor domestic and international travel. After gaining majority status in the 1994 elections, House Republican leadership instituted rules prohibiting members and staff from accepting meals or gifts valued above $50 from anyone registered as a lobbyist.

Protesting Too Much

Up to this point, the ethics reforms of the last century all made good sense. The behaviors they prohibited were readily objectionable, and the limits did not interrupt the ability of government leaders to do their jobs. But in the mid-2000s, the culture that has since come to be associated with Jack Abramoff prompted yet a third round of reforms. In this case, the effort to root out the infection badly harmed the patient.

First, let's acknowledge how the underlying evidence of corruption differed from that which had come before. Previous evidence of corruption had been so outrageous as to seem almost exotic. The Abscam scandal, what with its fake Arab sheikhs and grainy surveillance video, seemed like something out of a bad spy novel. Most members of Congress were able to express their disgust and disassociate themselves from the bad apples. The "franking" scandal, often described as members abusing their

Post Office privileges, seemed bizarrely pathetic; while the complex money laundering scheme was a prison-worthy breach of public trust, it did not besmirch the integrity of the entire institution.

The Abramoff scandal was different. Though sophisticated in execution, Abramoff's graft was jarringly unoriginal, crude even. The lobbyist and his associates used out-and-out bribes to secure desired outcomes from elected and appointed officials. He regularly promised congressional staffers lucrative jobs with the expectation that, until the staffer jumped to Abramoff's firm, the lobbyist would be able to exact favors. Abramoff orchestrated schemes in which his clients would put tens of thousands of dollars into consulting firms owned by the spouses of congressional staffers—even if the payee never delivered any service whatsoever. He took members of Congress and Bush Administration appointees on exotic trips—often to tropical Pacific islands and, most famously, to play golf in Scotland—with the expectation that when he needed a favor they would lend a hand.

Maybe even worse than Abramoff's criminal behavior was the effect it had on Washington as a whole. By the 2000s, the generational shift from those who fought in World War II (and tended to revere government) to those scarred by Watergate and Vietnam (and less impressed with public service) had already begun to take a toll on the public's faith in Washington. Americans were already increasingly suspicious of what might be happening inside the Beltway. And so when the Abramoff imbroglio went public, it didn't merely expose a presumed outlier; it affirmed America's worst fears about Washington.

Suddenly, everyone was suspect. Nearly every member of Congress had taken a fact-finding trip. Every member had dined with a lobbyist. Every power player had formed some sort of relationship with a non-profit group or lobbying firm that had helped him or her raise money. In essence, Abramoff's crimes called into question not only a few bad apples, but the barrel itself.

In light of the public's outrage, incumbents immediately began to conjure up the attack ads their opponents would produce in upcoming campaigns. Savvy challengers (and Super PACs) would surely run ads splicing pictures of Abramoff golfing in Scotland with footage of incumbent members boarding a plane. The scripts wrote themselves: "Congressman Smith took four trips last year—one to a four-star resort. Call him up and ask why he is spending your tax dollars for his vacations...."

It wouldn't matter if the "resort" stay was nothing more than a sleepover on the journey to monitor elections in Myanmar. It wouldn't matter if the lobbyist who had helped a senator raise campaign funds represented no one but a cancer research institution in the senator's home state. Abramoff bathed everyone in a negative light, and suggested that corruption pervaded the whole scene. Not surprisingly, senators and representatives threw themselves behind any legislative effort that promised to help cleanse them of the stink. They expressed outrage at their colleagues' transgressions. And they voted on the House and Senate floors for invasive and unnecessary restrictions. While recognizing that these rules were not in the best interest of the institution, they simply could not go on the record voting against them. This unfortunate outcome calls to mind a riff by the hilariously sardonic comedian Lewis Black:

> *The only thing dumber than a Republican or Democrat is when these pricks work together. We have a two party system. The Democratic Party—which is a party of no ideas. And the Republican Party—which is the party of bad ideas. And the way it works is that the Republican stands up in Congress and goes, "I've got a really bad idea" and the Democrat says "and I can make it shittier."*

As the founder and president of the Bipartisan Policy Center, it is important for me to acknowledge that some bipartisan legislation is just awful. When principled partisans reconcile differences with courage and creativity, it is the best that America has to offer. However, when Democrats and Republicans come together in the frenzied attempt to protect their shared incumbency, Mr. Black gets it just about right.

THE ILLEGAL MUG

After regaining the majority in the 2006 midterm elections, Democrats imposed a new regime for regulating the House of Representatives. The new rules eliminated the $50 threshold and instead prohibited members and staffers from accepting *any* gift, item, meal, or memento from a lobbyist or an organization that employs lobbyists, unless it was of "nominal" value. (Members and their staff can still receive gifts of $50 or less from non-lobbyists if the gift giver works for a company that employs no lobbyists, and presuming that they not exceed $100 in a calendar year.)

Many heralded the new rules as the dawn of a new era of clean government. At face value, they seem reasonable enough. Unfortunately, the reality has turned out to be far more muddled. As some predicted, the new rules were so overly broad as to create all sorts of odd questions and cumbersome interpretations. Mitch McConnell, the Senate Republican leader (who voted for the bill) asked at the time: "Does that mean I have to refuse the key to a city since cities have their own lobbyists? . . . How about a 22-year-old staff assistant who has to wait tables to make ends meet? What happens when they wait on a lobbyist, do they have to refuse their tips?"

For practical purposes, the ban on gifts from anyone associated with a lobbyist has become particularly confusing. An employee of a fifty-thousand-person company is confined by the same restrictions as a full-time lobbyist, if that corporation employs a single lobbyist. The same holds true for an employee of a nonprofit organization working to reduce toxic chemicals or improve product safety.

The previous ban on items and meals valued at over $50 was fairly reasonable, having been in accord with social norms of most professional relationships. It is common, for example, for hometown companies to express their pride by sending small gifts to their representatives—often for display in their offices. Members of Congress from Georgia might have had a bottomless bowl of homegrown peanuts on hand; various local candies were regularly on offer in member waiting rooms. A local sports team might have handed a team jersey or cap to a member who came by to catch a weekend game. Even in cases where an actual lobbyist sent over a bottle of wine at the holidays with a friendly note, it strains credibility to argue that a $40 gift would influence a legislator who was simultaneously raising millions each year in advance of their next campaign.

But by the standards imposed in and after 2007, it is hard to differentiate between a friendly gift and a flat-out bribe. Those working in Washington have to wonder whether the cumulative value of those peanuts has exceeded $100 in the current calendar year. Does the company sending the candy or the league associated with the team's jersey employ any registered lobbyists? And that is the most pernicious effect: Members and staffers now spend hours figuring out how to do their jobs without stepping over what are a series of fairly absurd lines.

You needn't come up with hypothetical examples on your own. A 2007 effort to explain the new requirements to members and staff offered a host of illustrations in the hope that they might brighten the lines of acceptability. A memo was circulated with the following examples:

- *Example 10:* A company in a Member's district that employs lobbyists offers the Member a $15 baseball cap with the corporate logo. The Member may accept as "an item of a nominal value such as . . . a baseball cap."
- *Example 11:* A company in a Member's district that employs lobbyists offers the Member a coffee mug worth $12. The Member may not accept the mug. Under Committee precedent, members and staff should not rely on the "items of a nominal value" provision in accepting any item having a value of $10 or more (except for a greeting card, baseball cap, or T-shirt).

So a $15 baseball cap is apparently an ethical all-American gift to be worn proudly by House members and staff, but a $12 coffee mug simply crosses the line. Take a sip from that unscrupulous vessel and there could be no turning back from a life of political grifting.

The Obama Administration has similarly embraced over-the-top restrictions that have undermined efficiency and provided little tangible benefit. In this example of reform gone wild, the protagonist is once again an unassuming coffee mug.

A former Treasury Department official recently relayed the following story: While working in the first Obama Administration, he was invited by the Brookings Institution to give a talk. After delivering his lecture, and participating in a question and answer session, he was presented by his hosts with a coffee mug emblazoned with "Brookings Institution" on the front, and he accepted it, as he was trained to do.

Small gifts like coffee mugs often fall below the *de minimus* exceptions for regular government officials. However, as an Obama Administration appointee, he had waived many of those exceptions. Nevertheless, there were still circumstances in which he could ethically accept the mug—he just needed to get approval. Upon returning to his office, he followed the proper protocol by handing the mug over to his assistant.

The process of vetting the mug began in earnest when his assistant filled out a form indicating when it had been received, where, and for what. The coffee mug was shipped to the Treasury General Counsel's office where an ethics official (such officials are often attorneys paid around $100,000 a year) began to comb through the public records to determine whether Brookings was a lobbying organization, employed any federal lobbyists, or was in any way in violation of the rules regarding who could give acceptable gifts.

The official's search turned up nothing and confirmed that Brookings, as a think tank established in 1916 in Washington, was an acceptable bearer of gifts. Then another staffer in the office was assigned the job of estimating the value of the coffee mug so there could be an independent valuation in addition to the official valuation. Once those two valuations were received, a third official, this time someone at a managerial level, had to make a formal decision as to whether the official could keep the mug. In this case, he was allowed to retain his gift as it was determined that Brookings was not a lobbying entity, the value of the mug was below the acceptable limit, and there were no strings attached to the mug.

The entire process took about three months, at which point the mug was returned by the counsel's office. The official estimates that it took at least ten hours of staff time, potentially more, to complete the process. Depending on how you value that time, checking the ethical nature of the mug cost the government upwards of $500 to $1,000. At a moment when the Treasury Department was working around the clock to avert a financial catastrophe, was this a reasonable use of the department's scarce resources?

TOOTHPICKS OF MORALITY

The gift ban is hardly the only place where the more recent rules affected the normal course of Washington business. The old laws, by almost any stretch, would have prevented members of Congress from enjoying a free meal at Jack Abramoff's expensive Pennsylvania Avenue eatery, Signatures. But the ban on "free lunches" with lobbyists is not the issue. Reducing the gift limit down to zero has created confusing obstacles that discourage members of Congress and their staff from attending policy dinners and even receptions.

Consider how the new rules have affected my organization, the Bipartisan Policy Center. Our board of directors convenes three times a year, usually in DC. The night before each meeting, we hold a casual dinner to share ideas and build relationships—- something American businesses have been doing since John Winthrop formed the Massachusetts Bay Company in 1629. Consistent with thousands of books on organizational effectiveness and basic common sense, strengthening the friendships among board members and familiarity with BPC staff increases the candor and value of our meetings. At many of these dinners, we host sitting members of Congress for conversations on policy challenges; recent discussions have covered the federal budget, debt ceiling, education policy, and technology investment. The events are animated and substantive. But when members come to dinner, they frequently run into a problem: They're not sure whether they're allowed to eat.

The confusion stems from the fact that despite attending briefings on the current rules, members are worried about getting into trouble for tucking into the wrong plate of food. Even though the BPC employs no lobbyists (so the members are permitted to sit and eat), many would rather not risk it. Some members have offered us money for the "fair value" of the dinner. One senator ate only after pulling me aside and confirming we do not employ lobbyists. Most just politely opt to go hungry.

Though this sounds like a minor and almost comical annoyance, for those thousands of organizations that *do* employ lobbyists—from the American Petroleum Institute to the American Lung Association—the restrictions present barriers to meaningful interaction with elected officials and staff. A great deal of work in Washington gets done at breakfast, lunch, and dinner. When Congress is in town, members are attending meetings and casting votes. Try to schedule a roundtable discussion and you'll be generally pointed to mealtime. What is gained by preventing a member of Congress from having a sandwich because one of the immigration reform advocates or technology company staff work for an organization that lobbies? There are creative ways to work around these restrictions, but doing so is a waste of time and energy. Creating sterile environments and regulated interactions is at odds with the give and take of good decision-making.

And this theater of the absurd doesn't end at the lunch table. There is a regulation in force that is commonly known as the "toothpick rule." In an effort to ensure that lobbyists are not wining and dining elected leaders, Congress raised the ethical bar in 2007 by adding criminal penalties for providing food to a member of Congress that requires a fork and knife. Once again, the requirement applies not only to lobbyists, but also to anyone who works for a corporation or organization that employs a lobbyist.

Fortunately, there's a catch: The "toothpick rule" exempts food or refreshments of a nominal value offered other than as part of a meal. In essence, the ethics committees currently distinguish the provision of "food" from the sharing of a "meal." And that means that a reception where the attendees consume food or drink standing up—like a continental-style breakfast with coffee and doughnuts, or a reception with roving hors d'oeuvres—is permissible through the toothpick exemption.

Over the past few years, ethics lawyers have become experts on portion size. In 2007, when the rule was just taking effect, I went to a reception thrown by some corporation or trade association at a DC hotel. It was a reception like most any other in DC. But there was one unforgettable aspect of this otherwise unremarkable event: After accidentally arriving early, I was struck by the sight of several men in $1,200 suits hacking somewhat frantically at the food tables. They had their sleeves rolled up and were cutting away with serving spoons and plastic knives while the catering staff looked on in horror. I wandered over to ask what was going on and discovered a scene out of a *Seinfeld* episode: The corporate attorneys had determined, after arriving at the event, that the servings were unethically large. And because there was no one else to do it, they were busy dicing up the appetizers into morally acceptable portions.

That's not even the worst of it. A colleague of mine once attended a DC birthday celebration for a now retired public servant. Consistent with the norms of the DC reception circuit, the toothpick rule was in full force, so there were very few tables to entice the attendees to piece the hors d'oeuvres together into an offending meal. It was apparently a lovely event but for one unanticipated challenge: Many of the guests were elderly. After greeting one another for a while, they needed a place to sit down. With scarce seating, it appears that many guests were compelled to leave early—but at least no skullduggery transpired during a seated meal.

The good news is that, for those willing to "lawyer-up," one can sometimes find exceptions to this toothpick hegemony. Each year, for example, the American Meat Institute holds a National Hot Dog Day on Capitol Hill. Dave Ray, a spokesman for the Meat Institute, indicated that they had received a waiver from the ethics committees to serve full-size hot dogs, corn dogs, and sausages because National Hot Dog Day is "a widely attended event," and not a reception. The "widely attended event" waiver requires that attendance by members and staff be in connection with the performance of their duties. Presumably the thousand people who attend each year are doing research for a new food safety bill or possibly expressing their opposition to First Lady Michelle Obama's Let's Move Initiative.

If these were simply humorous examples of a bureaucracy missing the big picture, they would be worth little more than trivia. But the stories laid out above expose a culture of public disdain and congressional self-loathing that is at the core of our current dysfunction. Our big challenges can only be solved in an environment capable of collaboration, trust, and compromise—the absurd fork and knife rule is a symptom of inherent distrust. We're fostering a work environment premised on the notion that our elected officials might at any moment sell us out for a seated meal or an afternoon of sightseeing. With this degree of distrust for Congress, it is little surprise that they don't trust one another.

If the latest round of ethics requirements were actually preventing real corruption, the costs to collaboration could be justified. But there's not much good to point to. There have always been and will always be some number of dishonest people in high office. Some arrive that way and others are seduced by the power and opportunities that come with great authority. For these people we have the Federal Bureau of Investigation and the Federal Bureau of Prisons. Abramoff, James Traficant—a Democratic congressman convicted of bribery and racketeering in 2002—and William "Cold Cash" Jefferson, who was caught with graft proceeds were, in a word, criminals.

Their crimes would not have been deterred by the obligatory return of coffee mugs or the requirement that they not accept a $38 dinner. Yet it was their malfeasance and other extreme acts that spurred Congress to enact the overwrought set of rules that now burdens every member of Congress. Breaking bread with a member of Congress isn't "gateway graft." However, it is a crucial element of the collaborative process. The last decade has seen Congress board up all its windows because of a leaky sink. The post-scandal antidotes were adopted out of fear. They are examples of how an angry nation and frightened legislature have colluded in harming Washington's ability to govern.

THE STIGMA OF ST. ANDREWS

There has been another unfortunate casualty of the Abramoff scandal: congressional travel. Long a mainstay of critical insights, personal interaction, and bipartisan collegiality, official and privately funded travel have been in decline since pictures of Tom DeLay golfing at St. Andrews appeared in newspapers around the country. Once again, fearful of political blowback, Congress sought to diminish its guilt by limiting its associations. While exact figures for taxpayer-supported travel are difficult to obtain, there is no question that official travel has been in decline. At the beginning of 2013, Speaker Boehner eliminated taxpayer-supported travel altogether (though this edict was moderately loosened a year later).

The reduction in official travel has been exacerbated by limitations on privately supported trips. Under rules passed in the aftermath of the Abramoff scandal, senators were prohibited from accepting travel expenses from any organization for anything more than a three-day domestic or seven-day foreign trip. In both houses of Congress, organizations, including nonprofits that retain lobbyists, were prohibited from supporting, planning, organizing, or arranging any type of congressional travel. But even then the veneer of corruption persisted. In 2010, after the *Wall Street Journal* revealed instances of taxpayer money being used to buy alcohol and underwrite sightseeing opportunities, Speaker Nancy Pelosi explicitly forbade House members and staffers from spending travel funds on personal expenditures or on business and first class seats on flights under fourteen hours.

For casual observers, these may seem like entirely reasonable prohibitions. Stories of Abramoff flying members of Congress to exotic locations and putting them up in luxury hotels were egregious. But those excesses are not all that these new rules interrupt. The flight from Washington, DC to Moscow takes ten hours. The flight to Israel takes twelve. If you're a member of Congress and want to learn more about Russia's efforts under the newly negotiated START Treaty or gauge for yourself whether Hamas leadership seems ready to embrace a two-state solution, or help negotiate a trade deal, should you really be forced to spend a sleepless night in row 48? No one thinks members of Congress should be pampered, but a full quarter of US senators are over seventy years old. With the number of global crises threatening our nation, do we really want to discourage senators from engaging other global leaders because we are averse to them flying business class? I for one would also like our nation's leaders to show up at international negotiations moderately well rested and in decent moods. It is a question of priorities and we have misplaced ours.

So much is lost by discouraging members of Congress from traveling with one another. In years past, the bonds established between our leaders on long journeys have enabled ongoing collaboration and even some notable public policy achievements. Senator Lindsey Graham (R-SC) often tells a story about traveling with Vice President Biden. According to Graham, he sat with the vice president on a flight to Afghanistan when they were in the midst of a heated disagreement about the timing and framing of the withdrawal of US forces. Shortly after take-off, in an effort to break the ice, Graham asked Biden, "So Joe, how did you get into politics?"

Twenty-two hours later, as the plane neared the runway in Kabul, Vice President Biden leaned over and said, "Lindsay, I guess we'll have to leave it there for now, but I'd be happy to tell you the rest on the flight home."

Even short trips outside of Washington provide a break in the routine and opportunity for personal connection. The relationship that President Clinton developed with Senator Pete Domenici (the Republican chairman of the Senate Budget Committee through much of the 1990s) on a flight from New Mexico to Washington laid the groundwork for the balanced federal budget that emerged in the years that followed. In a telling anecdote about the value of congressional travel and unusual friendships, Bob Dole recently told the *Washington Post* about a trip he took with his longtime friend and frequent combatant Senator George McGovern (D-SD) in the 1970s. Dole explained that he had initially voted against the creation of Medicare, believing that most retirees were basically receiving adequate health care. "I was a skeptic . . ." Dole said. "But after being with Senator McGovern for three days, I knew we had a problem in America." White House meetings or conversations off the Senate floor are often rushed, stilted, or transactional. But conversations had over the course of several hours and days absent distractions and cameras often build a different type of connection.

Unfortunately, there are now two significant barriers to congressional trips: resources and optics. It takes time, logistics, high-level international connections, and often considerable security to conduct international trips and substantive programs. In general, the best institution to develop these programs is government itself. The taxpayer expense is minuscule relative to the national benefit, and all questions about undue private influence would be eliminated.

However, in the absence of an effective federal program, we should not preclude organizations from sponsoring travel simply because they employ lobbyists. Under current rules, a charter school organization that has worked to secure federal subsidies for inner city schools is prohibited from flying members to see those students in action. An organization trying a novel way to combat child hunger in Africa is prohibited from showing senators how the program works because they sought congressional funding to create it. A major technology company that has developed a safer means to drill for natural gas has essentially no opportunity to bring committee staff to evaluate the new process in the field.

EVERYBODY'S SPECIAL

All organizations have interests, which seems fine unless those interests are, God forbid, "special." Special enjoys positive connotations in practically all arenas except politics. In political rhetoric, those with mundane and average interests reign supreme—which is bizarre for a nation that extols exceptionalism. Regardless of the character or caricature of different interests, it would be preferable to have them out in the open. Under the current rules, financial resources are either disguised and funneled through permissible nonprofit organizations or the opportunity is lost.

The far greater problem is that members of Congress fear political retribution for participating in taxpayer-funded travel. In the current atmosphere of mistrust, it is easy to presume that the Treasury is being fleeced when a member is reported to have joined a fact-finding trip on the public dime. Concerned that a future opponent might exploit this, many members of Congress have decided it is better to stay close to home.

Instead of fanning these flames with self-reproach, congressional leadership should be encouraging official travel. One way to diminish political risk would be to create the expectation that all members take at least one trip a year with their colleagues. Each committee chairman and ranking member should sanction several trips each calendar year—domestic or foreign—bearing on pressing issues within the committee's jurisdiction. The established expectation should be that any member who neglects to participate is committing the same dereliction of duty ascribed to missing votes or ignoring committee responsibilities. Traveling should be understood to be a requirement of the job, rather than a perk. For committees with chronic delinquents, leadership should consider docking the committee budgets.

Moreover, it should matter less if the trips are financed publicly or by private institutions like the Aspen Institute. This is beside the point. The journeys should be of sufficient time and duration that members actually interact. We should care less about the accommodations and more that the members actually spend some quality time together. Finally, we should design the rules to enable and encourage members to bring a family member. If Washington no longer provides natural opportunities for meaningful personal interaction, the long flight to Indonesia, a couple of decent meals, two full days of meetings on combating extremism, and a tour of the Borobudur Temple would be a wise use of public or private resources.

KOSHER PORK

A final area where overzealous reform has exacerbated political gridlock is the largely successful effort to eliminate congressional earmarks. Under Article I, Section 9 of the United States Constitution, the legislative branch is empowered to pass legislation directing all appropriations of money drawn from the US Treasury. In addition to passing a broad federal budget and funding government agencies, Congress is also empowered to direct more specifically—or "earmark"—funds from an agency's budget to support a specific program or project.

It is critical to understand that congressional earmarks do not increase federal spending. Agency budgeting is a zero sum game. If Congress adds $10 million in earmarks to a $1 billion agency appropriation, that agency then has $990 million left to allocate. For this reason, earmarks have always been resented by Executive Branch agencies that believe they are better equipped to determine how best to allocate public funds. Fortunately for cabinet secretaries, earmarks have never been a big drain on the Treasury. In 1996, earmarks claimed little more than half a percent of the federal budget.

Of greater concern than overwhelming Executive Branch prerogatives is the worry that earmarks are too easily subject to an unethical quid pro quo. The argument is that members might be tempted to earmark legislation to enrich their friends and supporters—or worse, themselves. Indeed, this has happened: Around the time that Jack Abramoff's misdeeds came to light, Randy "Duke" Cunningham, a congressman from California, was sentenced to prison for having exchanged Defense Department earmarks for luxuries like "a sport utility vehicle, a Tiffany statue, Bijar rugs and candelabras."

The general concern over earmarks went viral after the *New York Times* published an article asserting that the federal government was financing the construction of a "bridge to nowhere" in Alaska. What insiders termed "special member projects" and what many others continue to call "pork" became the ire of good government reformers. That such a focus emerged is fairly understandable. As Citizens Against Government Waste's *Pig Book* has detailed, over the dozen years that preceded Abramoff's unveiling, earmarking had grown exponentially, emerging to become something of an epidemic.

Even those, like me, who believe the conventional picture of earmarks isn't entirely accurate, have to concede that the process got out of control in the mid-2000s. A report done by the Transportation Department's inspector general revealed that between 1996 and 2005, infrastructure earmarks had increased in number by a factor of ten. Simultaneously, the annual bill that funds social programs—a piece of legislation that included not a single earmark in 1994—contained more than three thousand earmarks little more than a decade later. In total, the four most earmarked bills increased more than 1,000 percent over the same period, rising from a hearty 764 earmarks to a full 8,600. And that rise in number drove a rise in cost: Between 1997 and 2005, the annual earmarked total rose from $13.2 to $27.3 billion.

At first, the reforms designed to stem the epidemic were well intentioned and well crafted. Beginning in 2006, House leadership required members to submit lists of their earmark requests, along with certifications that they had no personal financial interest in any earmarked project's completion. Then, as a House Appropriations Committee synopsis of earmark reform explains, "in 2009, all Members were required to post online their earmark requests and justification, and the executive branch was directed to review all earmark requests." The following year, in 2010, "the House Appropriations Committee announced that it [would] not approve requests for earmarks that [were] directed to for-profit entities . . . and that an online 'one-stop' link to all House Members' appropriations earmark requests [would] be established to help the public easily view them."

These process improvements were all salutary. After all, it wasn't that earmarks were inherently suspect; it was the fact that so many were hidden from public view. Members on the Appropriations Committee and in other positions of influence could simply slip two lines into a 1,200-page committee report and direct a substantial sum of public money to a favorite cause with no debate and few people even noticing. It didn't pass the smell test. The public rightly felt entitled to know how its money was being spent. Consistent with Justice Scalia's view about owning one's speech, members of the public began to demand that Congress own its own spending.

But as has been the pattern in Washington, reformers then went a step too far. In 2011, with the backing of an unusual coalition of budget hawks and transparency advocates, House Republicans placed a moratorium on earmarks. The Senate joined soon thereafter in eliminating the practice altogether. Earmark spending fell from a little less than 1 percent of the budget in 2005 to a little below a tenth of one percent in 2012. And so today, while some still complain that there are backdoor ways for members to get special projects funded through the legislative process, the number of earmarks has fallen by more than 98 percent.

A BRIDGE TO SOMEWHERE
At first glance, the elimination of special projects seems like a positive development. But this is not the case. Far from turning Congress around, the elimination of member projects has driven the institution further into the ditch. First, on the most basic level, elected representatives often have as much or more knowledge than agency bureaucrats of where funds are most needed and best spent. As former senator Ben Nelson (D-NE) once said: "The arguments being made to ban earmarks are that it's going to reduce spending. That's nonsense. It's not. It just changes who decides—from elected officials, on the basis of what they're hearing from local folks, to nameless, faceless bureaucrats."

Special projects were also once used as an incentive to encourage and enable reluctant legislators to take hard votes that served the greater good. Unpopular votes are sometimes referred to by insiders as "leadership taxes." No member of Congress gains local support for voting to increase the debt ceiling or reducing the growth rate of entitlement spending. But the country depends on Congress's ability to make responsible choices when facing these kinds of critical issues. And that is where earmarks played an important role in the larger legislative picture.

The budget may allocate trillions of dollars, but local citizens are often concerned about their own community. Our federal republic can only function if legislators balance local and national interests. There is absolutely nothing wrong with the occasional package deal. If preventing the financial catastrophe of a debt default requires renovating three aging libraries, keeping a local airport open, and funding a few research labs—that's a no-brainer: We'll take it. If securing resources to build a brand new senior center and improved sidewalks gives a Democrat the political courage to reform Social Security, we should happily pour the concrete. This is the balance required to govern a vast and diverse nation—it is the glorious mess of American democracy. While this deal-making might strike some as unseemly, as explained in chapter 1, the Framers of the Constitution designed a system that obligated members of Congress to honor both national and local concerns. Earmarks were crucial ballast in modern-day efforts to strike that elusive balance. If they have nothing to bring back home to brag about, members are now more reluctant to vote for anything that might be unpopular.

Former Senate majority leader and BPC senior fellow Trent Lott (R-MS) once explained: "trying to be a leader where you have no sticks and very few carrots is dang near impossible [because] members don't get anything from you and leaders don't give anything. They don't feel like you can reward them or punish them."

Democratic Majority Leader Reid was apparently feeling that loss of leverage in 2011, when he stated that the president is "absolutely wrong" about earmarks and "should back off" his opposition. And no matter how distasteful that formula may be, a certain quid pro quo is a key element of nearly any important legislative achievement.

Andy Card, chief of staff to George W. Bush, recalls a night in 2003 when he was awakened at 3:00 a.m. and summoned by the Republican House Speaker to help find the nineteen votes needed to pass an overhaul of Medicare Part D, a program to provide prescription drug coverage to millions of elderly Americans. The legislation was a top priority for the Bush Administration, but it was a tough vote for many Republicans because it expanded Medicare, an entitlement program, at significant tax-payer cost. To secure the necessary support, Mr. Card worked through the night striking deals to improve a VA hospital and a variety of other local projects. In the end, it was close, but given something positive to run on in the next election, the votes were secured and the legislation was adopted.

FROM WEST LAFAYETTE TO BIRMINGHAM

The notion of easing tough votes with local favors is not a new concept in American history. In fact, I challenge anyone to identify a major legislative accomplishment that was not enabled by addressing local needs with federal largesse—including the grand moral ones. There are few more consequential pieces of modern legislation than the 1964 Civil Rights Act. While its passage required countless negotiations, concessions, and actual profiles in real courage, it also required a variety of strategic local investments including the location of a major NASA research center at Purdue University. In early 1964, President Johnson believed that the legislative effort was once again stalling out in the House of Representatives. Judge Howard Smith (D-VA), chair of the powerful House Rules Committee, was an avid opponent of the legislation. Due to prior success in blocking the legislation, the Rules Committee was often referred to as "Judge Smith's Graveyard."

President Johnson realized he was running out of time and decided to try to force the legislation to the floor over the objection of the chair. To succeed in circumventing the committee process, he needed Republican votes and he appealed to the House leader, Charles Halleck (R-IN). After much pleading, lobbying, and badgering, Johnson asked Halleck what he needed to get behind the bill. The answer was a new research facility at Halleck's beloved Purdue University. They cut the deal. Purdue gained a world-class research center, millions of Americans gained justice, and our nation gained a measure of dignity.

The inclusion of unique interests isn't just about necessary trade-off. It is about *ownership*. As any effective leader understands, people need to feel invested in an outcome even if they had little if any role in the development. Politicians are not above this. Special projects enable most rank-and-file members of Congress to prove that they exist and are capable of exerting some influence. Once they get their three lines in the one-thousand-page bill—it becomes *their* bill. In BPC projects, we call this "hanging ornaments on the tree." No matter how estranged one of our project participants might be from the core of a deal, if they get their unique idea into the mix, they will almost always support the consensus.

As is often the case, overzealous requirements often do nothing but drive necessary (and fruitful) political activity further underground. In 2012, Daniel Inouye, the longtime chairman of the Senate Appropriations Committee, noted that the desire for what he deemed "essential funding" often forced "unseemly bargaining" with the Executive Branch, stating, "In the end, the Congress will have to choose between an open and transparent method for allocating targeted funding, or one that is done with phone calls, conversations, winks and nods. One method allows for accountability and another leaves us all at the whim of unelected bureaucrats."

I don't want to minimize the risk of outright coercion: You don't want members of Congress to feel as if they can't vote their conscience because leadership might deny resources to their constituents. But the risks here are modest as congressional leaders gain nothing by creating enemies within their own caucus. If we truly want Congress to solve big national problems, our leaders must have some aboveboard tools to balance local interests and national priorities. Earmarks, despite the bad press and "pork" jokes, are a crucial ingredient for effective collaboration that serves the national interest. Rather than outlaw them entirely, we ought to embrace their continued existence, but with clear transparency and responsible limits.

IMMACULATE DYSFUNCTION

There's no real mystery as to how we got here. In an environment as broken as Washington appears to be, it is logical to conclude that some nefarious influence is screwing things up. If public servants aren't serving the public interest, better to separate them from the influences that have led them astray. And that is what the advocates of good government have tried, and often succeeded at, doing. There's no denying that, to a point, raising the ethical bar provides real benefits. The reforms that mark the bulk of the decades that followed the Second World War—to campaign finance laws, ethics rules, and earmark protocol—all marked steps in the right direction. As efforts to influence government have evolved, the rules have had to keep pace.

But we can't shy away from a simple fact: All ethics reforms are not created equal. Like any medicine, too much reform can be harmful to the body politic. The tendency of Congress to adopt new requirements and restrictions in the shadow of an embarrassing scandal is not surprising. But the propensity for excess during periods of public recrimination remains high. All too frequently, the scandals that fuel reform are evidence of truly repugnant criminality, which the new restrictions do little to address.

We want an ethical government—but not a government so burdened and pristine that it is incapable of working at all. My father likes to tell the story of a Cornell research effort to produce the perfect tomato. After years of effort they produced a simply gorgeous product: round, red, and firm. It resisted pests and lasted for weeks in shipping crates. It was perfect except for one problem—it had no taste. The "tasteless tomato" is a cautionary tale for those bent on perfecting our democracy to the point of dysfunction. Given the option, we must choice a political process that bursts with flavor, character, and spirit—even if it produces an occasional rotten tomato.

As the Abramoff story illustrated, there are innumerable reasons to be disillusioned with American government. Our expectations of Washington have melded into some combination of the very high and the very low. We've come to expect that Washington will deliver a bevy of services—health care, education, retirement security—well beyond the scope of what any previous American government had on offer. At the same time, we've come to assume that politicians are both incompetent and self-serving. It is always tempting to demand more of the people who have the honor to serve. But when you find, as we at the BPC have, that a certain course of action just isn't working, we must summon the courage to try something different.

It is time for us to rethink how we regulate the ethics of public service more broadly. Rather than tasking the institutions responsible for policing Washington—the House and Senate Ethics Committees, most specifically—with a singular mandate to crack down on questionable behavior, we ought to ask them to balance the benefits of regulation with the costs it imposes on the culture of collaboration. It is easy to look at Washington with a hunger to expose the dirty deal. But what we need in Washington today is more meeting of the minds. A cleaner political sphere needs also to incubate an environment where people who disagree also know one another well enough to have a spirited and productive debate.

Otto von Bismarck, the first chancellor of Germany, wisely called politics the art of the possible, and the possible simply does not happen without trade-offs. Representative democracy depends on people with different visions finding common ground. There is no such thing as "Immaculate Collaboration" and it is fruitless to fight corruption if the ends produce a dysfunctional government. The American public is right to deal harshly with those who abuse the public trust. But we must be equally vigilant in sustaining a political environment that enables collaboration and rewards creativity. These are the traits that have enabled our nation to overcome great challenges in the past. In the face of our spiraling debt, sputtering economy, broken immigration system, and changing global climate, we must look past our frustrations and let democracy do what it was designed to do.

CHAPTER 8

The Best and the Brightest?

THE GENERAL LAMENT OVER THE "LACK OF LEADERSHIP" IN WASHINGTON is so common that it has become a cliché. We yearn for principled people like Ronald Reagan, Ted Kennedy, Everett Dirksen, and Tip O'Neill—leaders who had the capacity to transcend our tangled legislative process and unite disparate factions. We're adamant that politicians reflect the will of the people, but we don't have much affection for spineless push-overs. O'Neill understood that all politics are local, but he didn't sit back, stick a finger in the air, and wait for his constituents to tell him what to do. There was no confusion about Kennedy or Reagan's core values. Our great leaders have been proud partisans—fierce negotiators and not above "playing politics," grandstanding, or exploiting an opponent's mistake. They have been pragmatists who recognized the legitimacy of different views and had the confidence to shape—not simply heed—public opinion. Washington today seems inundated with politicians who are too willing to demand "all" and accept "nothing." The result is the least productive Congress in memory and a national "to-do" list that is growing in scope and urgency.

I have argued that it is possible to create an environment in DC that is more conducive to collaboration. By enabling greater personal connection and creating more deliberative environments, legislators will have renewed opportunities to work together and get things done. But we now must confront something closer to the source: Are we electing and appointing people who want to work together? Even more fundamental: Are the "best and brightest" in our society still attracted to government service?

Much as there are legions of committed and talented individuals working in Washington today, a whole series of factors are diluting the political gene pool. The realities of our current elections system, the indignity of the vetting and appointment process, and the imposition of bans on whole classes of experts are just some of the things discouraging many from government service.

Recent polling done by the Bipartisan Policy Center and *USA Today* reveals what many likely assumed: Many of the most qualified among us are choosing not to enter the public arena. Only 14 percent of Americans have ever considered running for elected office. Among those who have considered politics, a sizable chunk admits to demurring because they believe campaigns have become too nasty. While a full 94 percent of people ages 18–29 describe "giving back" as at least somewhat important, they don't see government service as an expression of this desire. A disheartening 64 percent of young people today are not at all interested in serving in public office. Fortunately, this is not a lost cause. There are a series of practical things that can be done to attract more great people back into service—and to help us hold on to the ones we already have.

VOTING IN A SHALLOW POOL

In the aftermath of the 1960 Kennedy-Nixon presidential contest—a campaign tarred by allegations that John F. Kennedy's father had purchased the outcome for his son—the president-elect quipped: "I have just received the following telegram from my generous Daddy. It says, 'Dear Jack: Don't buy a single vote more than necessary. I'll be damned if I'm going to pay for a landslide.'" It was wry commentary from the most debonair of our leaders. Despite the self-deprecating wit, by today's standards Kennedy's aside is pretty offensive. The fear today, that money is regularly the deciding factor in American elections, is at the heart of contemporary disillusionment. It is no longer acceptable fodder for even wry jokes.

Fortunately, the kind of vote-fixing and ballot-box stuffing believed to have handed Kennedy Illinois's electoral votes in the 1960 election has declined dramatically over the last fifty years. Elections today—particularly after the Florida debacle of 2000—are vastly more scrutinized, regulated, and professionalized than they were in 1960. But no one has seemingly told the public. The same BPC/*USA Today* poll cited above, taken in 2013, revealed that only 35 percent of likely voters think our elections are actually conducted fairly. Combine this with the legions choosing not to vote and you unearth a troubling statistic: Less than one-quarter of voting age adults are participating in what they believe to be legitimate elections. And this is not just an Election Day problem. After all, if you don't trust the legitimacy of the election, it is hard to trust the legitimacy of the elected.

Disillusionment about our election process also influences who turns out to vote. Despite incredible gains in education, information, and access to voting, fewer Americans are voting now than a century ago. While four in five eligible voters cast ballots in the presidential election of 1860, we haven't bested three in five in a presidential contest since 1968. This sad commentary is not just an indication of civic indifference; it bears directly on the type of candidates we elect. In a system plagued by negative campaigns, inconvenient polling places, long lines, and general mistrust, many casual voters simply stay home. Why go through all the hassle if your allegiances are divided and you're not even sure if your vote will be counted?

As the voting pool shrinks, the imperative on Election Day becomes turning out the party faithful. As a result, "rallying the base" with an aggressive and hard-hitting campaign has become the dominant strategy particularly in low-turnout primary contests. These ideologically driven campaigns exacerbate voter alienation, rewarding extreme partisanship on the left and right. If our current election system is increasing polarization and reducing government legitimacy, the obvious response is to get more people engaged in an election system that they trust. But how?

Electoral reform is tangled in partisan interests. Conservatives tend to focus on the threat of voter fraud by seeking to clean up registration lists and requiring identification at the polls. Progressives cast these concerns as pretext designed to keep away traditionally Democratic voters, while focusing their energies instead on *increasing* registration and improving access to the polls. These are obviously not mutually exclusive desires. There are opportunities to increase voter access *and* ballot integrity. The *USA Today*/BPC poll conducted in 2013 revealed that Americans, by nearly a two-to-one margin, believe that expanding access to the vote was more important than preventing voter fraud. And in the same survey, 80 percent of respondents—including a majority of Democrats—supported requiring that voters show some sort of ID. What Americans want, in essence, is an "all of the above" approach: We want to make it easier to vote in an election system that has ever-greater integrity.

LET'S GET DIGITAL

The first step is comparably easy: *Improve the voter lists.* Democrats fear that too many eligible voters are being left off the lists. Republicans fear that lists fraught with duplicate registrations, dead, and incarcerated voters can lead to fraud. Both sides agree that the current system is a mess. Recent efforts in states like Florida to make the lists more accurate have raised hackles of a partisan purge as legitimate voters were prevented from casting ballots.

While I don't love the sound of a state culling its voter lists to improve accuracy, I have to admit to being part of the problem. Despite being a politically engaged citizen with a reasonably strong sense of social contract, I have never taken the time to contact my local county board of elections before moving out of state. So it is entirely possible that I am currently registered to vote in New York, Rhode Island, Massachusetts, the District of Columbia, and finally Maryland, where I now exercise the franchise.

Apparently, my plight is fairly common. According to the Pew Charitable Trusts, approximately 2.75 million people have registrations in more than one state. Overall, fifty-one million citizens (one in four) were eligible to register to vote but were not registered, and over twenty-four million names (one in eight) on the existing lists were "significantly inaccurate or no longer valid," including nearly two million deceased individuals who remain on active voter lists. So by at least one measure, the conservative critique is correct. There isn't enough being done to make sure that voting rolls are up to date. Concern over the accuracy of the voter rolls is also inflamed by highly partisan registration efforts. Rather than seeing access to voting as a basic good, the system encourages groups to try to register voters they expect to support their side. A whole spate of controversies has emerged as a result. Often, those registering new voters are paid per application, which strikes many observers as perverse because it motivates inaccuracies, carelessness, and fraud.

An obvious step is to move away from the outmoded technologies that dominate our registration systems. In 2014, no one should have to visit a voter registration office—or God help them, a DMV—to fill out a paper registration form. Online voter registration tools are far easier to access and can prevent the entry of most incorrect information. Over twenty states presently or will soon install online registration systems. In addition to making voter registration more accurate, technology can dramatically reduce its expense. In Maricopa County, Arizona (which includes the city of Phoenix), the cost of processing a registration dropped from almost $1 per paper registration to less than a nickel for those completed online. Canada moved its entire registration process online and reports recouping the full cost of the investment in a single election cycle. For a system already stretching every dime, these savings should provide ample motivation to move everything online.

Some states have decided to cross check their voter rolls with information that is already available. Colorado, Delaware, Maryland, Nevada, Utah, Virginia, and Washington have joined to make their lists more accurate by matching voter registration and motor vehicles data with other sources that some states already use, such as national change of address data from the Postal Service, as well as other databases, such as death records from the Social Security Administration. These states have committed to using the information to notify eligible voters and reach out to people who remain on the rolls but appear no longer valid.

In the age of Amazon, Google, and Facebook, the fact that our state governments are struggling to identify eligible voters is kind of pathetic. Amazon CEO Jeff Bezos wants to deliver packages to your door by drone and the county election board doesn't know if you exist or not. There's no lack of information out there on where we live, how old we are, and a whole lot more. This information is secured, curated, and heavily marketed. It's time for the public sector to catch up.

In 1993, Congress passed the National Voter Registration Act, commonly referred to as the "Motor Voter" law. Many thought that bill would compel states to automatically register anyone obtaining a driver's license.

But the law actually required only that individuals have the *opportunity* to register, and so the law's effectiveness has varied widely between locales. A 2005 survey of people leaving an agency office in Ohio identified that only three people out of every one hundred were given registration forms. Of course, the natural desire to leave the DMV as quickly as possible may prevent people from hanging around to fill out additional forms.

One attractive option would be to coordinate voter enrollment with the Selective Service system. A majority of states register eighteen-year-old men to vote when they sign up for the (presently dormant) military draft. In January 2013, Defense Secretary Leon Panetta lifted limitations on women serving in combat operations and established a goal of full gender-neutrality. Expanding the Selective Service requirements to include women is anticipated in this transition. There is a certain logic to engaging young Americans in the political franchise at the moment we make them available for military service; it is why we passed the Twenty-Sixth Amendment, which lowered the voting age to eighteen from twenty-one. We should take that sentiment a step further, not only offering young people the opportunity to vote, but presuming that they will want to use it. Most democracies around the world rely upon an even more comprehensive approach: They automatically register voters. In Automatic Voter Registration (AVR) systems, the government essentially pre-registers all eligible voters, and the voters need to "opt out" if they do not want to be in the system.

Increasing Access and Integrity

An idea that stems from the current debate over voter ID laws is to allow Election Day Registration (EDR) for anyone who can furnish a government-issued picture identification card. EDR has been shown to increase voter turnout—presumably among procrastinators and voters who tune in during the final campaign stretch. By restricting same-day voting to people with sanctioned identification, this approach also addresses integrity concerns and improves the accuracy of voter lists. And that then turns us back to the question of electoral integrity. As part of any program to expand voter registration, we should provide every registered voter with a free government-issued identification card. IDs are helpful when cashing a check, getting a prescription drug, or renting an apartment. New IDs would enable all registered voters to prove their identity at the polls. It would also diminish the unpleasant and anti-democratic perception that eligibility requirements are motivated in part by a desire to disenfranchise certain voters. Perhaps the most compelling aspect of these proposals is that they engage concerns expressed by both the left and the right—a prerequisite for progress too often ignored.

Finally, the long lines that plagued the 2012 election brought new attention to issues of voter access and convenience. In response to wait times of up to *six hours* (which required polls to stay open until midnight), President Obama created a bipartisan Presidential Commission on Election Administration (PCEA) led by Bob Bauer, Obama's counsel and top campaign lawyer, and Ben Ginsberg, his counterpart on the Romney campaign. In January 2014, the PCEA made a series of recommendations that avoided hot-button issues while offering a series of practical steps to improve the accuracy of voter rolls, increase access to polling places, and improve their efficiency.

Consistent with the PCEA recommendations, we should make it easier for voters to cast ballots before and after working hours during the week before the election. Some states have already adopted some such policy, but fifteen states still offer no opportunities to cast votes before the day of any given election, and many others only allow early voting at a limited number of polling places.

A more significant change would be to move Election Day from a Tuesday to a Saturday. The logic for Tuesday voting is anachronistic. In 1845, it was decided that there should be a uniform voting day to diminish the potential for election fraud. In the agrarian society of the time, Sunday was not a viable option because of religious observance and Monday didn't provide enough time for people from outlying areas to travel to their county seat. Congressional elections were similarly standardized in 1872. Thus, we have been voting on Tuesday for the last 150 years.

There's little question that Tuesday voting is inconvenient for many. Comedian Chris Rock thinks the rationale for the current schedule is simple: "They don't want you to vote. If they did, we wouldn't vote on a Tuesday. You ever throw a party on a Tuesday? No. Because nobody would come." Switching Election Day to the weekend would make it that much easier for many eligible voters to get to the polls.

If our goal is to encourage the election of pragmatic leaders, we must increase voter participation and improve the integrity of our elections. If we want Americans to give their leaders greater latitude to compromise, we need to first give voters greater confidence that their opinions will count, especially once every two years when they matter most.

PRIMARY PASSION

On the election front, even more can be accomplished by revamping state primaries. Because so many states and congressional districts vote reliably for one party or the other, the primary election process is often more consequential than the general election in determining who serves in Congress. Despite the reality that the primaries often matter more than the general election, they are valued decidedly less by the voters.

Voter participation in primary elections is abysmal: Over the past six midterm elections, participation has hovered between 16 and 21 percent; several states still employ caucuses and conventions, which significantly restrict opportunities for voter participation. And the result is a roster of leaders in Washington who aren't really representative of the broader public mandate. By comparison, a study by the Bipartisan Policy Center estimated that 57.5 percent of eligible voters cast ballots in the 2012 general election. That figure was down from 60.4 percent turnout in the 2008 election, but higher than the 54.2 percent turnout in 2000. Political scientist Norm Ornstein describes the predictable result of low-turnout primary elections: "The unhappy effects of low turnout are clear: ever-greater polarization in the country and in Washington, which in turn has led to ever-more rancor and ever-less legislative progress."

The problem here cannot be overstated. Even if most states and congressional districts are bright blue and deep red, the type of Democrats and Republicans chosen to serve these jurisdictions makes all the difference. Just ask former House Majority Leader Eric Cantor, who was resoundingly defeated in a 2014 primary in which less than 14 percent of eligible voters participated. Hardly a moderate, Cantor was routed by a Tea Party challenger who attacked him for contemplating even modest immigration reform and for being too accommodating in ending the 2013 government shutdown. Professor Geoffrey Layman from Vanderbilt has studied the increasing role that party activists play in driving polarization. "When a party is populated by ideologically-extreme single-issue activists," he writes, "the rational strategy of candidates for the party's nominations may be to take non-centrist positions on all major issues." If the only way to win a primary is to glorify ideological rigidity, sign zealous pledges, and brag about how you won't collaborate, many voters in the general election have no option to express a preference for pragmatism and collaboration.

Of course, instituting reforms that benefit more moderate candidates will be strongly opposed by the ideologues that currently control the party apparatus in many states. But now is the perfect time to press this debate. Commenting on the 2012 election cycle, conservative strategist Steven Law asserted, "There is a broad concern about having blown a significant number of races because the wrong candidates were selected." From Christine O'Donnell in Delaware to Ken Buck in Colorado to Richard Mourdock in Indiana and Todd Akin in Missouri, the GOP has lost senate seats that it might well have claimed had they nominated a more mainstream candidate. Democratic Party leaders are also chafing against their diminished authority in the primary process. As these proposed changes do not seek to advantage one party over the other, there's a real chance for them to be accepted.

There are other simple ways to get the public voting in primaries. As a starting point, many voters simply don't even realize a primary election is taking place. This sad reality is particularly acute during midterm elections where four out of five eligible voters don't bother to participate. When the race for the White House is particularly heated, primaries become a big deal and turnout remains comparably high despite the fact that the primaries are spread over several months. In 2008, over 30 percent of eligible voters participated in choosing among presidential hopefuls. Tellingly, in states that held 2008 primaries for Congress on different days than the presidential contest, less than 15 percent of eligible voters turned out.

The fix is relatively easy. In presidential election years, states should hold congressional primaries on the same day presidential candidates are selected. In midterm elections all states should agree to a common or "National Primary Day" to increase awareness and participation. Absent a presidential contest, states have no reason to compete for early primaries—making a single coordinated primary possible.

Next, caucus and convention systems—an all-too-common alternative to primaries—should be eliminated altogether. These antiquated processes concentrate power among a subset of party faithful and lead to results that can be out of step with the interests of the broader electorate. Consider one particularly egregious example: Despite serving three terms in the Senate and enjoying a 93 percent approval rating within the party in 2006, Senator Bob Bennett of Utah was ousted from his position as part of a party convention in 2010 that included only 3,500 Utahans in a state of roughly two million people of voting age.

In a surprising move, the Virginia Republican Party chose to swim against the current in 2012 and switched from a primary to a nominating convention. The convention predictably chose the more ideologically conservative candidates for governor, lieutenant governor, and attorney general. (All lost to their Democratic challengers.) The last two winners of the Iowa Republican caucuses (Mike Huckabee in 2008 and Rick Santorum in 2012) have failed to capture the party's nomination. This disconnect has led some party leaders to question the wisdom of Iowa's oversized role in the nominating process. According to the leading political analyst Charlie Cook, "The [Iowa] process has become increasingly contrived and manipulated, losing its effectiveness of being a surrogate for voters across the country."

A FORCE FOR MODERATION

In addition to all states holding actual primaries, these contests should allow participation by independent voters. A larger fraction of Americans than ever before are choosing to not affiliate with either party when they register to vote. A 2013 Gallup poll put the figure at 42 percent, marking the largest slice ever recorded in the poll's sixty-year history. In states with "closed" primaries, only registered and declared party voters can participate, thereby excluding a significant portion of the engaged electorate. That leaves the growing legions of independent voters without an opportunity to shape the roster of candidates left standing for the general election.

Our political system would only benefit by drawing less doctrinal voters into the candidate selection process, as more moderate candidates would stand a better chance of winning each nomination. A relatively modest change being embraced by about half the states is to allow people to choose which primary to vote in on Election Day. In states allowing "semi-closed" primary voting, individuals can declare their party affiliation at the polls. In states with "semi-open" primaries, voters simply request the ballot they wish to fill out. Either way, a larger fraction of the electorate is welcomed into the process.

———

The most prominent effort under way to change primary voting is the open primary, also described as the top-two primary, the nonpartisan blanket primary, or the "Cajun primary" (due to its early Louisiana roots). The practice has recently garnered significant attention, having been adopted by California and Washington State in public referenda. This new system allows multiple candidates from all parties (and independents) to be on the ballot during a primary open to all voters. The top two advance to the general election regardless of their affiliation. This approach is designed to increase participation by independent voters and create incentives for candidates to appeal to the broad electorate. Senator and Washington elder statesman Slade Gorton (R-WA) believes that the top-two primary "takes some of the teeth away from the more extreme elements of each party." While some in California see signs that the new system is having an impact, it is too early to determine if the experiment, implemented in 2012, will increase voter participation or opportunities for more moderate candidates.

Finally, to avoid serious conflicts of interest, states should move away from having partisan officials set and administer election rules. While the vast majority of election problems are caused by bureaucratic incompetence and a lack of resources, supporters of losing candidates often complain that partisan trickery did them in. A few states rely on bipartisan commissions to administer local elections. Some others vest authority in civil servants who are shielded from partisan officials. When it comes to building confidence in the integrity of the election system, hiring a referee that is not betting on (or employed by) either team makes a whole lot of sense.

None of these electoral reforms is meant to represent a panacea nor would any by itself restore America's faith in the electoral system. But taken together, they offer the blueprint to elect, from both parties, a better roster of American leaders. With a little more trust in the system, ordinary citizens might feel less inclined to believe that legislators need always to be monitored and parented while governing. And given that extra bit of latitude, the collaborative spirit that is so important to the nation's long-term interests may begin to take hold again within the Washington Beltway.

THE PRIVILEGE TO SERVE

The road to Washington doesn't begin and end with the electoral process. Article II, Section II of the Constitution states that the president

shall nominate, and by and with the Advice and Consent of the Senate, shall appoint Ambassadors, other Public Ministers and Counsels, Judges of the Supreme Court, and all Other Officers of the United States, whose appointments are not herein otherwise provided for, and which shall be established by law.

The process of recruiting top talent into our government is one place where the executive and legislative branches simply must collaborate. Of late, the choreography imposed by the Constitution has been more mosh pit than ballet.

In the run-up to the use of the so-called "nuclear option" in November 2013—the proposed change to significantly hinder filibusters—efforts to install presidential appointees were regularly at loggerheads. The effect not only hobbled the government, it discouraged many qualified individuals—particularly those without prior government experience—from considering public service at all. While there are challenges to address in the nominating and vetting processes, the crucible of the conflict is clearly Senate confirmation.

In many ways, the Senate confirmation process is the canary in the congressional coal mine. It is a barometer of the relationship between the president and the opposing party and a recurring opportunity for the parties to reward or punish one another. Presidential nominations have rarely been rubber-stamped, as some might have us believe. President John Tyler was so unsuccessful with getting his own nominees confirmed by the Senate during the 1840s that he eventually let the Congress decide who he'd appoint. Nevertheless, over the course of our democracy, the general understanding has been that a president should be able to fill his cabinet (if not his judicial appointments) as he sees fit, as long as the nominees are of reasonable moral character and basically qualified. Even when opposing a particular individual, senators allowed the nominee to receive an up or down vote on the Senate floor. And, in general, that led to a fairly expeditious confirmation process. During the Kennedy Administration, for example, most appointees were confirmed within three months of being nominated.

Since then, however, things have become far more contentious and freighted with unrelated conflicts. Senators began to see confirmations—or, more specifically, the threat of holding up a nomination—as leverage against the White House on all matters. A senator might put a "hold" on a nomination until an administration agreed to turn over documents or approve a controversial permit. As a result, during the Clinton Administration, nominees were being made to wait eight months—or nearly three times as long as they had during the 1960s. Before Senate Democrats invoked the "nuclear option" in late 2013, the wait had grown to a full ten months. When the Department of Housing and Urban Development was formed in 1965, it took the Senate an average of six days to hold hearings and confirm a top department official. But, when the Department of Homeland Security was formed in 2002, it took the Senate an average of sixty-seven days to scrutinize and confirm its top leaders. In light of the previous year's attacks on 9/11, the inability to act with urgency to fill these critical positions forecast a growing problem.

While members of Congress came to view the nominations process as a means of pressuring the White House, this strategy exacted a high toll on those caught in the middle. Many chose to drop out rather than spend more months in professional purgatory. Consider the experience of Connie Newman, whom President George H. W. Bush nominated to be the director of the Office of Personnel Management in 1989. Assured by the White House that her nomination would sail through the Senate, she sold her privately owned business to move to Washington. But then, in an attempt to pressure the White House on an entirely tangential concern, a Democratic senator put a hold on her nomination, single-handedly putting her in limbo for months without a salary. She was eventually confirmed six months later—but only after racking up a sizable debt of tens of thousands of dollars to pay for her basic living expenses.

BIG DESKS, EMPTY CHAIRS

Beyond the costs borne by any one individual is the toll the delays have on the government's capacity to do its work. More than two years after President Obama's 2008 election, nearly a quarter of the top five hundred Senate-confirmed positions in his administration were either vacant or filled by a temporary stand-in. The resulting morass is painfully revealed in moments of crisis. The 9-11 Commission Report took pains to note President George W. Bush's national security team was not confirmed and on the job until more than six months after he took office. Treasury secretary Tim Geithner had to operate without other senior appointees during the midst of the financial meltdown. The question is what set us down the path toward this dysfunction.

While there may not be any "original sin," few can dispute that the mood began to shift in 1968 when the Senate blocked Lyndon Johnson's effort to elevate Supreme Court justice Abe Fortas to chief justice. Conflict over Executive Branch appointments began to increase even more abjectly during the 1980s, when President Reagan started appointing more unabashedly political nominees to even lower ranking posts. The Republican's approach led to increased scrutiny from Democrats who had previously been accustomed to confirming technocrats in these deputy and assistant secretary roles.

The growing tension finally boiled over in the late 1980s and early 1990s during the battles to confirm Supreme Court nominees Robert Bork and Clarence Thomas. These two cases demonstrated that, beyond issues of qualification, the Senate was then inclined to consider questions of ideology when confirming Supreme Court justices. For a time this level of scrutiny was reserved for the nation's highest court. Several years later, however, when Democrats filibustered Miguel Estrada's nomination to the DC Circuit Court of Appeals (considered the second-highest court in the nation), similarly ideological battles began to form around lower-level appointments. From that point forward, progressives and conservatives would use nominees as pawns to achieve a variety of unrelated ends. And thus the dysfunction that has become now sadly common first began to take root.

On November 21, 2013, fifty-two Senate Democrats voted in favor of the "nuclear option," essentially eliminating the filibuster in all but Supreme Court confirmations. The direct result of this unilateral action is that the nominees can now be confirmed by a simple majority of fifty votes. If able to maintain support from its own members, there is no longer any obligation for the majority party to gain support—or even consult—across the aisle. This fundamental breakdown in the culture of the Senate did not occur in a vacuum. Senator Reid and McConnell's failure to work out a resolution epitomized the much deeper crisis facing the institution. Unfortunately, the toothpaste is now out of the tube and the tenor of the appointments process is certain to remain highly contentious. Accepting this reality, there remain a number of practical steps that can make the process more effective. If nomination battles are going to be "nasty and brutish" we should at least honor Thomas Hobbes and try to keep them "short."

First of all, we force way too many people through the Senate confirmation process. Between 1972 and 2004, the number of confirmable appointments grew by 26 percent, to 586. Far more dramatic, since 2004, the number has almost doubled again, to 1,152. Some of that growth is due simply to the expansion of the Executive Branch, like the Department of Homeland Security. But that is only a portion of the story.

Over the last several decades, the Senate has decided to require formal confirmation for many positions the president was once able to fill absent input. As late as the second Nixon Administration, none of the positions inside the Office of Management and Budget were subject to Senate confirmation. Nowadays, the number of appointments needing confirmation has reached the point of absurdity. Do we really need the entire US Senate to vote on each of the ten members of the National Institute for Literacy Advisory Board or for the Alternate Federal Co-Chairman of the Appalachian Regional Commission? Hundreds of confirmations are required for people who serve on part-time advisory boards, people with only the power to recommend action to a federal agency or commission. Even in the best of times, this would be an ineffective use of Senate time and energy.

INNOCENT UNTIL APPOINTED

Fortunately, this problem has not entirely escaped the Congress itself. As Senator Lamar Alexander (R-TN) lamented quite succinctly: "Too often the appointments process has degenerated into a time-consuming, unfair ordeal that creates an 'innocent until nominated' syndrome." As the cliché goes, knowing you have a problem is the first step toward solving it. Before retiring Senator Joseph Lieberman (I-CT) remarked, "If we don't fix what is broken in this system, I fear we risk discouraging some of our nation's most talented individuals from accepting nominations, thus leaving important positions unfilled."

In 2011 the Senate began to diminish their own burden. They passed a resolution to expedite consideration of nominees to part-time boards, a promising start that could affect over 250 nominees. Additionally, Congress passed the Presidential Appointments and Efficiency and Streamlining Act, which reduced the breadth of positions that require confirmation by over 150.

These were good initial steps—but they're not nearly enough. More should be done to free mid-level positions from the discouraging and inefficient confirmation process. An appropriate goal would be to reduce the number of confirmable positions by half—returning Washington to the roughly five hundred officials who required confirmation just a decade ago. Not only would this enable the next administration to get mid-level officials in place more quickly, it would also allow the Senate to focus its attention on those posts of greatest significance.

Of course, no one in Washington gives up power easily. It will be difficult for Senate committees to voluntarily limit their authority—particularly if they feel they are being singled out. But there is a model that has been used successfully in the past that would increase the chance for success.

In the wake of the Cold War and the advent of new defense systems, the United States had far more military bases than it needed. To modernize our military and reap the benefits of the "peace dividend," Congress had to close a significant number of military installations. As these bases play a significant role in the local economies and cultures of many congressional districts, efforts to close bases have always been met with fierce local opposition. To navigate these difficult politics, Congress created the Defense Base Closure and Realignment (BRAC) Commission in 1988. The commission made a package of recommendations that were then subject to an up-or-down vote without amendment. By making an all-or-nothing package of unpopular decisions at once, the BRAC diminished the sense that any individual member of Congress had failed to protect his or her local interests. A similar independent commission could be effective in realigning the confirmation process.

The 2011 Streamlining Act also acknowledged the overwhelming and inefficient paperwork that now accompanies any nomination, and authorized a working group to study the question. The working group suggested numerous fixes to reduce the number of speeches, former neighbors, financial transactions, and vacation itineraries that would-be nominees must track down. Senator Alexander, who was appointed to the working group, described the problem:

> We take some self-respecting U.S. citizen, and the president invites them to come take a position in the federal government of honor and dignity, and suddenly they find themselves immersed in a series of duplicative interrogations from all directions in which they must fill out forms that define words such as "income" in different ways, all of which is designed to lead them before a committee, not to really assess their qualifications but to see if they can be trapped and turned into an apparent criminal.

It is a bait and switch of epic proportion. Within hours of being announced as the president's choice for a position of great responsibility and stature, nominees find themselves on the phone with tax attorneys and digging through boxes in their basements to track down the Social Security number for their landscaper from twenty years prior. In an effort to streamline the arduous and often degrading process, the working group also made sensible recommendations to reduce duplicative questions, create a new computerized "smart form," form joint committees to provide one-stop confirming for nominations, and trim the scrutiny of nominees for part-time boards or commissions.

These ideas were gaining momentum, and there was even growing interest in a proposal to give each nomination an "expiration date" (at which point nominees stuck in the queue would be considered confirmed). However, the majority's recent decision to neuter their opposition has poisoned this well, making it unlikely that the Senate can have constructive conversations on anything to do with the confirmations process—at least for a while.

THE "VET" OFFENSIVE

The plight of nominees in the Senate, however, marks only part of the story. The White House has had a hand in this mess as well. Before the Senate can drag its feet, the president has to first select a nominee. And what has become apparent of late is that the vetting process *before* each nomination is a growing part of the problem. While it is impossible to come up with an exact tally, stories abound about highly qualified candidates passed over, abandoned mid-stream, or frustrated into submission. When combining an unnecessarily cumbersome process with unnecessary restrictions and undue hostility, it is no wonder we are not drawing the full breadth of American talent into government service.

The stories are maddening. At the outset of the Obama Administration, confusion over the obligation to pay employment taxes for part-time help like house cleaning and yard work took down several highly qualified candidates. The questions boiled down to the tax law minutia of whether a cleaning person was an "individual contractor" (whose employer has no obligation to pay employment taxes) or an "employee." The distinction turns on a variety of naunced factors. If the cleaning person brings her own equipment and materials and has latitude about when to arrive and what order to clean the house, nominees were good to go. If however, the cleaning person comes every other Wednesday and used the nominee's vacuum and Lysol, failure to pay employment taxes on time became one of the more consequential errors in his or her professional career.

Take the case of Nancy Killefer, nominated by President Obama in 2009 to serve as the administration's chief performance officer—a newly created position designed to cut government waste. Killefer had already served as the chief financial officer at the Treasury Department. Nevertheless, the White House felt compelled to withdraw her nomination after it was discovered that a lien had been placed on her property for failure to pay certain taxes due in 2005. Killefer had made an honest mistake; she paid the taxes as soon as she was alerted to the mishap, years before she was nominated. Nevertheless, she was deemed unfit to serve despite the fact that she spent four years in a leadership role at the place responsible for all of the nation's money.

Of course we want our government officials to be honest and ethical. And of course there are many non-criminal acts that should disqualify someone from high public office. But, as has been on particularly dramatic display recently, we've turned the desire for integrity into a puritanical crusade. The understandable fear of humiliation or abandonment is keeping legions of skilled people away from government service.

Even those whose background checks produce no red flags find the process a burden—and there are ways to make the whole ordeal more expeditious. For example, the forms that candidates are required to fill out when being vetted by the Executive Branch should be streamlined and made to emulate the forms that are required by the Legislative Branch. (Some progress on this front was made in 2011, but the process remains tortuous.) The basic form is a staggeringly unnecessary 127 pages long. Respondents must include such information as the birthplaces of divorced spouses, every country visited in the last seven years (with explanation), and the phone numbers of all work supervisors over the past decade. Potential nominees must also respond to the question, "Have you ever knowingly engaged in any acts of terrorism?" It is obviously critical that we don't place terrorists in senior government positions, but I doubt this question is effective at rooting them out.

There are three additional Executive Branch questionnaires, including a financial disclosure form that often requires nominees to divest financial holdings. Once you survive Executive Branch vetting, nominees are then required for fill out one or more of seventeen different Senate committee questionnaires and respond in writing to hundreds of questions posed by individual senators.

If the answer to any given question cannot reasonably be thought to bear on whether a candidate would be able to perform the duties of the job at issue, the question should not be asked.

THE SCARLET L

In addition to disqualifying nominees for errors of conduct that have nothing to do with character, the Obama Administration has championed its decision to exclude lobbyists from serving in the White House or appointed positions elsewhere in the administration. The caricature of lobbyists as influence-peddling insiders has been seized upon to symbolize all that is wrong with Washington. The administration's opprobrium has also served as a convenient foil to differentiate itself from the public's disdain for institutional DC.

While the administration's posture is popular across the country, these political points come at a cost. Beyond the obvious shrinking of the talent pool, the stigmatization of lobbyists discourages engaged advocacy and overlooks the great diversity of individuals and interests seeking to shape public policy. Under the current rules, advocates for health clinics, coal miners, drug companies, wind energy, the insurance industry, and the fight to end global hunger are all lumped together as an "untouchable" caste that need to be kept outside the White House fence.

It's not that lobbyists are just misunderstood altruists. Many lobbyists do play on the edges of propriety and most seek to transparently advance the narrow capitalist interests of their employers. In progressive administrations, it is reasonable to assume that being a corporate lobbyist will be seen as a liability for Executive Branch positions. But a blanket disqualification of anyone who has recently (i.e., over the prior two years) sought to influence policy doesn't make any sense. Should a lobbyist against drug abuse be banned from working in the drug czar's office? Should someone who has lobbied on behalf of torture victims be banned from heading up the State Department's Bureau on Human Rights? (This actually happened.) If the FBI can brag about hiring former convicted hackers to improve the security of its computer systems, one would think the Treasury Department might welcome a former tax lobbyist who understands the baffling intricacies of tax loopholes—and how to close them.

Many of these individuals want to work in government for all the right reasons. And to do so they have to "get clean," quit their jobs, and terminate their lobbying registration for two years. One Democratic lawyer described the process as having to enter "purgatory before the pearly gates of heaven."

I can't deny having some personal stake in this issue through my work at the Bipartisan Policy Center. Our goal is to develop pragmatic solutions and influence public policy. After a BPC task force spends two years hashing out a detailed policy compromise on immigration reform or climate change, we don't just hit "print" and wait for the policy to change. It is difficult, to the point of illogical, to try to influence public policy without influencing public policy makers: what is called "lobbying." As such, the administration's disapproval of lobbying poses a direct challenge to our work.

By definition, the BPC belongs to neither party and is no one's home team. To deeply entrenched partisans, BPC proposals are inherently suspect—after all, they are developed with input from the "other side." Effective lobbyists help soothe these suspicions and ensure that our ideas get a fair hearing. If we weren't able to promote our recommendations with a wide array of politicians, the BPC's studies would remain just that—studies. Lobbyists play a critical role overcoming the mistrust and tribal resentments that often prevent meaningful dialogue. Far from being agitators and obstacles, lobbyists often serve the role of special envoys and peacemakers.

Washington does not lack for ideas. It lacks the trust to consider new ones. This is why BPC formed an affiliated organization, the Bipartisan Policy Center Action Network (BPCAN). While BPC does not employ any lobbyists, BPCAN is staffed by a team of four full-time lobbyists and contracts with lobbying firms that have unique expertise and relationships with key legislators. In Washington, it is often true that people who know the most accomplish the least and vice versa. The knock against experts and think tanks is they don't want to sully themselves with political relevance. Conversely the trade associations and interest groups that thrive in the political trenches are not supposed to advance the broad public interest. BPC's combination of analysis and advocacy bridges this divide.

It is extremely effective to have the head of the Natural Resource Defense Council's Energy Program and a senior vice president of Exxon Mobil meet with a member of Congress to explain a joint proposal on energy production. It is compelling to have leading banking and consumer advocates make a detailed case together for how to fix the home mortgage system. As unpaid members of BPC's policy projects, these individuals can meet with anyone without triggering lobbying issues. But the nuts-and-bolts work to enable these interactions to occur is another matter. A staff member employed by our advocacy arm has to arrange these meetings, accompany our task force members, and provide follow-up analysis. In supporting these conversations, he or she is enmeshed in the dark art of lobbying and therefore barred from even contemplating a position with the administration.

It gets even quirkier. Despite the fact that BPC's Advocacy Network employs registered lobbyists, the administration rules do not exclude me, as head of the organization, from public service. However, my staff must proudly wear the "Scarlet L." They have sophisticated knowledge of key policy issues, credibility with ideologically diverse groups, a unique ability to identify workable solutions—and they are barred from even contemplating a position with the administration.

LATTE LOBBYING

It's not just that lobbyists have been banned from serving in government; the Obama Administration has also restricted its employees from conferring with lobbyists and excluded lobbyists from the vast array of federal advisory boards, committees, and working groups that exist to expand the government's perspective and expertise.

On June 18, 2010, President Obama issued a presidential memorandum designed to further limit special interest influence by barring lobbyists from a suite of activities. A memo from the National Institutes of Health exhibits the breadth of these restrictions:

> *The entities or groups covered include any board, commission, council, delegation, conference, panel, task force, or other similar group or subgroup regardless of whether it is subject to the Federal Advisory Committee Act (FACA). At NIH, this includes, but is not limited to all NIH/HHS National Advisory Councils (NACs), Program Advisory Committees (PACs), Boards of Scientific Counselors (BSCs), Initial/ Integrated Review Groups (IRGs), Special Emphasis Panels (SEPs), and any subcommittee or workgroup of one of these committees.*

Taken out of context, that may not seem so draconian. Few of these advisory groups exert a great deal of influence. Still, it is a broad exclusion motivated more by political expediency than fairness or ethics. Former solicitor general Charles Fried captures its broad implications:

> *The anti-lobbying measures of our day do not usually gainsay the right of lobbyists to ring the officials' bell; but some of them come quite close to decreeing that no one in the executive branch may come to the door. And this comes perilously close to infringing the very right the First Amendment establishes. Quite apart from that, some of these initiatives express a disdain for a whole class of persons, many of whom perform a useful and important function.*

Several lobbyists even recently brought suit in federal court alleging that the ban preventing them from serving on advisory boards represented a violation of their First Amendment rights. Initially dismissed, a judge on the Court of Appeals reinstated the lawsuit.

❧

White House staff are caught in the middle. They are eager to gain expert insights but reluctant to get caught cavorting with a suspect class. Many have adopted the habit of "bumping into" lobbyists at the Caribou Coffee across the street from the White House where these encounters are not recorded in official government visitor logs. Jim VandeHei, an editor at *POLITICO*, summarized the Executive Branch's ambivalent relationship with lobbyists: "The White House wants to enlist their help, wants to get their advice on legislation. But doesn't want the public to know about it."

Finally, the White House attitude toward lobbyists is at odds with the White House pledge of openness and transparency. It turns out that people are less inclined to scrupulously report their activities if they are penalized for doing so. Over the past few years, scores of former lobbyists have chosen to recast themselves as "strategic advisors" and de-registered without substantially altering the work they do. A similar dynamic is occurring among senior officials upon leaving government. Upon taking office, President Obama issued an Executive Order barring appointees from lobbying the administration when they return to the private sector.

In a Bloomberg article titled, "Obama Alumni Join Ranks of Unlobbyists Selling Washington Wisdom," Sarah Byner, the research director of the Center for Responsive Politics, asserts "The influence industry is moving underground." Her organization has identified eighty-six former administration officials who are now working as "unlobbyists." Their jobs are to influence government policy, but they have not registered as lobbyists and thus fly under the restrictions.

Howard Marlowe, a veteran lobbyist and former president of the American League of Lobbyists, believes that there is only one meaningful distinction between strategic advising and lobbying. "We in the lobbyist profession register," he says, "and the public and media can at least find out who we work for, what the issues are that we're hired to work on, and what we're getting paid." In a sign of the times, in 2013 the American League of Lobbyists changed its name to the Association of Government Relations Professionals.

The broader issue here is not just about lobbyists, and it is not just about nominations. The real concern is that good people from all facets of life are being shunted from public service. It has been roughly two decades since President Clinton, frustrated by the morass of installing people into government positions lamented: "[I]t's time to have a bipartisan look at the whole appointments process. It takes too long to get somebody confirmed. It's too bureaucratic. You have two and three levels of investigation. I think it's excessive."

And things have only gotten worse. Today, at a moment when it is clear that we've gone further afield, it may be time to switch the way we approach the nominations and confirmation processes. Rather than asking how we keep bad people out of government, we ought to consider how we get good people in.

DIALING FOR DOLLARS

There's one further way that Washington repels talented public servants—and it harks back to a subject covered in chapter 7: fundraising. While Super PACs are playing an increasing role in national elections, the money raised by the candidates themselves is far more important to their electoral prospects. Having acknowledged that there is little that can be done to stanch the amount of money in our political system, we can't ignore another part of the equation: how much time our elected officials devote to chasing down donations.

The sheer number of hours a politician has to spend dialing for dollars has become a serious deterrent to public office. On average, it costs $1.5 million to win a House seat and $10.2 million to secure one in the Senate. While the current limit on donations is $2,600 per candidate per cycle, the average political gift is closer to $100. If you want to run for Senate and aren't able or willing to spend your own money, you will need to capture the imaginations and checkbooks of tens of thousands of supporters. If fortunate enough to prevail, your task will be to recruit around fifty new donors every day for six years. Though members have support from paid fundraisers and private "bundlers" who recruit donors for the thankful officials, there's no question that asking for money has become a principal part of serving in Congress.

If troubled by the idea that officials in Washington, DC live a life of grandeur, there is a surefire way to dispel that concern: Become a political fundraiser. Our nation's leaders are not shaking hands under crystal chandeliers and sipping fine wine in ornate drawing rooms. Senators and representatives spend a dreadfully large percentage of their lives in call centers raising money for their next campaign. Democratic senators hunker down for call time in tiny windowless rooms across the street from their offices. (It is illegal to raise money in a government building.) Republican House members are relegated to cubbies where they must listen to each other's weary pitches. "Campaign fundraising is much like Amway or Mary Kay," a senior Republican strategist says, "The best Members spend 2–3 hours per day—5–6 days per week building and cultivating their networks."

And there's no attempt to gloss over these obligations. Democrats elected to Congress for the first time in 2012 were told to expect nine- to ten-hour workdays while in Washington, with four hours for "call time," one hour for "'strategic outreach,'" which includes fundraisers and press work," one "hour ... to 'recharge,'" and three to four hours ... for the actual work of being a member of Congress." They are generally told to complete roughly thirty calls each hour, with members dialing numbers from sheets that have nothing but a single bullet of personal info (a birthday, for example) and a reminder of their last interaction with the donor. The pressure to raise money is constant. A fundraiser who has done work in the past for the BPC tells of members making fundraising calls from restaurant bathrooms, while exercising at the gym, and from personal events like weddings and graduations.

"They're no sooner elected and they're down there making phone calls for the [next] election," Representative John Larson, a senior House Democrat says, expressing sympathy for those new to the fundraising meat grinder. While the indignity and boredom of fundraising is often cited as a reason not to run for office, the bigger issue is more obvious: All that time spent chasing money is time that is not available for actual governing.

At a recent BPC forum, Senator George Mitchell (D-ME) described the competition between fundraising and legislating when he ran the Senate in early 1990s. One of the key responsibilities of the majority leader is to plan the Senate calendar and decide when to schedule votes. Mitchell recounted that every day requests would come into the leader's office asking to move a vote or block out two hours so as not to conflict with a senator's fundraising plans. While respectful of his colleagues fundraising obligations, the scheduling conflicts quickly became unmanageable. Senator Mitchell called a group of colleagues together in his office. Displayed on the wall was a big calendar depicting all the times members had asked that no votes be scheduled. Except for a thin sliver of white the entire calendar was black. Mitchell remembered, "I showed them that the only time in the next week we could hold a vote was Thursday morning between 2:00 a.m. and 3:00 a.m." He laughingly admitted that he exaggerated to make a point. By all accounts scheduling time to legislate has become even harder today.

A former Senate chief of staff confirmed that members regularly miss votes to attend fundraisers noting, "usually, staff reviews the voting schedule to see if it is a 'bed check vote' or a 'real vote' to determine whether the Member can withstand missing it or not. Some Members never miss votes, no matter what. Others, however, actively plan fundraisers that conflict with vote times and then make a game-day decision where to be."

Precious Time

The interactions that once defined the life of an elected official—meetings with colleagues, conversations off the floor, briefings from staffers in the Executive Branch, correspondence with constituents back home, and, maybe most important, frank and informal discussions of policy ideas— have become almost ancillary to a member's fundraising responsibilities. I've never seen a bumper sticker that read: I'D RATHER BE FUNDRAISING. Congressmen would all rather be spending time focused on issues and meeting with constituents, but absent a campaign war chest, many rightly believe that their status and their jobs are in jeopardy.

It raises a dispiriting question: If you're talented and eager to make a mark in the world, why spend your time in pursuit of an elected office that is often little better than a glorified telemarketing gig? If fundraising is strangling the legislative process, the reflexive answer might be to limit the amount of money a member can raise by reducing the maximum donation, say by half, from $2,600 to $1,300. If the donations were smaller, one might assume leaders would be less inclined to spend so much time in those cubicles.

Don't count on it. A stricter limit on individual political giving likely would have the opposite effect. Feeling compelled to raise the same sums, members would likely spend *more* time dialing for dollars—particularly if they feared a potential challenge from a wealthy, self-funded opponent. In essence, more restrictive limits would have the perverse effect of requiring leaders to devote more of their busy schedule to telemarketing.

While dialing for dollars is a part of elected life, there are some things that could lessen the compulsion. First, we should get rid of so-called "Leadership PACs," the fundraising organizations that ambitious party members form to support—and receive support from—their colleagues. When a rank-and-file member of the House aspires to a leadership post, she will try to curry favor with other members by forming a fundraising organization (namely a leadership PAC) whose proceeds *cannot* be used to support her own re-election. Rather, the PAC's largesse has to be doled out to colleagues (or state parties). And in return for the donation, those cutting the check expect other members to support their aspirations for re-election or leadership posts.

It is a pretty straightforward equation. We could do away with those extra fundraising arms if both parties simply precluded members from maintaining more than one PAC. The rule wouldn't affect whether members could hold onto their own campaign committees— but they would be banned from forming organizations designed explicitly to win over the support of their colleagues. Leadership PACs are a nonessential component of the fundraising arms race. No member of Congress actually wants to spend a lot of time raising money for anyone else, but no one wants to unilaterally disarm in the competition to curry favor with party leaders. If everyone had to drop their weapons at once—give up their leadership PACs—no one would object too strenuously.

Second, we should consider ways that would enable candidates to spend less time soliciting donations. This is tough, if only because most proposals to adjust fundraising rules are presumed to favor one party or the other. Former Republican senators Bob Bennett and Trent Lott each favor increasing the individual donation limit to $10,000. At a February 2014 meeting on election reform hosted at the BPC, Lott opined,

"$2,600 is unrealistic in today's economy. It ought to be raised to $10,000 so members have time to try and pass some laws." Senator Bennett concurred, noting, "If the limit was raised to $10k, you would spend a lot less time at the NRSC [National Republican Senate Committee] and wouldn't have to spend all six years raising money for the next campaign." However, it is assumed that on balance, Republican donors are wealthier and capable of making larger donations—hence, any increase in the limits is usually opposed by Democrats.

Conversely, Democrats tend to advocate for public financing, particularly matching programs that create incentives for small donors who are believed more likely to support progressive candidates. In New York City today, local donations up to $175 are matched with public funds, six to one. So if a resident of Queens gives $50 to a candidate for mayor, the candidate's campaign is given a total of $350. Understandably, efforts to expand this approach to all of New York State or other jurisdictions have yet to garner Republican support.

The opportunity to explore is whether a combination of increased giving limits, immediate disclosure, and small donor matching could generate bipartisan support from our harried elected leaders. Raising the gift limits to $10,000 and creating a national small donor-matching program seems an ambitious step, but the imperative to free up legislators' time cannot be overstated. There is a balance to be struck and we should try to find it.

. . . OF THE PEOPLE

Upon taking office in 1801, Thomas Jefferson noted the paramount importance of human capital: "There is nothing I am so anxious about as good nominations, conscious that the merit as well as reputation of an administration depends as much on that as on its measures."

The need for top talent in government is as high today as it was two hundred years ago. Yet our processes for recruiting and electing our leaders are a mess. Our nominations process excludes thousands of talented candidates, and the confirmation process deters many more. Voters do not trust our system of elections, which undermines the legitimacy of leaders elected by that system. Low voter turnout, especially in primaries, rewards rigid candidates who feed (and feed off of) the culture of gridlock. Finally, the quality of life of our elected leaders leaves much to be desired. With few opportunities for accomplishment, fear of attack from extreme Super PACs and constant fundraising pressure, many of our most skilled legislators have simply had enough.

No one thinks government service should be easy—or even fun. Those who enter the federal workforce shouldn't do it for their own good; they should be held to a higher standard than those in private life and should be subject to greater scrutiny. But we should be aware that those who are willing to make those sacrifices do it with the expectation that *impact* will be their reward. And the unfortunate truth is that the burdens of achieving influence, and the hampered latitude in which it can be exercised, discourage too many Americans from public life.

The most lasting effect, of course, isn't just on the quality of people who choose to enter public service—it's on the quality of the product Americans get from their government. The premise of the American experiment is that an engaged public, once having selected their representatives, will give those in positions of authority some room to make tough decisions. In our zeal to rein in special interests and fight corruption, we have created barriers to interaction and sabotaged deliberation. It is time to restore the allure of public service for top officials, junior staff, and everyone in between. We need a system that builds the electorate's faith in those selected to wield power. And we need the broadest swath of America engaged in elections and available for government service.

The solutions proposed above are "silver buckshot." None will achieve great progress in isolation and each comes at a certain cost. But these ideas can lay the foundation for a resurgence of interest in government work. Whether you believe our government does too much or not enough, we should all agree that what the government *does* do, it should do well. Our nation possesses a phenomenal diversity of experience and expertise and right now our government needs access to all of it.

CONCLUSION

Two Hands on the Wheel

IN MARCH 2012, THE BPC HAD THE PRIVILEGE OF HONORING TWO OF its founders: Senators Howard Baker and Bob Dole. Political combatants of all stripes had gathered in the Mellon Auditorium on Constitution Avenue to celebrate two figures whose public careers had combined to span more than a century of public life. The remarkable moment was a stark contrast to the caustic mood on Capitol Hill. Earlier that day, Republicans and Democrats had clashed angrily over the impending fiscal cliff and traded barbs over the upcoming anniversary of "Obamacare."

But inside the auditorium, everything was going beautifully: Senator Dole and Senator Baker were in good spirits; the Secret Service had moved the line quickly despite a broken metal detector; and Vice President Biden's remarks were moving and on point. Speakers shared a host of stories that weaved a compelling narrative of effective leadership. The vice president, for one, lauded Dole's habit of affording every "man or woman, whether a political foe or friend . . . the dignity they deserve," and contended that the Kansan's capacity to engage adversaries made him a great statesman. In a prepared video, former senators Pete Domenici, Bill Frist, Tom Daschle, and Lamar Alexander shared memories of Howard Baker's courage, including his decision to support the Panama Canal Treaty despite intense opposition from constituents, party leaders, and even Baker's longtime supporters.

The unquestionable—and slightly bizarre—high point was Senator Pat Roberts (R-KS) leading the crowd in song to honor fellow Kansan Senator Dole. The lyrics "Sweet Robert Dole" were sung to a hastily doctored version of the Neil Diamond hit "Sweet Caroline." It was not a particularly deft play on words: The cadence was off and the audience first seemed inhibited by the peculiarity of the moment. But by chorus number three, the six hundred people seated in the Mellon Auditorium were belting it out. The fervor would have made Mr. Diamond proud and the sheer silliness of the moment brought the room together.

But then present-day majority and minority leaders, Harry Reid and Mitch McConnell, brought the crowd back down to earth with their remarks. Each noted the dissonance between the bipartisan affection on display at the gala and the angry gridlock they had come from that day in the Senate chamber. While offering warm tributes to Dole and Baker, each described the tone on Capitol Hill with a combination of frustration and some resignation.

Reid went first:

> I've had so many people come to me and say, you know, the Senate is dysfunctional; it's just not working; it's the worst it's ever been. And if I have time, I tell them the following: The Senate is the way it is not because of McConnell and Reid, it's because of the Founding Fathers. That's the way they set up this country.

McConnell offered a similar explanation for the current state of affairs:

> If the founders had wanted an efficient government, they certainly would never have created the Senate. . . . The genius of the Senate is that it was designed to be slow and painful, so legislation would reflect a national consensus and thus have the durability to last.

It was a deflating moment.

At an event designed to honor two men who had helped to ensure that the Senate *did* work, their successors seemed to suggest that the Senate's gridlock was deeply embedded and, to a great extent, pre-ordained. There is of course some truth in Reid and McConnell's view of political history. The Founding Generation designed our legislative process to be an obstacle course of sorts. A variety of hurdles was established to ensure that legislation would be crafted carefully and that serious arguments would be considered on either side. This arduous process has served our nation well. It has prevented bad laws from being passed and good ones from being overturned. But a healthy challenge is a far cry from what has emerged over the last few years.

Our Founders imagined a Congress engaged, courageous, and connected—not one ducking the hard work solving the nation's problems. What was designed to be an energetic system of checks, balances, and debate has tumbled into a state of near paralysis. The Founders' intentions are not an acceptable excuse for gridlock; in fact, they should be an inspiration to get things moving again.

America's greatness has been fueled by our capacity to harness the collision of ideas and unite the divergent views of a diverse nation. Time and again, legislative achievement has been led by passionate and principled individuals who respect their colleagues' contrary views. At its best, our democracy has been partisan, antagonistic, adept, creative, and confident. We must embrace this history and fight the urge to scrub the contention, personality, and spirit out of the messy business of governing in a democracy.

Where have we gone wrong? What has disabled Washington's ability to be both partisan and productive? The conventional explanations fail to tell the whole story. The forces most often blamed for Washington's gridlock—the hostile media, the ideological sorting of voters, and the undue influence of moneyed interests—aren't new to the nation's political landscape. These features of our democracy may evolve, but they've been here since the beginning and they are undoubtedly here to stay.

That fact strikes some people as simply unacceptable. Despite all evidence to the contrary, these idealists insist on doubling down, buying more bleach, and working even harder to sterilize the political landscape. They complain bitterly about the media, pass laws that shift money from the front pocket to the back, and stoke public frustration over the fact that nothing seems to change.

The conventional diagnosis is not fixing Washington, but it is disillusioning the nation. Rather than cursing the headwinds that have always rattled our democracy, it is time to shift our focus to fortifying the structure that has withstood these stresses for centuries.

Fortunately, we do not need a constitutional convention, new social theory, or external calamity to get Washington working again. In fact, the answer is pretty straightforward. It turns out that running a country works a lot better if the key players know and trust one another. Contrary to public supposition that Congress is an elitist, self-dealing club, many members of Congress today don't even know each other's names. They certainly don't spend much time debating policy questions in committees or hashing through their governing philosophy over dinner.

The consequences of this alienation are profound. The ingredient that has long allowed the United States to balance short-term demands with long-term interests is the sense of community that was once a staple of life in the nation's capital. The sorts of interactions that happen at the "Century of Service" gala—at a colleague's birthday party or at a bar near the shadow of the Capitol—aren't the problem with Washington. In fact, we need to be creating more of them. These connections are a critical counterweight to anger and gridlock extremism.

We cannot restore the traditions of past generations. Times have changed. Few members today move their families to Washington. Our gadgets, tweets, polls, podcasts, and airplanes have forever altered the rhythms of political life. America is deeply divided ideologically, geographically, and demographically. But the decline in collegiality is not an inevitable result of these changes. That is the thing about democracy. We get to steer the ship. In fact, it is our duty to do so.

Watergate and Vietnam were turning points in our nation's history and most of the reforms enacted in their wake have been highly beneficial. These laws have identified real conflicts of interest, ensured public input into federal decisions, tracked private efforts to influence legislation, and increased transparency in campaign contributions. But over the course of the last decade, for reasons best personified by the Jack Abramoff scandal, the effort to reform Washington has careened out of control.

Even those most committed to the ideals of the old reform movement can't be pleased with the results of their efforts. Four decades after Common Cause's founding, Washington seems less effective, more gridlocked, and equally riddled with flawed characters as it has ever been. Reflecting the public's disdain, politicians have become experts in the art of strategic self-loathing. They campaign against the Congress, disparage any connection to DC, and enact laws that insulate themselves from political attacks while undermining the institution. While often stating it is a privilege to serve our country, too many politicians sell themselves as outsiders, abdicating the privilege and responsibility that comes with governing. Too many Americans don't vote, refusing to grapple with the contradiction of their love of country and contempt for those who run it.

Our challenge today isn't to fix Washington with one fell swoop—it is to initiate a process in which the bonds that once sustained American democracy are slowly rebuilt. A town of division and dysfunction can once again become a productive and dynamic City of Rivals. We know what the good ideas are. Members should spend more time in session, deliberate in committee, take trips together, and occasionally *turn off the cameras*. Incentives driving political money to Super PACs and away from political parties should be reversed. Election rules that discourage participation and reward rigidity must be changed. And the variety of restrictions that are keeping good people out of government must be undone.

The goal is to spark a virtuous cycle in which collegiality, achievement, and public trust enhance one another. We need not expect or desire miracles. To get the country back on track, Congress must pass a few meaningful laws each session; reauthorize several more; and conduct the basic business of adopting budgets, overseeing the Executive Branch, and exploring new challenges. It is well within our grasp to return to the productivity of the 1990s, a period when, despite acrimony and divided government, the legislative process functioned and only half the public disapproved of Congress. In our dynamic and plural nation, this would be enough.

More than forty years ago, at a moment that President Gerald Ford called our "long national nightmare," a class of more than seventy young progressives was elected to Congress. Long known as the Watergate

Babies, the Democrats elected during the midterm election of 1974 have had an outsized impact on the politics and policy of the last several decades. By most standards, they have been phenomenally successful. Now, four decades later, the last of the Watergate Babies—Max Baucus, Tom Harkin, George Miller, and Henry Waxman—are all poised to leave Capitol Hill.*

It is a noteworthy turning of the page. Instead of a government suffused with secrecy, the current generation of lawmakers must grapple with its opposite: a near-constant scrutiny that rewards inflexibility and penalizes collaboration. There is a healthy midpoint between waging a secret war in Cambodia and publishing the text messages of cabinet officials. We need to find it.

The 1970s also remind us that public anger is essential to the workings of a dynamic republic. It's the fuel that drives change and enables progress. But the force of the fury must be directed at a movable target. Our efforts to improve Washington must do more than monitor, restrict, and constrain. We must protect the essential character of the body politic and enable our leaders to act in the national interest. America's unique capacity to make repairable mistakes endures. It is time to grab the wheel. Our democracy depends on it.

---

* Senator Patrick Leahy (D-VT) remains.

ACKNOWLEDGMENTS

IN *CITY OF RIVALS*, I ARGUE THAT THE SYNTHESIS OF DISPARATE IDEAS IS difficult, inefficient, often frustrating, and ultimately exhilarating. There is nothing quite like writing a book to prove the point. *City of Rivals* is a collaboration about collaboration and I have many people to thank: some whose partnership is revealed on every page, others who have helped me build the Bipartisan Policy Center, and still others who have shaped my opportunities and insights over the past thirty years.

I must begin by thanking three people who helped me to fashion and refine my ideas, arguments, and prose. First is Marc Dunkelman who has been a gifted, opinionated, and essential ally throughout this project. Through hundreds of discussions—and almost as many drafts—Marc's partnership proves the concept of authentic collaboration. Ben Kramer provided invaluable and remarkably timely research and wisdom beyond his years. He is better than Wikipedia and will hopefully be running for public office before he turns thirty. My editor, Jon Sternfeld, is a superior human being. Jon was unfailingly supportive, appropriately challenging, and almost always right. He is also extremely clever and some of the very best lines in the book are his.

The experiences, examples, and occasional audacity that inform this book are drawn directly from my colleagues at the Bipartisan Policy Center. There is no greater indulgence than to be surrounded every day by exceptionally smart and spirited people. My colleagues at the BPC disagree about almost everything and come to work each day to try to help the country succeed. It is a unique alchemy that regularly produces outcomes that have both balance and edge. Like with all BPC projects, the tires holding up this book were kicked hard and the final product is much better for it. I hope that my colleagues see themselves across these pages and that my description does justice to their insights and courageous work. I also thank the BPC Board of Directors for their leadership of the organization, their pride in our accomplishment, and their pushing me to write about it.

The political leaders who work with me at the BPC are a dream team of insight, experience, and optimism. This book is anchored in the commitments and careers of the BPC founders Howard Baker, Bob Dole, Tom Daschle, and George Mitchell. Senators Trent Lott, Bob Bennett, and Byron Dorgan were exceptionally generous with their time and their stories. And I owe a great deal to Secretary Dan Glickman and Senator Olympia Snowe who lead the Bipartisan Policy Center's Commission on Political Reform (CPR) and have been a constant resource throughout this project.

In *City of Rivals*, I take the liberty of connecting three decades of personal experience to 250 years of American success. It is a unique pleasure to acknowledge a series of people who have been instrumental in the personal story that informs this book. At Brown University, Harold Ward taught me the power of connecting analysis to real-world problems and Ross Cheit made public policy seem incredibly cool. I also want to thank my dear friend and college debate partner Aaron Belkin. The challenge and thrill of the constructive collision of ideas has animated my career and this book.

My first real job was working in New York State's Department of Environmental Conservation in Albany, New York. I am forever indebted to Tom Allen and Dave Shaw for giving me real work to do and to Dick Gibbs for showing me the stubbornness of facts and the fun you could have sticking to them. I would also like to thank Michael Bradley and the state environmental officials who gave me an opportunity to run an organization (NESCAUM) several years before it probably made sense. I also want to thank Paul Brest at the Hewlett Foundation for inspiring and supporting the National Commission on Energy Policy, which was the predicate for the BPC. The growth and success of the BPC would not have been possible without the support and friendship of Mark Heising and Liz Simons. There are few people who have true passion for pragmatism and Mark and Liz are among the very best.

Finally, I want to thank my wife, Stephanie, and my three lovely children, Isabella, Julia, and Adam. The ability to write a book while holding a day job and raising a family is a gift bestowed upon authors by the people who do all the things that you would be doing if you weren't in the basement writing the "*&%#" book. Stephanie maintained unusual good charm even as the effort absorbed countless weekends and a couple of family vacations. She was also an honest and searing editor—as only a spouse can be. For Isabella (11), Julia (8), and Adam (6) I am appreciative of their best efforts to display the one thing they are completely and appropriately incapable of—patience. The word "soon" has lost all meaning and credibility. I have just been asked by a six-year-old in cleats if we can go play soccer. It is with considered joy that I can say "Sure, buddy."

ENDNOTES

PROLOGUE

XVII. *three-quarters of adults believe their kids won't enjoy the same opportunities that they have:* Ronald Brownstein, "The American Dream—Under Threat," *National Journal*, September 19, 2013, www.nationaljournal.com/magazine/the-american-dream-under-threat-20130919.

INTRODUCTION

1. *the banter careened past bipartisanship:* Somehow Broder translated the scraps of BPC relevant discussion into a thoughtful column. David S. Broder, "'Common Ground' Caucus," *Washington Post*, March 8, 2007, www.washingtonpost.com/wp-dyn/content/article/2007/03/07/AR2007030702042.html.

3. *Democrat Henry Waxman and Republican Tom Bliley entered into:* Henry Waxman and Joshua Green, *The Waxman Report: How Congress Really Works* (New York: Twelve, 2009), 134.

3. *Bliley and Waxman worked out a detailed agreement:* Ibid., 136.

3. *"If Waxman and Bliley are together on this":* Ibid.

6. *the 2007 Energy Independence and Security Act passed the Senate:* John M. Broder, "Bush Signs Broad Energy Bill," *New York Times*, December 19, 2007, www.nytimes.com/2007/12/19/washington/19cnd-energy.html?_r=0.

6. *Congress also passed, to surprisingly little fanfare, a major patent reform bill:* Zach Carter, "Patent Reform Bill Signed into Law after Years of Debate," *Huffington Post*, September 16, 2011, www.huffingtonpost.com/2011/09/16/patent-reform-obama_n_966136.html.

6. *the Violence Against Women Act was reauthorized:* Niraj Chokshi, "Congress Has Passed 13 Laws This Year—None of Them Have to Do With Jobs," *National Journal*, June 7, 2013, www.nationaljournal.com/nationalsecurity/congress-has-passed-13-laws-this-year-none-of-them-have-to-do-with-jobs-20130607.

7. *"one manufactured crisis to the next.":* Barack H. Obama, "Remarks by the President in the State of the Union Address," February 12, 2013, www.whitehouse.gov/the-press-office/2013/02/12/remarks-president-state-union-address.

7. *Poet Susan Stewart aptly describes nostalgia:* Susan Stewart, *On Longing: Narratives of the Miniature, the Gigantic, the Souvenier, the Collection* (Baltimore: Johns Hopkins University Press, 1984).

8. *embracing instead "a 'lets-find-out-the-facts'" approach:* Arthur Krock, "Sputnik Provides Fuel for President's Foes," *New York Times,* October 20, 1957.

CHAPTER I

11. *the Constitution wasn't universally embraced:* Herbert J. Storing, *What the Anti-Federalists Were For: The Political Thoughts of the Opponents of the Constitution* (Chicago: University of Chicago Press, 1981), 6.

12. *down the path to "a Monarchy, or a corrupt oppressive Aristocracy":* Charles R. Kesler, "Introduction," in *The Federalist Papers,* Clinton Rossiter, ed. (New York: Signet Classic, 2003), vii.

13. *"proper relation between republicanism and responsibility.":* Ibid., xxii–xxxi.

13. *No doubt, they were also motivated:* The Federalists often spoke with seeming derision for the common man. Hamilton once said: "Take mankind in general, they are vicious—their passions may be operated upon . . . Take mankind as they are, and what are they governed by? Their passions. There may be in every government a few choice spirits, who may act from more worthy motives. One great error is that we suppose mankind is more honest than they are, our prevailing passions are ambition and interest; and it will be the duty of a wise government to avail itself of those passions, in order to make them subservient to the public good." Moreover, the prevailing view among Federalists and anti-Federalists alike was to exclude the majority of the adult population from the political franchise. (Alexander Hamilton, "Speech to Constitutional Convention." Speech presented at the Constitutional Convention, Philadelphia, PA, June 22, 1787).

14. *A pure democracy, by which I mean a society consisting . . . :* James Madison, "Federalist No. 10," Library of Congress, The Federalist Papers, http://thomas .loc.gov/home/histdox/fed_10.html.

14. *"greater variety of parties and interests":* Ibid., 76.

17. *"the Constitution gave Jefferson no power . . . ":* Thomas Fleming, *The Louisiana Purchase* (Hoboken, NJ: John Wiley & Sons, Inc., 2003), 150.

17. *"and improving "the 'fertility of the country'":* Ibid., 147.

18. *That a pure democracy if it were practicable . . . :* Alexander Hamilton, Speech Urging Ratification of the Constitution (speech, New York, June 21, 1788), *Our Republic,* www.ourrepubliconline.com/Topic/15.

18. *As the cool and deliberate sense of the community . . . :* Charles R. Kesler, "Introduction," in *The Federalist Papers,* Clinton Rossiter, ed. (New York: Signet Classic, 2003), 382–83.

19. *Noting that very point, then–Senator John F. Kennedy:* John F. Kennedy, *Profiles in Courage* (New York: Harper Perennial, 2006), 18.

19. *As Kennedy pointed out, the Compromise, which Henry Clay pushed:* Ibid., 57–74.

20. *I'd learned while negotiating union contracts . . . :* Ronald W. Reagan, *An American Life: The Autobiography* (New York: Simon and Schuster, 1990), 171.

20. *the Greenspan Commission is . . . now remembered:* Matthew Dallek, "Bipartisan Reagan-O'Neill Social Security Deal in 1983 Showed It Can Be Done," *US News and World Report*, www.usnews.com/opinion/articles/2009/04/02/bipartisan-reagan-oneill-social-security-deal-in-1983-showed-it-can-be-done.

21. *"The test of a first-rate intelligence . . . ":* F. Scott Fitzgerald in Roger L. Martin, *The Opposable Mind: Winning through Integrative Thinking* (Boston: Harvard Business Review Press, 2009), 1.

21. *six "killer apps" are, together, largely responsible . . . :* Niall Ferguson, *Civilization: The West and the Rest* (New York: Penguin, 2012), 12.

21. *"it doesn't move very fast . . . ":* Biography of Everett M. Dirksen, The Dirksen Center, www.dirksencenter.org/print_emd_bio.htm.

21. *role as the "indispensable nation.":* Jules Witcover, "Should We Continue to Be the Indispensable Nation?" *Chicago Tribune*, September 28, 2013, http://articles.chicagotribune.com/2013-09-28/opinion/sns-201305091700--tms--poltodayctnyq-a20130510-20130510_1_chemical-weapons-barack-obama-president-obama.

23. *A prime minister, acting with the support of a majority:* Sudha Setty, "The President's Question Time: Power, Information, and the Executive Credibility Gap," *Cornell Journal of Law and Public Policy* 17, no. 2 (Spring 2008): 266.

24. *"because we had all fought the war together.":* Personal interview with Howard Baker, conducted by Jason Grumet, Washington, DC, March 2012.

24. *the so-called "Greatest Generation.":* Tom Brokaw, *The Greatest Generation* (New York: Random House, 2004), xii–xxix.

25. *federal programs intended to improve lives across the board:* John W. Gardner, "No Easy Victories," *American Statistician* 22, no. 1 (February 1968): 15–16.

26. *"to build a true 'citizens' lobby.":* Common Cause, "John Gardner's Letter That Launched Common Cause," www.commoncause.org/site/pp.asp?c=dkLNK1MQIwG&b=4860209.

26. *"revitalize politics and government [if] millions of American citizens.":* Ibid.

26. *"action to reduce the influence of money . . . ":* Michael Schudson, *Watergate in American Memory: How We Remember, Forget, and Reconstruct the Past* (New York: Basic Books, 1992), 158.

26. *"set of rules for public financial disclosure . . . ":* Ibid.

27. *"In this present crisis, government is not the solution . . . ":* Ronald W. Reagan, "First Inaugural Address" (speech, Washington, DC, January 20, 1981),

American Rhetoric, www.americanrhetoric.com/speeches/ronaldreagandfirst
inaugural.html.

27. *"the nine most terrifying words . . . "*: Ronald W. Reagan, "New Conference,"
The Ronald Reagan Presidential Library and Foundation video, 0:37, August 12,
1986, www.reaganfoundation.org/reagan-quotes-detail.aspx?tx=2079.

27. *"An honest man in politics shines . . . "*: Mark Twain, in Emily Heil, "Mark
Twain on Congress: Idiots, Criminals, Dumber than Fleas," *Washington Post*,
April 18, 2012.

CHAPTER 2

29. *Held at a new, iconic stadium:* "Beijing TV Coverage Drew 4.7 Billion Viewers Worldwide," Associated Press, September 5, 2008, http://sports.espn.go
.com/oly/news/story?id=3571042.

29. *As Tom Friedman has argued, in the absence of:* Thomas Friedman, *The World Is
Flat 3.0: A Brief History of the 21st Century* (New York: Farrar, Straus, and Giroux, 2005), 52.

30. *[The] sense of resignation, that sense that . . . :* Thomas L. Friedman and
Michael J. Mandelbaum, *That Used to Be Us: How America Fell Behind in the
World and How We Can Come Back* (New York: Farrar, Straus, and Giroux,
2011), 5.

31. *Goldman Sachs executive Jim O'Neill coined the term "BRICS":* Jim O'Neill,
"Building Better Global Economic BRICs," Global Economics Paper No. 66,
Goldman Sachs, November 30, 2001, www.goldmansachs.com/our-thinking/
archive/archive-pdfs/build-better-brics.pdf.

31. *Recent data also suggests that the BRICS are no longer growing:* Ruchir
Sharma, "Broken BRICs: Why the Rest Stopped Rising," *Foreign Affairs*,
November/December 2012.

31. *If only the federal deficit were smaller:* Robert Kagan, *The World America Made*
(New York: Alfred A. Knopf, 2012), 4.

32. *After all, America's political system didn't survive:* "Growing Old in America:
Expectations vs. Reality," Pew Research Center, A Social & Demographic
Trends Report, June 29, 2009, www.pewsocialtrends.org/files/2010/10/Getting
-Old-in-America.pdf.

32. *If de Tocqueville's famous admonition still applies:* Alexis de Tocqueville, in
Melissa Schwartzberg, *Democracy and Legal Change* (New York: Cambridge
University Press, 2007), 115.

33. *Despite a late 2013 amendment:* "What Is the Impact of the Defense Sequester
on the Economy," Bipartisan Policy Center, December 2013, http://bipartisan
policy.org/sites/default/files/Economic%20Impact%20Defense%20Sequester.pdf.

34. *Columbia political scientist Ian Bremmer, recently ranking:* "Top Risks 2013,"
Eurasia Group, www.eurasiagroup.net/pages/top-risks-2013.

34. *US median income declined:* Binyamin Applebaum, "Family Net Worth Drops to Level of Early '90s, Fed Says," *New York Times,* June 11, 2012, www .nytimes.com/2012/06/12/business/economy/family-net-worth-drops-to-level -of-early-90s-fed-says.html?_r=1.

34. *It's no secret that we're transitioning from the industrial:* "Bloomberg View: A Reality Check on American Manufacturing," *Bloomberg Business-week,* September 6, 2012, www.businessweek.com/articles/2012-09-06/ bloomberg-view-a-reality-check-on-american-manufacturing.

34. *The Information Technology and Innovation Foundation ranked the United States sixth:* Singapore ranked first in innovation and global competitiveness, and China, while placing 33rd in innovation and global competitiveness, was ranked first in progress made over the last decade. Robert D. Atkinson and Scott M. Andes, "The Atlantic Century: Benchmarking EU and U.S. Innovation and Competitiveness," The Information Technology and Innovation Foundation, February 2009, www.itif.org/files/2009-atlantic-century.pdf.

34. *The number of new startups created in the United States each year:* John Haltiwanger, Ron Jarmin, and Javier Miranda, "Business Dynamics Statistics Briefing: Where Have All the Young Firms Gone," Ewing Marion Kauffman Foundation, May 2012, www.kauffman.org/uploadedfiles/bds_2012.pdf.

34. *The American Society of Civil Engineers has awarded American infrastructure a grade:* "America's Infrastructure G.P.A.," 2013 Report Card for America's Infrastructure, American Society of Civil Engineers, www.infrastructurereport card.org.

34. *The nation's health care system, once considered the best in the world:* Jason Kane, "Health Costs: How the U.S. Compares with Other Countries," *PBS NewsHour,* October 22, 2012, www.pbs.org/newshour/rundown/ health-costs-how-the-us-compares-with-other-countries.

35. *Although our health care bill:* The World Bank, Russian Federation, http:// data.worldbank.org/country/russian-federation.

35. *the World Health Organization ranks us twenty-seventh in life expectancy:* Fareed Zakaria, "Are America's Best Days Behind Us?" *Time,* March 3, 2012, www.time.com/time/magazine/article/0,9171,2056723,00.html.

35. *Moreover, the high school dropout rate:* Robert J. Gordon, "The Great Stagnation of American Education," *New York Times,* September 7, 2013, http:// opinionator.blogs.nytimes.com/2013/09/07/the-great-stagnation-of-american -education/?_php=true&_type=blogs&_php=true&_type=blogs&_r=1.

35. *Roughly 30 percent of all Americans:* Frank Bruni, "America the Clueless," *New York Times,* May 11, 2013, www.nytimes.com/2013/05/12/opinion/sunday/ bruni-america-the-clueless.html?ref=frankbruni.

35. *"there's nothing wrong with America that together we can't fix":* Ronald Reagan, Address Before a Joint Session of the Congress on the Program for Economic Recovery, February 18, 1981,www.presidency.ucsb.edu/ws/?pid=43425.

35. *Fewer than half of Americans believed that the nation:* Frank Newport, "Americans Downbeat on State of U.S., Prospects for Future," Gallup Politics, January 21, 2013, www.gallup.com/poll/160046/americans-downbeat-state-prospects -future.aspx?utm_source=alert&utm_medium=email&utm_campaign =syndication&utm_content=morelink&utm_term=All%20Gallup%20Headlines.

35–36. *Today, by contrast, those figures have dropped:* "Public Trust in Government: 1958–2013," Pew Research Center for the People and the Press, January 31, 2013, www.people-press.org/2013/10/18/trust-in-government-nears-record -low-but-most-federal-agencies-are-viewed-favorably.

37. *Cable television and talk radio have had . . .:* Interview with Byron Dorgan, Washington, DC, July 18, 2013.

37. *"Eli Pariser coined the term "filter bubble" . . . Our news is now prioritized for us"; it reinforces our existing worldview:* Eli Pariser, *The Filter Bubble: What the Internet Is Hiding from You* (New York: Penguin Press, 2011), 9–10.

37. *"murder, robbery, rape, adultery . . .":* Richard K. Scher, *The Modern Political Campaign: Mudslinging, Bombast, and the Vitality of American Politics* (Armonk, NY: M.E. Sharp, 1997), 31.

37. *By turn, a propagandist on Jefferson's payroll:* David McCullough, *John Adams* (New York: Simon and Schuster, 2008), 537.

38. *Soon thereafter, the United States took up arms against:* "Yellow Journalism," PBS, *Crucible of Empire: Spanish American War,* www.pbs.org/crucible/frames/ _journalism.html.

38. *no one would have wanted to watch a news program titled "Ceasefire":* Michael Kinsley, "Am I Blue," *Washington Post,* November 7, 2004, www.washingtonpost .com/wp-dyn/articles/A29470-2004Nov5.html.

39. *"the 93 seats held by Democrats in Republican districts . . .":* "2012 Redistricting: Will the House Be More Polarized Than Ever," Bipartisan Policy Center, October 2012, http://bipartisanpolicy.org/sites/default/files/Redistricting_Report.pdf.

39. *The overall level of congressional polarization . . . :* Ronald Brownstein, "Polling Apart," *National Journal,* February 24, 2011, www.nationaljournal.com/ magazine/congress-hits-new-peak-in-polarization-20110224.

39. *Former New York City mayor Michael Bloomberg said that political polarization:* Rebecca Shabad, "Bloomberg Vows to Fight Gerrymandering," *The Hill,* October 10, 2013, http://thehill.com/blogs/ballot-box/ redistricting/327725-bloomberg-plans-to-finance-nonpartisan-redistricting.

39. *"safe, lily white strongholds . . . "an alternate universe . . . ":* Charlie Cook, "The GOP Keeps Getting Whiter," *National Journal,* March 14, 2013, www.national journal.com/columns/cook-report/the-gop-keeps-getting-whiter-20130314.

40. *to create a "radical center" in American politics, Americans need to advocate:* Thomas L. Friedman, "A Tea Party Without Nuts," *New York Times,* March 23, 2010, www.nytimes.com/2010/03/24/opinion/24friedman.html.

40. *The phrase "gerrymander" originated:* "Why Do Politicians Gerrymander?" The Economist Explains, *The Economist,* October 27, 2013, www.economist.com/blogs/economist-explains/2013/10/economist-explains-17.

40. *The days of the moderate Rockefeller Republicans:* Ronald Brownstein, "Polling Apart," *National Journal,* February 24, 2011, www.nationaljournal.com/magazine/congress-hits-new-peak-in-polarization-20110224.

40. *The necessary result of these policies:* David Weigel, "The Voting Rights Act and the GOP's Gerrymandering Advantage," *Slate,* January 17, 2013, www.slate.com/blogs/weigel/2013/01/17/the_voting_rights_act_and_the_gop_s_gerrymandering_advantage.html.

40. *But in the decade since, the number dropped only to 101:* "2012 Redistricting: Will the House Be More Polarized Than Ever," Bipartisan Policy Center, October 2012, http://bipartisanpolicy.org/sites/default/files/Redistricting_Report.pdf.

41. *"the increase in the number of safe districts . . .":* Nicole McCarty, "Hate Our Polarized Politics? Why You Can't Blame Gerrymandering," *Washington Post,* October 26, 2012, www.washingtonpost.com/opinions/hate-our-polarized-politics-why-you-cant-blame-gerrymandering/2012/10/26/c2794552-1d80-11e2-9cd5-b55c38388962_story.html.

41. *Bill Bishop found that Americans are separating themselves into:* Bill Bishop, *The Big Sort* (New York: Houghton Mifflin Company, 2008), 42.

41. *The trend continued in 2010, as 82 percent:* David Wasserman, "Will the 2012 Election Be a Contest of Whole Foods vs. Cracker Barrel Shoppers?" *Washington Post,* December 9, 2011, www.washingtonpost.com/opinions/will-the-2012-election-be-a-contest-of-whole-foods-vs-cracker-barrel-shoppers/2011/09/28/gIQAMuXDiO_story.html.

42. *"redistricting matters a little. . .":* Phone Interview with Slade Gorton, March 3, 2014.

42. *Campaign spending at the federal level in presidential:* Patrick Bashman, "It's the Spending, Stupid! Understanding Campaign Finance in the Big-Government Era," Cato Institute, July 18, 2001, www.cato.org/sites/cato.org/files/pubs/pdf/bp64.pdf.

42. *The combined cost of the nation's biannual congressional races:* "The Money Behind the Elections," Center for Responsive Politics, www.opensecrets.org/bigpicture.

42. *"to lubricate the thirsty throats of [those] who may have trudged . . .":* Tracy Campbell, *Deliver the Vote: A History of Election Fraud, an American Political Tradition—1742–2004* (New York: Carroll & Graf Publishers, 2005), 5.

42. *The same dynamic persisted through the nineteenth century:* John F. Kennedy, *Profiles in Courage* (New York: Harper Perennial, 2006), 60–61.

43. *"never before was a candidate placed . . .":* Asawin Suebsaeng, Andy Kroll, and Aaron Ross, "250 Years of Campaigns, Cash, and Corruption," *Mother Jones,* August 9, 2012, www.motherjones.com/politics/2012/08/campaign-finance-timeline-dark-money.

43. *a few decades later, Lyndon Johnson used his control:* Robert Caro, *Master of the Senate* (New York: Alfred A. Knopf, 2002), 406.

43. *And in the 1968 and 1972 presidential elections the liberal philanthropist Stewart Mott:* "The Biggest Political Donors of All Time," *Slate,* January 27, 2013.

43. *Many, including former and current members of Congress:* Patricia Zengerle, "Most Americans Think Campaign Money Aids Right," Reuters, May 24, 2012, www.reuters.com/article/2012/05/24/us-usa-campaign-spending-idUSBRE84N1RB20120524.

43. *A recent CNN poll revealed that two-thirds of Americans believe that elections are generally for sale:* "CNN Poll: Two-Thirds Say Elections Are Usually for Sale," CNN, June 9, 2011, http://politicalticker.blogs.cnn.com/2011/06/09/cnn-poll-two-thirds-say-elections-are-usually-for-sale.

44. *It was McCain-Feingold in combination with subsequent Supreme Court rulings that:* Martina Stewart, "Super PACs' money could tip balance of power in Congress," CNN, January 26, 2012, www.cnn.com/2012/01/26/politics/super-pac-general/index.html.

44. *"God grant me the serenity . . . ":* The Serenity Prayer, reprinted with permission from Al-Anon Family Group Headquarters, Inc., Virginia Beach, VA.

46. *"human nature is really based on . . . social connections":* David Brooks, interviewed by Robert Siegel, March 7, 2011, National Public Radio.

47. *"headquarters building . . . that promoted "encounters and unplanned collaborations' . . . ":* Walter Isaacson, *Steve Jobs* (New York: Simon and Schuster, 2011), 431.

47. *"if a building doesn't encourage that . . . ":* Ibid.

47. *"Today's office is a wasteland . . . ":* "Beyond the Cubicle," *Wall Street Journal,* August 3, 2012, http://online.wsj.com/article/SB1000087239639044368750457756346248455008.html.

47. *I asked Tony Calabro:* Personal conversation with the author, April 2, 2014.

CHAPTER 3

50. *The sparingly used practice of "obstructing or delaying of legislative action . . .":* American Heritage Dictionary of the English Language, 5th ed, s.v. "Filibuster," http://ahdictionary.com/word/search.html?q=filibuster.

50. *In the process, our once proud Senate is now seen:* Richard A. Arenberg and Robert B. Dove, *Defending the Filibuster: The Soul of the Senate* (Bloomington: Indiana University Press, 2012), 1–2.

50. *We don't suffer anymore . . . :* "On Leadership" Speaker Series, Bipartisan Policy Center, January 19, 2012, http://bipartisanpolicy.org/sites/default/files/On%20Leadership%20Lott-Daschle%20Transcript.pdf.

51. *Signatories will exercise their responsibilities . . . :* "Text of Senate Compromise on Nominations of Judges," *New York Times,* May 24, 2005, www.nytimes.com/2005/05/24/politics/24text.html?pagewanted=print&_r=0.

52. *White House counsel Kathy Ruemmler opined that the move amounted:* Manu Raju, "Dems Warn: McConnell Will Regret These Filibusters," *POLITICO,* December 7, 2011, www.politico.com/news/stories/1211/70047.html.

52. *"We have a new start for this body.:"* Harry Reid, in Kathleen Hunter and Laura Litvan, "Senate Confirms Cordray Nomination Averting Rule Fight," July 17, 2013, Bloomberg Politics, www.bloomberg.com/news/2013-07-16/senate-nears-showdown-nominee-votes-as-leaders-seek-deal.html.

52. *"if you should feel really happy":* Garrison Keillor, in Jug Suraiya, "The Shrink and the Sage," *Times of India,* September 3, 2012, http://blogs.timesofindia.indiatimes.com/jugglebandhi/entry/the-shrink-and-the-sage?sortBy=RECOMMENDED&th=1.

52. *"This changes everything, this changes everything.":* John McCain, in Dana Bash, "Senate Democrats Go 'Nuclear,' Changing Filibuster Rules," CNN, *Erin Burnett OutFront,* November 21, 2013, http://outfront.blogs.cnn .com/2013/11/21/senate-democrats-go-nuclear-changing-filibuster-rules.

53. *"the measures of government must be injuriously suspended . . . ":* Alexander Hamilton, "Federalist No. 22: Other Defects of the Present Confederation," December 14, 1787, www.constitution.org/fed/federa22.htm.

53. *"no one is to speak impertinently . . . ":* Thomas Jefferson, *A Manual of Parliamentary Practice* (1801; reprint, Washington, DC: Government Printing Office, 1993), 40.

53. *The first recorded filibusters occurred:* Gregory Koger, *Filibustering: A Political History of Obstruction in the House and the Senate* (Chicago: University of Chicago Press, 2010), 46.

53. *1854's Kansas-Nebraska Act, a bill which empowered:* Ibid., 67.

53. *In total, there were fifty-six filibusters between 1861:* Ibid., 69.

54. *When the commission concluded that Hayes had won:* Hayes-Tilden Election (1876), *Jim Crow Stories,* PBS, www.pbs.org/wnet/jimcrow/stories_events_election .html.

54. *A negotiation ensued, and in the end, the Democrats:* Ibid.

54. *Tom Reed, launched a reform campaign that came to be known:* Ibid., 55.

54. *"the best system is to have one party govern . . . ":* Gary W. Cox and Matthew D. McCubbins, *Setting the Agenda: Responsible Party Government in the US House of Representatives* (New York: Cambridge University Press, 2005), 56.

54. *By eliminating the filibuster in the House:* Gregory Koger, *Filibustering: A Political History of Obstruction in the House and the Senate* (Chicago: University of Chicago Press, 2010), 55.

55. *Wilson's frustration was born in the fact that the use:* John C. Danforth and David L. Boren, "Danforth and Boren: It's Time for Filibuster Reform," *Roll Call,* January 4, 2013, www.rollcall.com/news/danforth_and_boren_its_time _for_filibuster_reform-220566-1.html?zkPrintable=true.

55. *But just because senators had given themselves the authority:* Gregory Koger, *Filibustering: A Political History of Obstruction in the House and the Senate* (Chicago: University of Chicago Press, 2010), 21.

55. *But that didn't sway Louisiana Democrat Huey Long:* Ibid., 157.

55. *Of the forty filibusters that occurred during:* Ibid.,159.

55. *Concerned that passage of the legislation would hand:* David R. Mayhew, "Supermajority Rule in the U.S. Senate," *Political Science and Politics* 36, no. 1 (2003): 32.

56. *if a single senator was willing to talk:* Gregory Koger, *Filibustering: A Political History of Obstruction in the House and the Senate* (Chicago: University of Chicago Press, 2010), 163.

56. *Fearing gridlock, in 1949 a broad array:* Ibid.,165.

56. *In 1959, the Senate addressed the problem of members:* Richard A. Arenberg and Robert B. Dove, *Defending the Filibuster: The Soul of the Senate* (Bloomington: Indiana University Press, 2012), 120.

56. *"There is nothing improper about [the filibuster . . . ":* Wayne Morse, in "The Fate of the Filibuster," Edward M. Kennedy Institute for the United States Senate, http://emkinstitute.org/updates/entry/the-fate-of-the-filibuster.

56. *In this spirit, even on issues as profound:* Richard A. Arenberg and Robert B. Dove, *Defending the Filibuster: The Soul of the Senate* (Bloomington: Indiana University Press, 2012), 120.

57. *Mike Mansfield, who took up the reins of Senate:* Ibid., 167–68.

57. *After a period of thirty-five years when:* Ibid., 169.

57. *But when the filibuster continued, sixty-seven senators:* Ibid., 64.

57. *Over the eleven years that followed:* Gregory Koger, *Filibustering: A Political History of Obstruction in the House and the Senate* (Chicago: University of Chicago Press, 2010), 171.

57. *Mansfield, the longtime Senate majority leader, grew to resent:* Ibid., 172.

57. *In 1975, the Senate responded to this exasperation:* Richard A. Arenberg and Robert B. Dove, *Defending the Filibuster: The Soul of the Senate* (Bloomington: Indiana University Press, 2012), 130.

58. *The limit was set at one hundred hours:* Library of Congress, CRS, *Proposals to Change the Operation of Cloture in the Senate*, by Christopher M. Davis and Valerie Heitshusen, CRS Report R42342 (Washington, DC: Office of Congressional Information and Publishing, January 3, 2013).

58. *From 2007 to the middle of 2014:* "Senate Action on Cloture Motions," The United States Senate, www.senate.gov/pagelayout/reference/cloture_motions/clotureCounts.htm.

58. *In the six years that marked the end of George W. Bush's:* Ibid.

58. *In December 1980, the Democratic majority leader:* Congressional Record, 112th Cong., 2nd Sess. (2012), S8027. Years later, Senate minority leader Tom

Daschle said in a speech on the Senate floor that he understood the first time a Senate majority filled the tree to be 1977, meaning that Byrd's use of this tactic in 1979 to ensure passage of the Tonnage Measurement Simplification Act was a novel and groundbreaking strategic move.

58. *If the Democrats weren't going to let the Republicans offer amendments:* Interview with Steve Bell conducted by Jason Grumet and Marc Dunkelman, Bipartisan Policy Center, Washington DC, September 13, 2012.

59. *Majority leader Harry Reid filled the tree:* Donald R. Wolfensberger, "A Brief History of Congressional Reform Efforts," Bipartisan Policy Center and the Woodrow Wilson Center, February 22, 2013, www.wilsoncenter.org/sites/default/files/brief_history_congressional_reform_efforts.pdf.

59. *"I filled the tree one time and Tom [Daschle] got mad . . .":* Meeting at the Bipartisan Policy Center, Washington, DC, February 4, 2014.

60. *but to that point, the cost had been borne exclusively:* T. R. Reid, *Congressional Odyssey: The Saga of a Senate Bill* (San Francisco: W.H. Freeman and Company, 1980), 10.

60. *Russell Long, protecting the Louisiana businesses dependent on commerce:* Interview with Pete Domenici and Steve Bell conducted by Jason Grumet and Marc Dunkelman, Bipartisan Policy Center, Washington, DC, January 31, 2013.

60. *Domenici devised a legislative workaround:* T. R. Reid, *Congressional Odyssey: The Saga of a Senate Bill* (San Francisco: W.H. Freeman and Company, 1980), 11.

60. *Domenici knew the legislative fight wouldn't be easy:* Ibid., 12.

60. *As he said later, reflecting on the fight:* Ibid., 60.

61. *"adroit parliamentary maneuvering . . .":* Ibid., 117.

61. *And so, when facing the last legislative hurdle:* Ibid.

61. *The longtime chairman told the freshman:* Interview with Steve Bell conducted by Jason Grumet and Marc Dunkelman, Bipartisan Policy Center, Washington, DC, January 31, 2013.

61. *To Long's dismay, within hours of Domenici's return:* T. R. Reid, *Congressional Odyssey: The Saga of a Senate Bill* (San Francisco: W.H. Freeman and Company, 1980), 119.

61. *"The Senate [can] only operate . . .":* Ibid.

62. *"The key is not allowing the Senate to become a majority institution . . .":* Meeting of the BPC Commission on Political Reform, February 5, 2014, Washington, DC.

63. *One reform, first introduced by Senator Jeff Merkley:* Gregory Koger, "The Past and Future of the Supermajority Senate," *The Forum* 9, no. 4 (2011): 12; Jeff Merkley, "Thoughts on the Reform of Senate Procedures," November 16, 2010, http://voices.washingtonpost.com/plum-line/Senate%20Procedures%20Reform%20Memo.pdf.

63. *Merkley's proposal has failed twice:* Gregory Koger, "The Past and Future of the Supermajority Senate," *The Forum* 9, no. 4 (2011): 12; Manu Raju and

Ginger Gibson, "Reid, McConnell Reach Filibuster Deal," *POLITICO*, January 24, 2013, www.politico.com/story/2013/01/reid-mcconnell-reach-senate-filibuster-deal-86674.html.

63. *The level of frustration among members . . . ":* Meeting of the Bipartisan Policy Center's Commission on Political Reform, Bipartisan Policy Center, Washington, DC, January 15, 2014.

64. *This is a small but significant step . . . :* Wesley Lowery and Ed O'Keefe, "Senate Passes Flood Insurance, Child-Care Bills," *Washington Post*, March 13, 2014, www.washingtonpost.com/blogs/post-politics/wp/2014/03/13/senate-passes-flood-insurance-child-care-bills.

64. *"Many members who've come here since 2006 . . . ":* Ed O'Keefe and Paul Kane, "Chuck Schumer, Lamar Alexander Might Have Solution to Fixing Senate," *Washington Post*, March 10, 2014, www.washingtonpost.com/politics/chuck-schumer-lamar-alexander-might-have-solution-to-fixing-senate/2014/03/10/d1635fd6-a302-11e3-a5fa-55f0c77bf39c_story.html.

CHAPTER 4

65. *Back then the dispute was over Medicare . . . :* Lisa Lerer, "Obama in Shutdown Politics Channels Clinton Who Scored Win," Bloomberg, October 1, 2013, www.bloomberg.com/news/2013-10-01/obama-in-shutdown-politics-channels-clinton-who-proved-a-winner.html.

67. *And so he approached the Senate Republican leadership:* "Investigating the Impact of the Year 2000 Problem," Senate Special Committee on the Year 2000 Technology Problem, www.gpo.gov/fdsys/pkg/GPO-CPRT-106sprt10/pdf/GPO-CPRT-106sprt10-6-3.pdf.

67. *Republican majority leader Trent Lott agreed to give Bennett the authority:* Special Committee on the Year 2000 Technology Problem, Investigating the Impact of the Year 2000 Problem, S. Rep. No. 105-S. Prt. 106-10 (1999), 13.

67. *Bennett, Dodd, and several colleagues held thirty-five hearings:* Special Committee on the Year 2000 Technology Problem, Y2K Aftermath—Crisis Averted Final Committee Report, S. Rep. No. 106-S. Prt. 106-XX (2000), 4.

67. *to examine the crisis's impact on the country's water supply:* Special Committee of the Year 2000 Technology Problem, Summary of Committee Findings, 106th Cong., 2d sess., 2000, S. Prt. 106-42, 52.

67. *to examine whether Oregon was prepared:* Special Committee of the Year 2000 Technology Problem, Summary of Committee Findings, 106th Cong., 2d sess., 2000, S. Prt. 106-42, 51.

67. *estimated $100 billion to head off the Y2K problem:* Special Committee on the Year 2000 Technology Problem, Y2K Aftermath—Crisis Averted Final Committee Report, S. Rep. No. 106-S. Prt. 106-XX (2000), 3.

68. *"the one period in which the government as a whole . . .":* National Commission on Terrorist Attacks upon the United States (Philip Zelikow, Executive Director; Bonnie D. Jenkins, Counsel; Ernest R. May, Senior Advisor). The 9/11 Commission Report. New York: W.W. Norton & Company, 2004, 358.

69. *In the evenings, literally every evening . . . :* John McCain, in Charles Gibson, "Restoring Comity to Congress," Harvard John F. Kennedy School of Government, Joan Shorenstein Center on the Press, Politics and Public Policy, Discussion Paper Series, January 2011, www.hks.harvard.edu/presspol/publications/papers/discussion_papers/d60_gibson.pdf.

69. *President Eisenhower would invite several members of both houses:* Tom Daschle, in Charles Gibson, "Restoring Comity to Congress," Harvard John F. Kennedy School of Government, Joan Shorenstein Center on the Press, Politics and Public Policy, Discussion Paper Series, January 2011, www.hks.harvard.edu/presspol/publications/papers/discussion_papers/d60_gibson.pdf.

69. *"Hell, if I lived up there . . . ":* Sam Rayburn, in Charles Gibson, "Restoring Comity to Congress," Harvard John F. Kennedy School of Government, Joan Shorenstein Center on the Press, Politics and Public Policy, Discussion Paper Series, January 2011, www.hks.harvard.edu/presspol/publications/papers/discussion_papers/d60_gibson.pdf.

69. *". . . on the Senate floor, put his arm around my dad's shoulder":* Evan Bayh, "Why I'm Leaving the Senate," *New York Times,* February 20, 2010, www.nytimes.com/2010/02/21/opinion/21bayh.html?pagewanted=all&_r=0.

70. *Senator Barry Goldwater (R–AZ), for example, once told:* Richard A. Arenberg and Robert B. Dove, *Defending the Filibuster: The Soul of the Senate* (Bloomington: Indiana University Press, 2012), 46.

70. *When he first moved to Washington in 1968:* Tom Price, "Crafting Policy to Bridge the Red-Blue Divide," *Pacific Standard,* December 12, 2011, www.psmag.com/navigation/politics-and-law/crafting-policy-to-bridge-the-red-blue-divide-38255.

70. *As late as the 1980s, as many as sixty senators would eat lunch:* Robert Kaiser, *Act of Congress: How America's Essential Institution Works, and How It Doesn't* (New York: Alfred A. Knopf, 2013), 231.

70. *And until Bob Dole ended the practice,:* Interview with Steve Bell conducted by Jason Grumet and Marc Dunkelman, Bipartisan Policy Center, Washington, DC, September 13, 2012.

70. *"I used to argue . . . ":* Melinda Henneberger, "Bob Dole Honored for Work in Helping to Feed the Poor," *Washington Post,* December 13, 2013, www.washingtonpost.com/politics/bob-dole-honored-for-work-in-helping-to-feed-the-poor/2013/12/12/667b36ac-635c-11e3-aa81-e1dab1360323_story.html.

70. *To read a biography of John Hay, the accomplished:* John Taliaferro, *All the Great Prizes: The Life of John Hay, From Lincoln to Roosevelt* (New York: Simon and Schuster, 2013), 187.

71. *"where laws are debated, where policies are . . . ":* Emily Langer, "Constantine Valanos, Capitol Hill Restaurateur, Dies at 93," *Washington Post*, April 5, 2012, www.washingtonpost.com/local/obituaries/constantine-valanos-capitol-hill -restaurateur-dies-at-93/2012/04/05/gIQAzejQyS_story.html.

71. *Robert Caro's multi-volume biography of Lyndon Johnson details:* Robert Caro, *Master of the Senate: The Years of Lyndon Johnson* (New York: Vintage, 2003), 208–10.

73. *A 1955 Gallup poll found that only 38 percent:* John Samples, "Term Limits and Popular Government," Cato Institute, September 27, 2011, www.cato.org/ blog/term-limits-popular-government.

74. *While previous Speakers, namely Democratic legend Tip:* Thomas P. O'Neill, *Man of the House: The Life and Political Memoirs of Speaker Tip O'Neill* (New York: Random House, 1987), 143; Jim Cooper, "Fixing Congress," *Boston Review*, May 2, 2011, www.bostonreview.net/cooper-fixing-congress.

74. *During the 1960s, members were only allowed:* Robert Kaiser, *Act of Congress: How America's Essential Institution Works, and How It Doesn't* (New York: Alfred A. Knopf, 2013), 231.

74. *Given the prevalence of more affordable plane tickets:* Randal C. Archibold, "Running (Late) for Mayor; Congressman in Primary Can't Catch His Breath," *New York Times*, May 21, 2005, http://query.nytimes.com/gst/fullpage.html?res =950DE7DE1539F932A15756C0A9639C8B63&pagewanted=all.

74. *As former senator Olympia Snowe:* Personal conversation with the author, Bipartisan Policy Center, November 18, 2013.

75. *Newsweek recently reached 46 of the 107 freshman:* Lisa Miller, "No More Washington Wives, and It's Our Loss," *Newsweek*, January 4, 2011, www.newsweek .com/no-more-washington-wives-and-its-our-loss-66761.

75. *The arrangement inspired:* Leslie Larson, "Three Congressmen Who Live in One DC House Inspire Series by Gerry Trudeau," *New York Daily News*, June 5, 2013, www.nydailynews.com/news/politics/ congressmen-house-inspire-tv-series-article-1.1364145#ixzz2vyGcq1pn.

75. *Rather than spend the money required to rent:* Natasha Lennard, "Wake-up Call on the Hill," *POLITICO*, February 15, 2011, www.politico.com/click/ stories/1102/wakeup_call_on_the_hill.html.

75. *But in a sign of just how dramatically the ethos:* Michael M. Phillips and Danny Yadron, "Pajama Party: New to Congress, Many Members Plan to Sleep Over," *Wall Street Journal*, November 29, 2010, http://online.wsj.com/news/ articles/SB10001424052748703559504575630661395762460.

75. *While earlier eras of legislators had been invested in Washington life:* Robert Kaiser, *Act of Congress: How America's Essential Institution Works, and How It Doesn't* (New York: Alfred A. Knopf, 2013), 105.

76. *Between 1961 and 1985, Congress was in session:* Thomas E. Mann and Norman J. Ornstein, *The Broken Branch: How Congress Is Failing America and How to Get It Back on Track* (New York: Oxford University Press, 2006), 170.
76. *Between 2000 and 2006, the average number of days:* Thomas E. Mann and Norman J. Ornstein, *The Broken Branch: How Congress Is Failing America and How to Get It Back on Track* (New York: Oxford University Press, 2006), 170.
76. *In 2013, the House spent a mere 118 days:* Jonathan Weisman, "House G.O.P Trims Agenda, Looking to Avert Election-Year Trouble," *New York Times*, January 5, 2014, www.nytimes.com/2014/01/06/us/politics/house-gop-trims -agenda-looking-to-avert-election-year-trouble.html?_r=0; James Warren and Dan Friedman, "Congress Finishes Out Least Productive Year in Its History as Productivity Dips," *New York Daily News,* December 22, 2013, www.nydailynews.com/news/politics/congress-finishes-productive-year -history-article-1.1555561.
76. *Moreover, certain days spent "in session":* Norman J. Ornstein, Thomas E. Mann, and Michael J. Malbin, *Vital Statistics on Congress* (Washington, DC: Brookings Institution Press, 2008), 124; Thomas E. Mann and Norman J. Ornstein. *The Broken Branch: How Congress Is Failing America and How to Get It Back on Track* (New York: Oxford University Press, 2006), 170.
76. *The percentage of midweek votes has steadily increased:* Timothy P. Nokken and Brian R. Sala, "Institutional Evolution and the Rise of the Tuesday-Thursday Club in the House of Representatives" (paper presented at the annual meeting of the American Political Science Association, Washington, DC, August 31– September 3, 2000).
77. *In her farewell remarks, she defined the threat in no uncertain:* www.bloomberg .com/news/2013-08-27/napolitano-u-s-risks-major-cyber-attack-in-the-future .html.
78. *Acrimony between the Democratic and Republican:* Ramsey Cox and Jennifer Martinez, "Cybersecurity Act Fails Senate Vote," *The Hill,* August 2, 2012, http://thehill.com/blogs/hillicon-valley/ technology/241851-cybersecurity-act-fails-to-advance-in-senate.
78. *And so in the end, the bill was put on ice:* Ed O'Keefe and Ellen Nakashima, "Cybersecurity Bill Fails in Senate," *Washington Post.* August 2, 2012, www .washingtonpost.com/world/national-security/cybersecurity-bill-fails-in -senate/2012/08/02/gJQADNOOSX_story.html.
79. *When I'm over here at the congressional . . . :* Chris Cillizza, "President Obama Is Older and Wiser This Time Around," *Washington Post,* January 20, 2013, www.washingtonpost.com/politics/president-obama-is-older-and-wiser-this -time-around/2013/01/20/39dfbc1a-631e-11e2-85f5-a8a9228e55e7_print.html.
79. *A moment of seemingly meaningful connection occurred:* Only senators Marco Rubio (R-FL) and Jeanne Shaheen (D-NH) were not

present at the meeting; they cited prior personal commitments.
Ed O'Keefe and Jenna Johnson, "No Filibuster Deal, but Senators Agree They Should Meet More Often," *Washington Post*, July 15,
2013, www.washingtonpost.com/blogs/post-politics/wp/2013/07/15/
no-filibuster-deal-but-senators-agree-they-should-meet-more-often.
79. *If one listened to the members' reactions:* Ibid.
79. *Senator Angus King (I-ME) reflected that the meeting:* Ibid.
79. *Senator Jeff Merkley (D-OR) noted that the closed door:* Niels Lesn-
iewski, "Ghosts of the Old Senate Chamber Leave Mark on 'Nuclear
Option' Deal," *Roll Call*, July 16, 2013, http://blogs.rollcall.com/wgdb/
ghosts-of-old-senate-chamber-leave-mark-on-nuclear-option-deal.
79. *After that, there was talk of making talking a regular:* Ed O'Keefe
and Jenna Johnson, "No Filibuster Deal, but Senators Agree
They Should Meet More Often," *Washington Post*, July 15, 2013,
www.washingtonpost.com/blogs/post-politics/wp/2013/07/15/
no-filibuster-deal-but-senators-agree-they-should-meet-more-often.
79. *Senators Martin Heinrich (D-NM) and Dean Heller (R-NV):* Niels Lesn-
iewski, "Senators Want More Bipartisan Meetings," Roll Call, July 19, 2013,
http://blogs.rollcall.com/wgdb/heinrich-heller-seek-more-joint-meetings.
79. *Senator Reid even suggested he might reach out:* Niels Lesn-
iewski, "Ghosts of the Old Senate Chamber Leave Mark on 'Nuclear
Option' Deal," *Roll Call*, July 16, 2013, http://blogs.rollcall.com/wgdb/
ghosts-of-old-senate-chamber-leave-mark-on-nuclear-option-deal.
80. *Some folks still don't think I spend enough time . . . :* Barack Obama,
CBS News, "Obama on Getting a Drink with Mitch McConnell:'Really?'"
April 30, 2013, www.cbsnews.com/videos/obama-on-getting-a-drink-with
-mitch-mcconnell-really.
80. *"I answered and heard":* Personal interview, October 8, 2013, Washington,
DC.
82. *The campus design he eventually:* Jon Gertner, "True Innovation," *New York
Times,* February 25, 2012, www.nytimes.com/2012/02/26/opinion/sunday/
innovation-and-the-bell-labs-miracle.html?pagewanted=all.
83. *"Back in the 1980s and 1990s . . . ":* Personal conversation with the author,
April 2, 2014.

Chapter 5

85. *"the most difficult task I have ever undertaken . . .":* George Mitchell, *Making
Peace* (New York: Alfred A. Knopf, 1999), ix.
86. *"It is a sad irony that we received these honors . . . ":* "Mitchell Knighted as
Accord Hits Crisis," *Sun Journal*, Lewiston, ME, July 16, 1999, http://news

.google.com/newspapers?nid=bcT4vkklUMwC&dat=19990716&printsec
=frontpage&hl=en.

86. *it made it impossible to avoid harmful leaks:* Nicholas Watt, "George Mitchell's Patient Diplomacy Shepherded Northern Ireland to Peace. Now for the Middle East," *The Guardian*, Politics Blog, www.theguardian.com/politics/blog/2009/jan/23/george-mitchell-interview.

86. *Senator Mitchell hunkered down with leaders:* "UK: Northern Ireland Mitchell Extends Review," BBC News, October 23, 1999, http://news.bbc.co.uk/2/hi/uk_news/northern_ireland/482990.stm.

87. *"The global coalition against corruption.":* "Overview," Transparency International, www.transparency.org/whoweare/organisation.

88. *"to forbid 'licentious publications of their proceeding'":* Richard Brookhiser, *James Madison* (New York: Basic Books, 2011), 51.

91. *Over the course of the following decades, a series of technological advances:* "Moving Toward a 21st Century Right-to-Know Agenda: Recommendations for President-Elect Obama and Congress," Center for Effective Government, November 2008, www.foreffectivegov.org/files/21strtkrecs.pdf.

91. *And one need look no further than C-SPAN:* Chris Pergram, "Who Controls the Cameras in Congress," FoxNews.com, February 6, 2011, http://politics.blogs.foxnews.com/2011/02/06/who-controls-cameras-congress.

91. *the wells of the House and Senate were places:* Interview with Steve Bell, Bipartisan Policy Center, Washington, DC, January 31, 2013.

92. *the "observer" effect:* http://psychology.about.com/od/hindex/g/def_hawthorn.htm. On a more technical level, this is Heisenberg's Uncertainty Principle, http://science.howstuffworks.com/innovation/science-questions/quantum-suicide2.htm.

92. *talk to cameras instead of each other:* E-mail from Steve Bell, December 2013.

92. *C-SPAN hasn't simply exposed dialogue:* Pete Davis, "C-SPAN Should Televise Most, But Not All Congressional Meetings," January 8, 2010, Stan Collender's Capital Gains and Games, http://capitalgainsandgames.com/blog/pete-davis/1385/c-span-should-televise-most-not-all-congressional-meetings.

92. *"You deliberately stood in that well . . . ":* David Osborne, "The Swinging Days of Newt Gingrich," *Mother Jones*, November 1, 1984, www.motherjones.com/politics/1984/11/newt-gingrich-shining-knight-post-reagan-right.

93. *But the experiment failed in large part:* Donald R. Wolfensberger, "Can Party Governance Endure in the U.S. House of Representatives?" (paper presented at 120th Anniversary Roundtable on Woodrow Wilson's Congressional Government, Washington, DC, November 14, 2005).

94. *Few would suggest that the pursuit of transparency:* It was reported in late 2013 that messages sent by Merkel, the German chancellor, had been intercepted by America's National Security Agency. Hendrik Hertzberg, "Obama's

Game of Telephone," *New Yorker*, November 1, 2013, www.newyorker.com/
online/blogs/comment/2013/11/how-much-did-president-obama-know
-about-the-nsa-eavesdropping-on-angela-merkel.html.
94. *critical arbiter of the lines between public and private:* Electronic Frontiers
Foundation, "History of FOIA," https://www.eff.org/issues/transparency/
history-of-foia.
94. *It's hard to dispute the altruistic motives:* Kenneth Chamberlain, "History: The Day the Freedom of Information Act Expanded," *National
Journal*, November 20, 2012, www.nationaljournal.com/congress-legacy/
history-the-day-the-freedom-of-information-act-expanded-20121120.
94. *"every portion of every meeting of an agency . . . ":* "The Government in Sunshine Act," Reporters Committee for Freedom of the Press, www
.rcfp.org/federal-open-government-guide/federal-open-meetings-laws/
government-sunshine-act.
95. *"Heavens, no! . . . It would get subpoenaed.":* Jeff Shesol, "The Clinton Documents and the Case for Writing It Down," *The New Yorker*, March 21, 2014,
www.newyorker.com/online/blogs/newsdesk/2014/03/the-clinton-documents
-and-the-case-for-writing-it-down.html.
95. *"The climate of fear . . . ":* Ibid.
96. *"CEI first asked for her texts on 18 . . . ":* Brian McNicoll, "CEI Seeks
Injunction Against Ongoing EPA Record Destruction," Competitive Enterprise Institute, October 3, 2013, http://cei.org/news-releases/
cei-suit-seeks-injunction-against-ongoing-epa-record-destruction.
97. *"enjoin and prevent the destruction of certain EPA text . . . ":* Ibid.
97. *The notion is all e-mails should be captured. . . . :* Lisa Rein, "U.S. Chief Records
Officer Details Federal E-Mail Record-Keeping Programs," *Washington Post*,
June 16, 2013, www.washingtonpost.com/politics/us-chief-records-officer
-details-federal-e-mail-record-keeping-programs/2013/06/16/a6995e92-d470
-11e2-a73e-826d299ff459_story.html.
97. *Two of its many slogans are, "secrets are lies" . . . :* Dave Eggers, *The Circle* (New
York: Knopf, 2013), 326.
98. *But the government hasn't been entirely flat-footed in the face:* Annual FOIA
Reports, United States Department of Justice, www.justice.gov/oip/reports
.html. This percentage was calculated by analyzing Annual FOIA Reports for
the Justice Department between FY2003 and FY2012.
99. *CEQ is a relatively nimble bureaucracy:* "Facing the Future: Recommendations on the White House Council on Environmental Quality," Henry M.
Jackson Foundation, October 2008, www.hmjackson.org/publications.
99. *One reason, a White House staffer privately told me:* Personal interview, July 12,
2013, Washington, DC.
100. *"Baucus and Hatch promised that any ideas written and transmitted
. . . ":* Brendan Greeley, "Senators' Tax Loophole Requests Will Get Special

Vault," *Bloomberg Businessweek*, August 1, 2013, www.businessweek.com/articles/2013-08-01/senators-tax-loophole-requests-will-get-special-vault.

100. *Roughly one thousand of these:* "The Federal Advisory Committee Act (FACA) Brochure," US General Services Administration, www.gsa.gov/portal/content/101010.

101. *For timely issues it is very difficult . . . :* Interview with EPA official, United States Environmental Protection Agency, Washington, DC, August 20, 2013.

102. *The FACA rules demanded . . . :* Interview with Paul Bledsoe, Bipartisan Policy Center, Washington, DC, February 2, 2014.

103. *While no one wanted to get too specific:* Personal conversations with four federal advisory committee members from three separate committees.

103. *From there, the deliberative work was largely:* Personal conversation between the author and Senator Gorton, March 3, 2014.

104. *But, for most everyone in public life, there's:* "Moving Toward a 21st Century Right-to-Know Agenda: Recommendations for President-Elect Obama and Congress," Center for Effective Government, November 2008, www.foreffectivegov.org/files/21strtkrecs.pdf.

104. *My Administration is committed . . . :* President Barack Obama to Heads of Executive Departments and Agencies, "Transparency and Open Government," www.whitehouse.gov/the_press_office/TransparencyandOpenGovernment.

105. *Americans have lost trust with their government . . . :* Ira Stoll, "Boehner's Backroom Deal," Reason.com, December 10, 2012, http://reason.com/archives/2012/12/10/boehners-backroom-deal/print.

105. *When a contractor working on HealthCare.gov:* Matthew Burke, "HealthCare.gov Contractor Rejects Illegal Obama HHS Request to Withhold Subpoenaed Documents from Congress," Tea Party News Network, December 13, 2013, www.tpnn.com/2013/12/13/healthcare-gov-contractor-rejects-illegal-obama-hhs-request-to-withhold-subpoenaed-documents-from-congress.

105. *Even fellow Democrats were troubled by a lack of:* Robert Parry, "Congress Denied Syrian Facts, Too," Consortiumnews.com, September 7, 2013, http://consortiumnews.com/2013/09/07/congress-denied-syrian-facts-too.

105. *"There's a complete disconnect between . . . ":* Lucas, "Obama Administration Transparency Faces Congressional Oversight," CNSNews.com, March 16, 2014, http://cnsnews.com/news/article/obama-administration-transparency-faces-congressional-oversight#sthash.zuvXkEUN.dpuf.

106. *"What I object to . . . is mak[ing] it impossible . . . ":* Elisabeth Bumiller, "Cheney Is Set to Battle Congress to Keep His Enron Papers Secret," *New York Times*, January 28, 2002.

106. *The result is a level of collegiality and collaboration:* This was demonstrated in 2013 when the Democratic chairwoman and Republican vice chairman of the Senate Select Committee on Intelligence (which operates along much the same lines) addressed the press together in the wake of leaked evidence that

the National Security Agency was surveying American phone activity. Dianne Feinstein and Saxby Chambliss, "Feinstein, Chambliss Statement on NSA Phone Records Program," United States Senate Select Committee on Intelligence, June 6, 2013, www.intelligence.senate.gov/press/record.cfm?id=343993.

106. *The atmosphere frequently promotes careful deliberation:* Interview with Michael Allen conducted by Jason Grumet, Marc Dunkelman, and Ben Kramer, February 17, 2014.

108. *people "poured their hearts out . . . they really talked . . . ":* "Lott, Daschle, Discuss Fiscal Cliff, Bipartisanship and Media," CNN, Interview with Dana Bash, December 13, 2012, http://politicalticker.blogs.cnn.com/2012/12/13/lott-daschle-discuss-fiscal-cliff-bipartisanship-and-the-media.

108. *"there are times when not having media . . . ":* Ibid.

110. *A longstanding criticism of the Act has been . . . :* "Reform of the Government in Sunshine Act," Report and Recommendation by the Special Committee to the Government in Sunshine Act, Administrative Conference of the United States, March 8, 2013, www.acus.gov/sites/default/files/documents/Special%20Committee%20Sunshine%20Act%20Recommendation%20%281995%29.pdf.

CHAPTER 6

111. *It is one of the happy incidents . . . : New York State Ice Co v Liebmann*, 285 U.S. 262, March 21, 1932, Brandeis Dissent.

111. *The better part of a century later, Brandeis's notion: New York State Ice Co. v. Liebmann*, 285 U.S. 262 (1932), http://caselaw.lp.findlaw.com/scripts/getcase.pl?navby=CASE&court=US&vol=285&page=262.

112. *A few of the members, as happens in all such assemblies . . . :* James Madison, Federalist #53, in *Classics of American Political Thoughts and Constitutional Thought: Origins Through the Civil War*, vol. 2, Scott J. Hammond, Kevin R. Hardwick, and Howard Leslie Lubert, eds. (Indianapolis: Hackett Publishing Company, 2007), 449.

112. "*The small-group principle is deeply . . . ":* Ken Segall, *Insanely Simple: The Obsession That Drives Apple's Success* (New York: Penguin Group, Inc., 2012), 26.

113. *"Congress in session is Congress on public exhibition . . . ":* Lee H. Hamilton, *How Congress Works and Why You Should Care* (Bloomington: Indiana University Press, 2004), 50.

113. *As explained in a Bain and Company report:* "Effective Organization Design Considers Five, Interrelated Components," Bain and Company Organizational Toolkit, in "Designing an Effective Organization," The Bridgespan Group, January 2009.

114. *The term, "Czar Speaker" emerged because:* Daniel J. Palazzolo, *The Speaker and the Budget: Leadership in the Post-Reform House of Representatives* (Pittsburgh, PA: University of Pittsburgh Press, 1992), 12.

114. *Motivated to rein in abuses of power:* Donald R. Wolfensberger, "Committee Leaders Through History, An Introductory Essay," Woodrow Wilson International Center for Scholars, Friday, February 8, 2002. The "King Caucus," which unlike the Czar Speakers, was the organ of the Democratic Caucus, had the same effect.

114. *House committees and committee chairs . . . :* Joseph Cooper, "The Twentieth-Century Congress," in *Congress Reconsidered,* 7th ed., Lawrence C. Dodd and Bruce I. Oppenheimer, eds. (Washington, DC, Congressional Quarterly Press, 2001), 339.

114. *As Washington's mandate grew:* Roger H. Davidson, "The Advent of the Modern Congress: The Legislative Reorganization Act of 1946," *Legislative Studies Quarterly* 15, no. 3 (August 1990): 360.

114. *The existing committee structure quickly proved:* Andrew Glass, "Truman Signs Legislative Reorganization Act, Aug. 2, 1946," *POLITICO,* August 2, 2010, www.politico.com/news/stories/0810/40522.html.

115. *After months of work and negotiation:* Michael H. Crespin, Anthony Madonna, Nathaniel Ament-Stone, "Senate Collection Action and the Legislative Reorganization Act of 1946" (paper presented at the Congress and History Conference, Providence, RI, June 9-10, 2011).

115. *and a limit was set on the number:* Library of Congress, CRS, *Committee Numbers, Sizes, Assignments, and Staff: Selected Historical Data,* by Carol Hardy Vincent and Elizabeth Rybicki, CRS Report 96-109 (Washington, DC: Office of Congressional Information and Publishing, February 1, 1996).

115. *people who would serve for a decade or more . . . :* Julian Zelizer, "The Culture of Congress, Yesterday & Today," Woodrow Wilson International Center for Scholars, Washington, DC, April 31, 2012, www.wilsoncenter.org/sites/default/files/cultureofcongresstranscript.pdf.

116. *In their eyes, this period was less about bipartisan collaboration:* After passage of the 1946 Legislative Reorganization Act, Republicans only controlled the Senate for four Congresses, and the House for one Congress, until the 1995 Republican takeover. And, the 80th Congress (1947–1949) was the only Congress, save for one in 1953–1954, between 1946 and 1995 for which Republicans simultaneously controlled both chambers.

116. *Democrats often defined the agenda:* Robert Kuttner, "Congress without Cohabitation: The Democrats' Morning After," *American Prospect,* December 4, 2010, http://prospect.org/article/congress-without -cohabitation-democrats-morning-after.

116. *Between 1947 and 1980, the number of laws:* One must be very careful when comparing the number of laws passed over time. For example, in the ("Do Nothing") 80th Congress, 906 public bills were enacted, totaling 2,236 pages for an average of 2.5 pages per statute. In the 111th Congress, 383 public bills

were enacted totaling 7,617 pages, for an average of 19.89 pages per statute: that's 523 fewer laws from 1947-1948 to 2009-2010—a 57.73 percent drop, but 5,381 more pages of law—a 240 percent increase. Norman J. Ornstein, Thomas E. Mann, Michael J. Malbin, and Andrew Rugg, "Vital Statistics on Congress," Brookings Institution, July 11, 2013, www.brookings.edu/research/reports/2013/07/vital-statistics-congress-mann-ornstein.

116. *Admittedly, not all of those laws were of real:* Lisa Mascaro and Richard Simon, "House May Ban Honorific Resolutions," *Los Angeles Times*, November 25, 2010, http://articles.latimes.com/2010/nov/25/nation/la-na-resolutions-20101125.

116. *The most recent Congress (112th) passed:* United States House of Representatives, Office of the Clerk, "Resume of Congressional Activity," http://library.clerk.house.gov/resume.aspx.

117. *From these unshakable perches:* Earl Black and Merle Black, *The Rise of Southern Republicans* (Cambridge, MA: Harvard University Press, 2003), 2–3.

117. *This reform package returned some power:* Donald R. Wolfensberger, "Can Party Governance Endure in the U.S. House of Representatives?" (paper presented at 120th Anniversary Roundtable on Woodrow Wilson's *Congressional Government*, Washington, DC, November 14, 2005).

118. *They pushed through a rule that:* Ibid.

118. *Then the reformers took a few scalps:* Donald R. Wolfensberger, "Can Party Governance Endure in the U.S. House of Representatives?" (paper presented at 120th Anniversary Roundtable on Woodrow Wilson's *Congressional Government*, Washington, DC, November 14, 2005).

119. *After leading the charge to install the first Republican:* Donald R. Wolfensberger, "Committee Leaders Through History, An Introductory Essay," Woodrow Wilson International Center for Scholars, February 8, 2002.

119. *A few years later, the Republican House majority leader:* Bruce Miroff, Raymond Seidelman, Todd Swanstrom, and Tom De Luca, *The Democratic Debate: American Politics in an Age of Change* (Boston: Cengage Learning, 2009), 259.

119. *But under Speaker Wright, the number of closed rules:* Steven E. Schier and Todd E. Eberly, *America's Dysfunctional Political System* (New York: Routledge, 2013), 74.

120. *To increase engagement, expertise, and shared:* Roger H. Davidson, "The Advent of the Modern Congress: The Legislative Reorganization Act of 1946," *Legislative Studies Quarterly* 15, no. 3 (August 1990): 366.

120. *But in the years that followed, committee rosters:* Louis P. Westefield, "Majority Party Leadership and the Committee System in the House of Representatives," *American Political Science Review* 68, no. 4 (December 1974): 1593.

120. *The number of committee seats:* Roger H. Davidson, "The Advent of the Modern Congress: The Legislative Reorganization Act of 1946," *Legislative Studies Quarterly* 15, no. 3 (August 1990): 366.

120. *Roughly the same thing happened in the Senate:* Ibid.

120. *In the Senate and the House the number:* Library of Congress, CRS, *Committee Numbers, Sizes, Assignments, and Staff: Selected Historical Data*, by Carol Hardy Vincent and Elizabeth Rybicki, CRS Report 96-109 (Washington, DC: Office of Congressional Information and Publishing, February 1, 1996).

120. *For example Appropriations has twelve separate subcommittees:* Committee System Rules Changes in the House, 110th Congress, Congressional Research Service, January 25, 2007.

120. *It was rarely clear whether the job of:* Donald R. Wolfensberger, "Can Party Governance Endure in the U.S. House of Representatives?" (paper presented at 120th Anniversary Roundtable on Woodrow Wilson's *Congressional Government*, Washington, DC, November 14, 2005).

120. *And the effect, according to Princeton professor Julian Zelizer:* Julian E. Zelizer, *On Capitol Hill: The Struggle to Reform Congress and Its Consequences, 1948–2000* (New York: Cambridge University Press, 2004), 199–200.

121. *director Robert S. Mueller III noted that while:* Thomas H. Kean and Lee H. Hamilton, "Homeland Confusion," *New York Times*, September 10, 2013, www .nytimes.com/2013/09/11/opinion/homeland-confusion.html?_r=0.

121. *"Congressional oversight for intelligence . . .":* *The 9/11 Commission Report: Final Report of the National Commission on Terrorist Attacks Upon the United States*, official government edition (Washington, DC: US Government Printing Office, 2004), 420–21.

121. *As of 2012, the department whose job:* "Comparatively, DOD reports to only 36 committees and subcommittees despite its budget equaling 10 times that of DHS. Many of these 108 committees, like Small Businesses, Financial Services, and Aging, are not readily sensible as homeland security overseers." Jessica Zuckerman, "Politics Over Security: Homeland Security Congressional Oversight In Dire Need of Reform," The Heritage Foundation, September 10, 2012, www.heritage.org/research/reports/2012/09/ homeland-security-congressional-oversight-in-dire-need-of-reform.

122. *In the 112th Congress, which ended in January . . . :* Thomas H. Kean and Lee H. Hamilton, "Homeland Confusion," *New York Times*, September 10, 2013, www.nytimes.com/2013/09/11/opinion/homeland-confusion. html?_r=1&.

124. *"It is with the help of our speakers at these . . .":* "Congressmen Paul Kanjorski and Scott Garrett Host Fourth Bipartisan Financial Regulatory Roundtable," Bipartisan Policy Center, June 2, 2009, http://bipartisanpolicy.org/news/press-releases/2009/06/ congressmen-paul-kanjorski-and-scott-garrett-host-fourth-bipartisan.

126. *"the result was a huge disappointment to those of us":* Interview with Byron Dorgan, Washington, DC, July 18, 2013.

132. *Senator Chuck Schumer (D–NY) and Lamar Alexander:* Ed O'Keefe and
Paul Kane, "Chuck Schumer, Lamar Alexander Might Have Solution to Fixing
Senate," *Washington Post,* March 10, 2014, www.washingtonpost.com/politics/
chuck-schumer-lamar-alexander-might-have-solution-to-fixing
-senate/2014/03/10/d1635fd6-a302-11e3-a5fa-55f0c77bf39c_story.htm.
132. *In early 2013, Congress took up an issue long mired:* Robert Pear and Carl
Hulse, "Immigration Bill Fails to Survive Senate Vote," *New York Times,* June 28,
2007, www.nytimes.com/2007/06/28/washington/28cnd-immig.html?_r=0.
133. *The unusual influence of this gang was enabled:* Members of the Gang of Eight
who were simultaneously serving on the Senate Judiciary Committee included
senators Chuck Schumer, Richard Durbin, Jeff Flake, and Lindsey Graham.
133. *the bill was reported to the Senate floor:* "S.744 Amendments," United States
Senate Committee on the Judiciary, www.judiciary.senate.gov/legislation/
immigration/amendments.cfm.

Chapter 7

137. *In 2006, he pled guilty to fraud:* Susan Schmidt and James V. Grimaldi,
"Abramoff Pleads Guilty to 3 Counts," *Washington Post,* January 4, 2006, www
.washingtonpost.com/wp-dyn/content/article/2006/01/03/AR2006010300474
.html.
138. *"men, women, rich, poor, young, old . . .":* "Poll: This Is a 'Do-Nothing'
Congress," CNN, December 26, 2013, http://politicalticker.blogs.cnn.
com/2013/12/26/poll-this-is-a-do-nothing-congress/?hpt=hp_t2.
140. *While Congress imposed a $1,000 cap:* Clyde Wilcox et al., "With Limits
Raised, Who Will Give More? The Impact of BCRA on Individual Donors," in
Life After Reform: When the Bipartisan Campaign Reform Act Meets Politics, Michael J.
Malbin, ed. (Lanham, MD: Rowman & Littlefield Publishers, 2003), 62.
140. *Even better, with certain exceptions, the law banned political:* Library of Congress, CRS, *Bipartisan Campaign Reform Act of 2002: Summary and Comparison
with Previous Law,* by Joseph E. Cantor and L. Paige Whitaker, CRS Report
RL31402 (Washington, DC: Office of Congressional Information and Publishing, January 9, 2004).
141. *Super PACs, while still being precluded from coordinating with any given
campaign:* There's no set definition for this newfangled term: Basically, candidates would solicit donors on behalf of Super PACs exclusively determined
to promote their own candidacies, thereby obviating the limits now put on
donations to any official campaign apparatus. Kim Barker and Marian Wang,
"Super-PACs and Dark Money: ProPublica's Guide to the New World of
Campaign Finance," ProPublica, July 11, 2011, www.propublica.org/blog/item/
super-pacs-propublicas-guide-to-the-new-world-of-campaign-finance.

141. *This outlay is slightly larger than the GDP of Bermuda:* "Gross Domestic
Product 2012," World Bank, http://databank.worldbank.org/data/download/
GDP.pdf.
142. *By 2012, state party average resources:* Byron Tau, "Last Call for State Parties?" *POLITICO*, February 17, 2014, www.politico.com/story/2014/02/last
-call-for-state-parties-103559.html#ixzz2tbmlLx2S. Analysis of the federal
data for all 100 state parties, conducted by *POLITICO* with assistance from the
law firm Sandler, Reiff, Young & Lamb. A separate analysis was conducted of
state finances, using numbers collected by the National Institute on Money in
State Politics.
142. *"more chaos and disequilibrium . . .":* Nicholas Confessore, "Big-Money
Donors Demand Larger Say in Campaign Strategy," *New York Times,* March 1,
2014, www.nytimes.com/2014/03/02/us/politics/big-money-donors-demand
-larger-say-in-party-strategy.html?_r=1.
142. *"It's obviously only an estimate. . . . ":* Tarini Parti, "$7 billion Spent on
2012 campaign, FEC Says," *POLITICO*, January 31, 2013, www.politico.com/
story/2013/01/7-billion-spent-on-2012-campaign-fec-says-87051.html.
142. *"If the First Amendment has any force . . .":* Adam Liptak, "Justices, 5–4,
Reject Corporate Spending Limit," *New York Times,* January 21, 2010, www
.nytimes.com/2010/01/22/us/politics/22scotus.html?pagewanted=all&_r=0.
143. *Limits on independent expenditures were dealt:* Speechnow.org v. FEC Case
Summary, Federal Election Commission, www.fec.gov/law/litigation/speechnow
.shtml.
143. *"Republicans will be far more interested in finding . . . ":* Tim Mak, "How
McCain-Feingold Empowered the Kochs," *FrumForum*, March 11, 2011, www
.frumforum.com/how-mccain-feingold-empowered-the-koch-brothers.
144. *Researchers at Wesleyan University tallied:* Erica F. Fowler, "Presidential Ads 70
Percent Negative in 2012, Up from 9 Percent in 2008," Wesleyan Media Project,
May 2, 2012, http://mediaproject.wesleyan.edu/2012/05/02/jump-in-negativity.
144. *The Susan B. Anthony List, a conservative Super PAC/501(c)4:* "National
Organization for Women: Spending by Cycle," Center for Responsive Politics,
www.opensecrets.org/pacs/lookup2.php?strID=C00092247.
145. *"We were always able to get every dollar . . . ":* Jack Abramoff, Radio
Interview with *The Kojo Nnamdi Show*, August 15, 2012, Washington, DC, http://thekojonnamdishow.org/shows/2012-08-15/
recipe-corruption-jack-abramoffs-restaurants/transcript.
145. *If you're a donor . . . :* Byron Tau, "Last Call for State Parties?" *POLITICO*,
February 17, 2014, www.politico.com/story/2014/02/last-call-for-state
-parties-103559.html#ixzz2tbmlLx2S.
146. *"The work can be easier, demanding . . . ":* Greg Giroux, "Why
Super PACs Make the Best Attack Ads," *Bloomberg Businessweek,*

July 26, 2012, http://mobile.businessweek.com/articles/2012-07-26/why-super-pacs-make-the-best-attack-ads.

146. *Now you get these terrible ads . . . :* Interview with Senator Bob Bennett (R-UT), Bipartisan Policy Center, February 5, 2014.

147. *"Undoubtedly I will give more to . . . ":* Nicholas Confessore, "Ruling Spurs Rush for Cash in Both Parties," *New York Times,* April 4, 2014, www.nytimes.com/2014/04/05/us/politics/ruling-sets-off-a-bipartisan-rush-for-campaign-cash.html?ref=todayspaper&_r=0.

147. *For example, the DNC and RNC are presently allowed:* "2013 Coordinated Party Expenditure Limits," Federal Election Commission, www.fec.gov/info/charts_441ad_2013.shtml.

148. *"A foolish consistency is the hobgoblin . . . ":* Ralph Waldo Emerson, "Self Reliance," in *Essays: First Series* (1841; repr., Stilwell, Kansas: Digireads.com Publishing, 2007), 21.

148. *"transparency enables the electorate . . . ":* Liz Cox Barrett, "This Transparency Enables Electorate to Make Informed Decisions," *Columbia Journalism Review,* October 28, 2010, www.cjr.org/campaign_desk/this_transparency_enables_elec.php.

148. *"Requiring people to stand up in public . . .":* Antonin Scalia, cited in: Ian Vandewalker, "Justice Scalia's Sense of Enlightenment," Brennan Center for Justice, July 20, 2012, www.brennancenter.org/blog/justice-scalia's-sense-entitlement.

148. *And there's movement afoot:* The other three states that allow unlimited campaign contributions are Missouri, Oregon, and Utah. Seven states—Alabama, Indiana, Iowa, Mississippi, North Dakota, Pennsylvania, and Texas—limit or prohibit contributions by corporations and unions, but allow unlimited contributions from all other sources. "Contribution Limits: An Overview," National Conference of State Legislatures, October 3, 2011, www.ncsl.org/research/elections-and-campaigns/campaign-contribution-limits-overview.aspx.

148. *Only foreign nationals and foreign businesses:* "The Virginia Way," The Virginia Public Access Project, www.vpap.org/about_us/thevaway.

148. *a candidate must disclose the name:* Ibid.

148. *At the federal level, the Securities and Exchange Commission may soon require:* Mike Ludwig, "Citizens United Opponents Cheer Corporate Disclosure Rule on SEC Agenda," Truthout, January 14, 2013, http://truth-out.org/news/item/13865-citizens-united-opponents-cheer-corporate-disclosure-rule-on-sec-agenda.

148. *In addition, there are two bills moving through Congress:* Rosalind S. Helderman, "DISCLOSE Act, New Donor Transparency Law, Blocked in Senate," *Washington Post,* July 16, 2012, http://thomas.loc.gov/cgi-bin/bdquery/z?d113:h.r.148; Paul Blumenthal, "Ron Wyden, Lisa Murkowski Unveil

Bipartisan Campaign Finance Bill," *Huffington Post,* April 23, 2013, www
.huffingtonpost.com/2013/04/23/wyden-murkowski-campaign
-finance_n_3141818.html.

149. *"there is no distinctly native American criminal class except Congress,":* Deal L.
Yarwood, *When Congress Makes a Joke: Congressional Humor Then and Now* (Lanham, MD: Rowman and Littlefield Publishers, 2004), 81.

149. *political corruption has, for good reason:* David Freed, "A Tale of Two Iden-
tities," *Harvard Political Review,* May 21, 2013, http://harvardpolitics.com/
books-arts/a-tale-of-two-identities.

149. *President Zachary Taylor's attorney general and secretary of the Treasury conspired:* John S. D. Eisenhower, *Zachary Taylor,* The American Presidents Series
(New York: Henry Holt and Company, 2008), 130–32.

150. *President Eisenhower's chief of staff, Sherman Adams, had: Congressional Ethics: History, Facts, and Controversy,* John L. Moore, ed. (Washington, DC: Congressional Quarterly, Inc., 1992), 146.

150. *In response, Congress enacted:* The Code of Ethics for Government Service
was adopted as a House Resolution on July 11, 1958, but was not formally
incorporated by way of executive order until 1989 pursuant to a recommendation of the President's Commission on Government Ethics.

150. *But it marked an important shift right at the dawn of the Cold War: Congressional Ethics: History, Facts, and Controversy,* John L. Moore, ed. (Washington,
DC: Congressional Quarterly, Inc., 1992), 146.

150. *In response, both the Senate and House established Ethics Committees:* The permanent Select Committee on Ethics replaced the Select Committee on Standards and Conduct in 1977.

150. *For example, members were permitted to accept payments: Congressional Ethics:
History, Facts, and Controversy,* John L. Moore, ed. (Washington, DC: Congressional Quarterly, Inc., 1992), 147.

150. *"I know it when I see it" definition:* Justice Potter Stewart, concurring opinion in *Jacobellis v. Ohio 378 U.S. 184 (1964),* regarding possible obscenity in *The
Lovers.*

150. *Deeply disturbed by Nixon's transgressions and fearful of angry voters:* Judy
Schneider, Christopher M. Davis, and Betsy Palmer, *Reorganization of the House
of Representatives: Background and History* (Hauppauge, NY: Nova Science
Publishers, Inc., 2003), 57–58; *Congressional Ethics: History, Facts, and Controversy,* John L. Moore, ed. (Washington, DC: Congressional Quarterly, Inc.,
1992), 150; Library of Congress, CRS, *The Senate Select Committee on Ethics: A
Brief History of Its Evolution and Jurisdiction,* by Mildred L. Amer, CRS Report
RL30650 (Washington, DC: Office of Congressional Information and Publishing, March 26, 2008).

151. *In the Abscam Scandal:* Alyssa Fetini, "A Brief History of the Keating Five," *Time*, October 8, 2008, http://content.time.com/time/business/article/0,8599,1848150,00.html.

151. *Then, in the early 1990s, after nearly two dozen House members:* Gary C. Jacobson and Michael A. Dimock, "Checking Out: The Effects of Bank Overdrafts on the 1992 House Elections," *American Journal of Political Science* 38, no. 3 (August 1994): 601–24. President Clinton pardoned Rostenkowski in 2000.

151. *The second wave of reforms began in the late 1980s, when: Congressional Ethics: History, Facts, and Controversy,* John L. Moore, ed. (Washington, DC: Congressional Quarterly, Inc., 1992), 156.

151. *To address growing public concern about congressional travel:* Ibid., 157–58.

151. *After gaining majority status in the 1994 elections:* Juliet Eilperin, "House GOP Softens Its Ethics Rules: Democrats Fear Abuse of Gift Limits," *Washington Post*, January 8, 2003. Fifty years earlier, Congress had enacted lobbying disclosure requirement though it included loopholes enabling advocates to obscure their specific interests and clients. Craig Holman, "Origins, Evolution, and Structure of Lobbying Disclosure Act," *Public Citizen*, May 11, 2006, www.citizen.org/documents/LDAorigins.pdf.

151. *above $50 from anyone registered as a lobbyist:* Ironically, Republicans weakened these rules in 2003 when they instituted the "pizza rule," allowing special interests to purchase perishable food and drinks, like pizza, up to $50 per person, for members and their staff (Ryan Lizza, "The Nation; Reform? Republicans Reconsider," *The Nation*, January 12, 2003). That same year, House Republicans also enacted a rule allowing "any charity certified by the Internal Revenue Service to reimburse members for 'travel and lodging expenses' for events where the net proceeds go toward the charity" (Juliet Eilperin, "House GOP Softens Its Ethics Rules: Democrats Fear Abuse of Gift Limits," *Washington Post*, January 8, 2003).

152. *He regularly promised congressional staffers:* Lee Fang, "Jack Abramoff Explains How He 'Owned' Members of Congress and Their Staff," Think Progress, November 7, 2011, http://thinkprogress.org/special/2011/11/07/362392/abramoff-owned-congress.

152. *Abramoff orchestrated schemes in which his clients:* R. Jeffrey Smith, "Former DeLay Aide Enriched by Nonprofit," *Washington Post,* March 26, 2006, www.washingtonpost.com/wp-dyn/content/article/2006/03/25/AR2006032501166.html.

152. *Bush Administration appointees on exotic trips:* Associated Press, "A Look at the Abramoff Scandal and Where It Goes Next," *USA Today*, January 4, 2006, http://usatoday30.usatoday.com/news/washington/2006-01-04-abramoff-q-a_x.htm.

153. *The only thing dumber than a Republican or a Democrat . . . :* "Lewis Black on Political Bipartisanship," Youtube, posted April 12, 2012, www.youtube.com/watch?v=IzVGdibTQHU.

153. *The new rules eliminated the $50 threshold:* Library of Congress, CRS, *Gifts and Ethics Rules: Side-by-Side Comparison of Provisions of S. 1 and H. Res. 6, 110th Congress,* by Jack Maskell, CRS Report (Washington, DC: Office of Congressional Information and Publishing, February 20, 2007).

154. *Many heralded the new rules:* Louise Slaughter, "Slaughter Applauds Passage of Honest Leadership, Open Government Act," Press Release, July 31, 2007, Reprinted by Project Vote Smart, http://votesmart.org/public -statement/286825/slaughter-applauds-passage-of-honest-leadership -open-government-act#.Us20mf2Rhg0.

154. *"Does that mean I have to refuse the key to a city . . . ":* Jeff Zeleny and Carl Hulse, "Congress Backs Tighter Rules on Lobbying," *New York Times,* August 3, 2007, www.nytimes.com/2007/08/03/washington/03lobby.html.

155. *Example 10: A company in a Member's district:* "Summary of Activities: One Hundred Tenth Congress," A Report of the Committee on Standards of Official Conduct, United States House of Representatives, https://ethics.house.gov/ sites/ethics.house.gov/files/documents/Summary_of_Activities_110th _Congress.pdf.

157. *something American businesses have been doing:* Franklin A. Gevurtz, "The Historical and Political Origins of the Corporate Board of Directors," *Hofstra Law Review* 33, no. 1 (January 2004), 114.

157. *Even though the BPC employs no lobbyists:* BPC is a 501(c)(3) charitable organization with no registered lobbyists on staff. BPC has an affiliated organization, the Bipartisan Policy Center Advocacy Network (BPCAN), which is a 501(c)(4). BPCAN employs lobbyists who advocate for the policy solutions developed by the BPC.

159. *The good news is that:* Rob Hotakainen, "A Stand-Up Routine for Hungry Lawmakers and Lobbyists," *McClatchy DC,* January 15, 2008, www .mcclatchydc.com/2008/01/15/24749/a-stand-up-routine-for-hungry .html#storylink=cpy.

160. *official and privately funded travel have been in decline since pictures of Tom DeLay:* Danielle Kurtzleben, "Anti-Lobbyist Rules Have Grounded Some Congressional Travel," *US News and World Report,* September 22, 2010, www.usnews.com/news/articles/2010/09/22/ anti-lobbyist-rules-have-grounded-some-congressional-travel.

160. *The reduction in official travel:* Library of Congress, CRS, *Gifts and Ethics Rules: Side-by-Side Comparison of Provisions of S. 1 and H. Res. 6, 110th Congress,* by Jack Maskell, CRS Report RL33893 (Washington, DC: Office of Congressional Information and Publishing, February 20, 2007).

160. *Under rules passed in the aftermath of the Abramoff scandal:* Senators and Senate staff also may not attend trips sponsors by lobbyists' clients. United States Senate Select Committee on Ethics, "Senate

Select Committee on Ethics' Regulations and Guidelines for Privately Sponsored Travel," www.ethics.senate.gov/public/index.cfm/files/serve?File_id=d821533f-d956-4984-8027-3c7d0805b191.

161. *Speaker Nancy Pelosi explicitly forbade House members:* Brody Mullins, "Congress Reins In Its Perks for Travel," *Wall Street Journal,* May 14, 2010, http://online.wsj .com/article/SB10001424052748703950804575242751142413016.html.

161. *Stories of Abramoff flying members of Congress to exotic:* Associated Press, "Travel Records Made Public in Abramoff Scandal," NBC News, May 26, 2006, www.nbcnews.com/id/12993256/ns/politics/t/travel-records-made -public-abramoff-scandal/#.UvY5sP2RJg0.

162. *The relationship that President Clinton developed:* Interview with Steve Bell, former chief of staff to Senator Pete Domenici, September 17, 2013, Washington DC. Bell served on Senator Domenici's staff from 1974 to 1986 and again from 1996 to 2009.

162. *In a telling anecdote about the value of congressional travel and unusual friendships:* www.washingtonpost.com/politics/bob-dole-honored-for -work-in-helping-to-feed-the-poor/2013/12/12/667b36ac-635c-11e3-aa81 -e1dab1360323_story.html.

164. *In 1996, earmarks claimed little more than half a percent:* "Congressional Pig Book 2012," Citizens Against Government Waste, http://cagw.org/ reporting/pig-book#historical_trends; "The Federal Budget, 1993–2013," The Heritage Foundation, August 20, 2013, www.heritage.org/multimedia/ infographic/2013/08/federalspendingbynumbers2013/page-1-chart-1.

164. *Duke Cunningham, a congressman from California, was sentenced to prison:* Walter Pincus, "Pentagon Orders Investigation of Cunningham's MZM Earmark," *Washington Post,* March 24, 2006, www.washingtonpost.com/wpdyn/ content/article/2006/03/23/AR2006032301605.html; Randal C. Archibold, "Ex-Congressman Gets 8-Year Term in Bribery Case," *New York Times,* March 4, 2006, www.nytimes.com/2006/03/04/politics/04cunningham.html.

165. *What insiders termed "special member projects":* Perry Bacon Jr., "The Senator Fighting Pork," *Time,* May 2, 2006, http://content.time.com/time/nation/ article/0,8599,1190071,00.html.

165. *As Citizens Against Government Waste's Pig Book:* "Congressional Pig Book 2012," Citizens Against Government Waste, http://cagw.org/reporting/ pig-book#historical_trends.

165. *A report done by the Transportation Department's inspector general:* Conn Carroll, "A Brief History of Earmarks," The Foundry, The Heritage Foundation, December 23, 2010, http://blog.heritage .org/2010/12/23/a-brief-history-of-earmarks.

165. *Simultaneously, the annual bill that funds social programs:* "Recent History of Earmark Reform," Committee on Appropriations, US House of Representatives,

March 2010, www.taxpayer.net/user_uploads/file/Appropriations/FY2011/
House_Approps_2010_Earmark_Reforms_Fact_Sheet_3_10_2010.pdf.
165. *In total, the four most earmarked bills increased:* "Recent History of Earmark
Reform," Committee on Appropriations, US House of Representatives, March
2010, www.taxpayer.net/user_uploads/file/Appropriations/FY2011/House
_Approps_2010_Earmark_Reforms_Fact_Sheet_3_10_2010.pdf.
165. *And that rise in number drove a rise in cost:* "Congressional Pig Book
2012," Citizens Against Government Waste, http://cagw.org/reporting/
pig-book#historical_trends.
165. *Beginning in 2006, House leadership required:* "Recent History of Earmark
Reform," Committee on Appropriations, US House of Representatives, March
2010, www.taxpayer.net/user_uploads/file/Appropriations/FY2011/House
_Approps_2010_Earmark_Reforms_Fact_Sheet_3_10_2010.pdf.
165. *"all Members were required to post online their earmark . . . ":* Ibid.
165. *"the House Appropriations Committee announced that it [would] not approve
requests . . . ":* Ibid.
166. *Consistent with Justice Scalia's view about owning:* Ian Vandewalker, "Justice
Scalia's Sense of Enlightenment," Brennan Center for Justice, July 20, 2012,
www.brennancenter.org/blog/justice-scalia's-sense-entitlement.
166. *The Senate joined soon thereafter in eliminating:* "Earmark Data," Taxpayers for Common Sense, November 7, 2012, www.taxpayer.net/library/article/
earmark-data.
166. *Earmark spending fell from a little less than 1 percent:* "Congressional
Pig Book 2012," Citizens Against Government Waste, http://cagw.org/
reporting/pig-book#historical_trends; "The Federal Budget, 1993–2013,"
The Heritage Foundation, August 20, 2013, www.heritage.org/multimedia/
infographic/2013/08/federalspendingbynumbers2013/page-1-chart-1.
166. *the number of earmarks has fallen by more than 98 percent:* Sean Kennedy,
"Earmark Moratorium: Earmarks Live On, Transparency Does Not," Citizens
Against Government Waste, November 27, 2011, http://cagw.org/media/
wastewatcher/earmark-moratorium-earmarks-live-transparency-does-not;
"Congressional Pig Book 2012," Citizens Against Government Waste, http://
cagw.org/reporting/pig-book#historical_trends.
166. *"The arguments being made to ban earmarks . . . ":* J. Taylor Rush-
ing, "Senate Dems Defend Earmarks as GOP Votes to Ban Practice," *The Hill,* November 16, 2010, http://thehill.com/homenews/
senate/129519-senate-dems-defend-earmarks-as-gop-bans-practice.
167. *"trying to be a leader where you have no sticks . . . ":* Trent Lott, cited
in: Dan Merica, "Longing for Pork: Could Earmarks Help Congress Get
Things Done?" CNN, October 17, 2013, www.cnn.com/2013/10/17/politics/
earmarks-help-congress.

167. *when he stated that the president is "absolutely wrong":* http://firstread.nbcnews
.com/_news/2011/01/26/5925377-reid-to-obama-on-earmarks-back-off?lite.

167. *Andy Card, chief of staff to George W. Bush:* Author interview, Boston, MA,
March 25, 2014.

168. *also required a variety of strategic local investments:* Michael O'Donnell,
"How LBJ Saved the Civil Rights Act," *The Atlantic,* March 19, 2014,
www.theatlantic.com/magazine/archive/2014/04/what-the-hells-the
-presidency-for/358630.

168. *Due to prior success in blocking the legislation:* Susan Bre-
itzer, "Civil Rights Act of 1964," *Encyclopedia Virginia,* Virginia
Endowment for the Humanities, www.encyclopediavirginia.org/
Civil_Rights_Act_of_1964#start_entry.

169. *"In the end, the Congress will have to choose . . . ":* Steven T. Dennis, "As
Inouye Extends Earmark Ban, Senate Votes Against Permanent Measure," *Roll
Call,* February 2, 2012, www.rollcall.com/news/as_inouye_extends_earmark
_ban_senate_votes_against_permanent_measure-212080-1.html.

171. *Otto Von Bismarck, the first chancellor of Germany:* Interview (11 August
1867) with Friedrich Meyer von Waldeck of the *St. Petersburgische Zeitung;*
reprinted in *Fürst Bismarck: neue Tischgespräche und Interviews,* Vol. 1, 248.

CHAPTER 8

174. *Among those who have considered politics, a sizable chunk:* Susan Page,
"Poll: Public Service Valued; Politics—Not So Much," *USA Today,*
July 22, 2013, www.usatoday.com/story/news/nation/2013/07/21/
public-service-valued-politics--not-somuch/2573743.

174. *While a full 94 percent of people ages 18–29 describe:* "Bipartisan Policy Cen-
ter/*USA Today* National Survey of Adults Regarding Public Service," Bipartisan
Policy Center and *USA Today,* June 24–27, 2013, http://bipartisanpolicy.org/
sites/default/files/BPC%20Public%20Service%20Toplines.pdf.

174. *A disheartening 64 percent of young people:* "Bipartisan Policy Center/*USA
Today* National Survey of Adults Regarding Public Service," Bipartisan Policy
Center and *USA Today,* June 24–27, 2013, http://bipartisanpolicy.org/sites/
default/files/BPC%20Public%20Service%20Toplines.pdf.

174. *"I have just received the following telegram . . . ":* Joslyn Pine, ed., *Presidential
Wit and Wisdom: Memorable Quotes from George Washington to Barack Obama*
(Mineola, NY: Dover Publications, 2009), 258.

174. *The same BPC/USA Today poll cited above:* "35% Think U.S. Elections Are
Fair," *Rasmussen Reports,* November 4, 2013, www
.rasmussenreports.com/public_content/politics/general_politics/
october_2013/35_think_u_s_elections_are_fair.

175. *While four in five eligible voters cast ballots:* "Voter Turnout in Presidential Elections: 1828– 2008," The American Presidency Project, www.presidency .ucsb.edu/data/turnout.php.

175. *Democrats spin these concerns as pretext:* As one former GOP official told the *Palm Beach Post*: "The Republican Party, the strategists, the consultants, they firmly believe that early voting is bad for Republican Party candidates . . . It's done for one reason and one reason only . . . 'We've got to cut down on early voting because early voting is not good for us.'" Jamelle Bouie, "Republicans Admit Voter-ID Laws Are Aimed at Democratic Voters," *Daily Beast*, August 28, 2013, www.thedailybeast.com/articles/2013/08/28/republicans-admit -voter-id-laws-are-aimed-at-democratic-voters.html.

175. *The USA Today/BPC poll conducted in 2013 revealed:* Susan Page, "Poll: Americans Support Fine-Tuning Election Policy," *USA Today*, October 14, 2013, www.usatoday.com/story/news/politics/2013/10/14/ americans-election-policy-usa-today-bipartisan-policy-center-poll/2983159.

176. *Recent efforts in states like Florida to make the lists more accurate:* Steve Bousquet and Michael Van Sickler, "Renewed 'Scrub' of Florida Voter List Has Elections Officials on Edge," *Tampa Bay Times,* August 3, 2013, www.tampabay.com/news/publicsafety/crime/ renewed-scrub-of-florida-voter-list-has-elections-officials-on-edge/2134695.

176. *According to the Pew Charitable Trusts, approximately 2.75 million people:* "Inaccurate, Costly, and Inefficient: Evidence That America's Voter Registration System Needs an Upgrade," The Pew Center on the States, February 2012, www.pewstates.org/uploadedFiles/PCS_Assets/2012/Pew_Upgrading_Voter _Registration.pdf.

176. *Often, those registering new voters:* Amy Bingham, "9 Florida Counties Report Faked Voter Registration Forms from GOP-Backed Firm," ABC News, October 2, 2012, http://abcnews.go.com/Politics/OTUS/voter -registration-fraud-gop-backed-firm-spreads/story?id=17370445; Stephanie Saul, "Man Aiding G.O.P. Voter Registration Drive Is Charged," *New York Times*, October 19, 2012, www.nytimes.com/2012/10/20/ us/politics/man-aiding-gop-voter-registration-drive-is-charged. html?_r=1&; "Sacramento Elections Officials: GOP Voter Drive 'Suspicious,'" ABC News, www.news10.net/news/article/192033/2/ GOP-voter-drive-raises-questions-about-company-laws.

177. *Over twenty states presently or will soon install:* "Voter Registration Modernization in the States," Brennan Center for Justice, January 16, 2014, www .brennancenter.org/analysis/voter-registration-modernization-states.

177. *Canada moved its entire registration process online:* Ibid.

177. *Colorado, Delaware, Maryland, Nevada, Utah, Virginia, and Washington— have joined:* "David Becker: Upgrading Voter Registration," The Pew Charitable

Trusts, State and Consumer Initiatives, February 28, 2012, www.pewstates.org/ research/analysis/david-becker-upgrading-voter-registration-85899377178.

177. *In 1993, Congress passed the National Voter Registration Act:* "Reviewing the Motor Voter Law," *New York Times*, April 10, 2009, www.nytimes .com/2009/04/11/opinion/11sat4.html.

178. *A 2005 survey of people leaving an agency office:* Ibid.

178. *January 2013, Defense secretary Leon Panetta:* "Backgrounder: Women and the Draft in America," The Office of Public and Intergovernmental Affairs, Selective Service System, February 25, 2014, www.sss.gov/wmbkgr.htm.

179. *New IDs would enable all registered voters:* The failure to effectively assist people in acquiring qualifying identification is one of the reasons the Pennsylvania Voter ID Law was recently invalidated by the courts.

179. *President Obama created a bipartisan Presidential Commission:* Jennifer Epstein, "Obama Signs Executive Order Creating Election Commission Administration," *POLITICO*, March 28, 2013, www.politico.com/ politico44/2013/03/obama-to-sign-order-creating-election-reform -commission-160422.html.

179. *In January 2014, the PCEA made a series:* Nathaniel Persily et al., "The American Voting Experience: Report and Recommendations of the Presidential Commission on Election Administration," Presidential Commission on Election Administration (January 2014).

179. *Some states have already adopted some:* "Absentee and Early Voting," National Conference of State Legislators, www.ncsl.org/research/elections -and-campaigns/absentee-and-early-voting.aspx

179. *Congressional elections were similarly:* Peter Grier, "Election Day 2010: Why We Always Vote on Tuesdays," *Christian Science Monitor*, November 2, 2010, www.csmonitor.com/USA/DC-Decoder/Decoder-Wire/2010/1102/Election -Day-2010-Why-we-always-vote-on-Tuesdays .

179. *"They don't want you to vote . . . ":* Chris Rock, in Jacob Soboroff, "Chris Rock on Why We Vote on Tuesday," *Huffington Post*, May 4, 2008, www .huffingtonpost.com/jacob-soboroff/chris-rock-on-why-we-vote_b_100081.html . (My wife and I have an Annual Fat Tuesday party. I now feel better about the occasional low attendance.)

180. *Voter participation in primary elections is abysmal:* "Electoral Reform Systems," paper presented to Bipartisan Policy Center's Commission on Political Reform, 14.

180. *By comparison, a study by the Bipartisan Policy Center:* "2012 Election Turnout Dips Below 2008 and 2004 Levels: Number of Eligible Voters Increases by Eight Million, Five Million Fewer Cast Votes," Bipartisan Policy Center, November 8, 2012, http://bipartisanpolicy.org/news/press -releases/2012/11/2012-election-turnout-dips-below-2008-and-2004-levels -number-eligible.

180. *"The unhappy effects of low turnout are clear . . . "*: Norman Ornstein, "Vote—Or Else," *New York Times,* August 10, 2006, www.nytimes.com/2006/08/10/opinion/10ornstein.html.

180. *Just ask former House Majority Leader Eric Cantor . . . "*: Virginia State Board of Elections, http://sbc.virginia.gov/index.php/resultsreports/election-results/2014-election-results.

180. *"the rational strategy of candidates . . . "*: Geoffrey C. Layman and Thomas M. Carsey, "Ideological Realignment in Contemporary American Politics: The Case of Party Activists," paper presented at annual meeting of Midwest Political Science Association, April 27–30, 2010, www.unc.edu/~carsey/research/workingpapers/mw_2000_1.pdf.

181. *"There is a broad concern about . . . "*: Jeff Zeleny, "Top Donors to Republicans Seek More Say in Senate Races," *New York Times,* February 2, 2013, www.nytimes.com/2013/02/03/us/politics/top-gop-donors-seek-greater-say-in-senate-races.html?pagewanted=1&_r=3&partner=rss&emc=rss.

181. *Tellingly, in states:* "The Primary Turnout Story: Presidential Races Miss Record High," American University, Government and Politics, October 1, 2008, www.american.edu/media/news/20081001_Primary_Record.cfm.

181. *Next, caucus and convention systems:* "Congressional and Presidential Primaries: Open, Closed, Semi-Closed, and 'Top Two,'" FairVote, www.fairvote.org/congressional-and-presidential-primaries-open-closed-semi-closed-and-top-two.

182. *Despite serving three terms in the Senate:* Amy Gardner, "Tea Party Wins Victory in Utah as Incumbent GOP Senator Loses Bid for Nomination," *Washington Post,* May 9, 2010, www.washingtonpost.com/wp-dyn/content/article/2010/05/08/AR2010050803430.html.

182. *(All lost to their Democratic challengers.):* David Sherfinski, "Va. GOP Switches from Primary to Convention to Make 2013 Gubernatorial Nomination," *Washington Times,* June 15, 2012, www.washingtontimes.com/news/2012/jun/15/va-gop-switches-primary-convention-make-2013-guber.

182. *"The [Iowa] process has become increasingly contrived . . . "*: Mark Z. Barabak, "Republicans Question Iowa's Key Role in Presidential Balloting," *Los Angeles Times,* March 7, 2014, http://articles.latimes.com/2014/mar/07/nation/la-na-iowa-caucuses-peril-20140308.

182. *Gallup poll put the figure at 42 percent:* Jeffery M. Jones, "Record-High 42% of Americans Identify as Independents," Gallup, January 8, 2014, www.gallup.com/poll/166763/record-high-americans-identify-independents.aspx.

183. *The most prominent effort under way:* Lyle Brown, Joyce A. Langenegger, Sonia R. Garcia, Ted Lewis, and Robert E. Biles, *Practicing Texas Politics,* 15th ed. (Boston: Cengage Learning, 2012), 199.

183. *Senator and Washington elder statesman Slade Gorton:* Interview with Slade Gordon conducted by Jason Grumet, March 3, 2014.

183. *While some in California see signs:* Adam Nagourney, "California Sees Gridlock Ease in Governing," *New York Times,* October 18, 2013, www.nytimes .com/2013/10/19/us/california-upends-its-image-of-legislative-dysfunction .html?_r=0; Douglas J. Ahler, Jack Citrin, and Gabriel S. Lenz, "Do Open Primaries Help Moderate Candidates? An Experimental Test on the 2012 California Primary," paper presented at annual meeting of Western American Political Science Association, March 28–30, 2013, Los Angeles, CA, http:// wpsa.research.pdx.edu/papers/docs/ahlercitrinandlenz.pdf.

184. *shall nominate . . . :* US Constitution; Article II, Section 2, Clause 2.

184. *President John Tyler was so unsuccessful:* Library of Congress, CRS, *Evolution of the Senate's Role in the Nomination and Confirmation Process: A Brief History*, by Betsy Palmer, CRS Report RL31948 (Washington, DC: Office of Congressional Information and Publishing, May 13, 2009); "Senate Rejects Clinton Nominee," CBS News, October 5, 1999, www.cbsnews.com/news/ senate-rejects-clinton-nominee.

185. *Nevertheless, over the course of our democracy:* Library of Congress, CRS, *Evolution of the Senate's Role in the Nomination and Confirmation Process: A Brief History*, by Betsy Palmer, CRS Report RL31948 (Washington, DC: Office of Congressional Information and Publishing, May 13, 2009).

185. *As a result, during the Clinton Administration:* Twentieth Century Fund Task Force on Presidential Appointments, Obstacle Course: Report of the Twentieth Century Fund Task Force on Presidential Appointments (New York: Twentieth Century Fund Press, 1996), 72.

185. *Before Senate Democrats invoked the "nuclear option":* Peter Baker, "Unshackling the Presidency to Fix the Government," *New York Times,* July 13, 2012, www.nytimes.com/2012/07/14/us/politics/no-labels-group-offers-ideas-for -more-effective-presidency.html.

185. *But, when the Department of Homeland Security was formed:* Library of Congress, CRS, *The Appropriate Number of Advice and Consent Positions: An Analysis of the Issues and Proposals for Change*, by Henry B. Hogue, CRS Report RL32212 (Washington, DC: Office of Congressional Information and Publishing, March 14, 2005).

185. *Consider the experience of Connie Newman:* Story as relayed by Alvin S. Felzenberg, Executive Director, President's Commission on the Federal Appointments Process.

186. *Nearly a quarter of the top five hundred Senate-confirmed positions:* Tevi Troy, "Fixing the Confirmation Process," *National Affairs*, no. 7 (Spring 2011): 82–97.

186. *The 9-11 Commission Report took pains:* National Commission on Terrorist Attacks, *The 9/11 Commission Report: Final Report of the National Commission on Terrorist Attacks Upon the United States* (New York: W.W. Norton & Company, 2004), 422.

186. *She was eventually confirmed:* Barbara Gamarekian, "Washington Talk; Defending the Federal Bureaucracy, by the New Chief of the Bureaucrats," *New York Times,* June 13, 1989, www.nytimes.com/1989/06/13/us/washington-talk -defending-federal-bureaucracy-mew-chief-bureaucrats.html.

186. *Treasury secretary Tim Geithner had to operate without: Eliminating the Bottlenecks: Streamlining the Nominations Process: Hearing Before the S. Comm. on Homeland Sec. and Governmental Affairs,* 112th Cong. 36 (2011) (statement of Max Stier, president and CEO, Partnership for Public Service).

187. *From that point forward, progressives and conservatives:* For example in 1999, Republican senators refused to allow Richard Holbrooke's nomination for US ambassador to the United Nations to move forward unless President Clinton appointed a conservative to serve on the Federal Election Commission. More recently, Senator Lindsey Graham sought to block President Obama's nominees across the board unless the White House conceded to have the survivors of the Benghazi attack testify before Congress. Rebecca Kaplan, "Lindsey Graham Doubles Down on Threat to Block Nominees over Benghazi," CBS News, November 10, 2013, www.cbsnews.com/news/ lindsey-graham-doubles-down-on-threat-to-block-nominees-over-benghazi.

187. *This fundamental breakdown in the culture:* Paul Kane, "Reid, Democrats Trigger Nuclear Option; Eliminate Most Filibusters on Nominees," *Washington Post,* November 21, 2013, www.washingtonpost.com/politics/senate-poised-to -limit-filibusters-in-party-line-vote-that-would-alter -centuries-of-precedent/2013/11/21/d065cfe8-52b6-11e3-9fe0-fd2ca728e67c _story.html. There were sixty-eight individual nominees blocked prior to Obama taking office and seventy-nine (so far) during Obama's term. "Harry Reid Says 82 Presidential Nominees Have Been Blocked under President Barack Obama, 86 Blocked under All Other Presidents," *Tampa Bay Times,* PolitiFact, www.politifact.com/truth-o-meter/statements/2013/nov/22/ harry-reid/harry-reid-says-82-presidential-nominees-have-been.

187. *we should at least honor Thomas Hobbes:* Thomas Hobbes, *Leviathan,* Richard Tuck, ed. (Cambridge, England: Cambridge University Press, 1991), 89.

187. *Between 1972 and 2004, the number of confirmable:* Library of Congress, CRS, *The Appropriate Number of Advice and Consent Positions,* by Henry B. Hogue, CRS Report RL32212 (Washington, DC: Office of Congressional Information and Publishing, March 14, 2005).

187. *Far more dramatic, since 2004, the number:* "Streamlining Paperwork for Executive Nominations," Working Group on Streamlining Paperwork for Executive Nominations, November 2012, www.rules.senate.gov/public/?a=Files .Serve&File_id=823659d3-b173-40b6-8afa-a261d561eba3.

187. *As late as the second Nixon Administration:* Library of Congress, CRS, *The Appropriate Number of Advice and Consent Positions: An Analysis of the Issues and*

Proposals for Change, by Henry B. Hogue, CRS Report RL32212 (Washington, DC: Office of Congressional Information and Publishing, March 14, 2005).
187. *Do we really need the entire US Senate:* Library of Congress, CRS, *Presidential Appointments, the Senate's Confirmation Process, and Changes Made in the 112th Congress*, by Maeve P. Carey, CRS Report R41872 (Washington, DC: Office of Congressional Information and Publishing, October 9, 2012).
188. *"Too often the appointments process . . . ":* "Schumer, Alexander, Lieberman, Collins Announce House Passage of Bipartisan Deal to Streamline Senate Confirmation Process," US Senate Committee on Homeland Security and Governmental Affairs, July 31, 2012, www.hsgac.senate.gov/media/majority -media/lieberman-collins-schumer-alexander-announce-house-passage-of -bipartisan-deal-to-streamline-senate-confirmation-process.
188. *"if we don't fix what is broken in this system . . .":* 157 Cong. Rec. S1978, 1989 (daily ed. March 30, 2011) (statement of Senator Joseph Lieberman).
188. *These were good initial steps:* Since 2011, 272 less senior positions have been made subject to a less stringent congressional vetting: for those nominees, unless a senator objects, committee consideration is bypassed, and the full Senate considers them immediately. At the same time, the Senate eliminated 163 executive positions from the confirmation process altogether. Library of Congress, CRS, *Presidential Appointments, the Senate's Confirmation Process, and Changes Made in the 112th Congress*, by Maeve P. Carey, CRS Report R41872 (Washington, DC: Office of Congressional Information and Publishing, October 9, 2012).
189. *The working group suggested numerous fixes:* "Streamlining Paperwork for Executive Nominations," Working Group on Streamlining Paperwork for Executive Nominations, November 2012, www.rules.senate.gov/public/?a=Files .Serve&File_id=823659d3-b173-40b6-8afa-a261d561eba3.
189. *We take some self-respecting citizen . . . :* Charles S. Clark, "Consolidate Paperwork for Presidential Appointees, White House Group Urges," *Government Executive*, November 12, 2012, www.govexec.com/management/2012/11/ consolidate-paperwork-presidential-appointees-white-house-group-urges/59448.
189. *In an effort to streamline the arduous:* Ibid.
191. *Nevertheless, the White House felt compelled:* Huma Khan, "Another Tax Problem for Obama Nominee," ABC News, February 3, 2009, http://abcnews .go.com/blogs/politics/2009/02/another-tax-pro.
191. *Killefer had made an honest mistake:* Ibid.
191. *For example, the forms that candidates are required to fill out:* "Commission to Reform the Federal Appointments Process," Aspen Institute, March 23, 2012, www.aspeninstitute.org/sites/default/files/content/images/fed-appts/Aspen%20 Commission%20to%20Reform%20the%20Federal%20Appointments%20 Process%20White%20Paper.pdf.

191. (*Some progress on this front was made:* "Questionnaire for Completion by Presidential Nominees," United States Senate, Select Committee on Intelligence, www.intelligence.senate.gov/130207/questionnaire2.pdf.

191. *"Have you ever knowingly engaged . . .":* "Questionaire for National Security Positions," US Office of Personnel Management, https://www.opm.gov/forms/pdf_fill/sf86.pdf.

191. *Once you survive Executive Branch vetting, nominees are:* Robert Rizzi and Jason Abel, "Senate Confirmation Process Goes 'Nuclear,' but Some Burdens Remain," *Roll Call,* January 3, 2014, www.rollcall.com/news/senate_confirmation_process_goes_nuclear_but_some_burdens_remain_commentary-229914-1.html.

192. *Should someone who has lobbied on behalf of torture victims:* "Only in Washington: Obama's Lobbying Ban Leads to More Corruption," *Republic Report,* March 9, 2012, www.republicreport.org/2012/obama-lobby-ban-corruption-ricchetti/#sthash.mVWbk1hk.dpuf.

192. *If the FBI can brag about:* Keith Johnson, "'I WANT YOU:' Uncle Sam Hiring Criminal Hackers," *American Free Press,* July 4, 2012, https://americanfreepress.net/?p=4863.

193. *One Democratic lawyer described the process:* Jonathan Martin, "Lobbyist Ban Limits Obama's Options," March 13, 2009, *POLITICO,* www.politico.com/news/stories/0309/19961_Page2.html.

195. *The entities or groups covered include . . . .:* Office of Federal Advisory Committee Policy implementing ban on lobbyists serving on advisory committees, December 2011. PDF document, 4 pages: www.ofacp.od.nih.gov/policies/policies.asp (cached).

195. *The anti-lobbying measures of our day . . . .:* "Lobbying Law in the Spotlight: Challenges and Proposed Improvements," American Bar Association, Task Force on Federal Lobbying Laws, Section of Administrative Law and Regulatory Practice, January 3, 2011, www.americanbar.org/content/dam/aba/migrated/2011_build/administrative_law/lobbying_task_force_report_010311.authcheckdam.pdf.

195. *Initially dismissed, a judge on the Court of Appeals:* Andy Sullivan, "Obama Lobbying Ban Faces Setback in Court," Reuters, January 17, 2014, www.reuters.com/article/2014/01/17/us-usa-courts-lobbying-idUSBREA0G1JU20140117.

195. *Many have adopted the habit of "bumping into" lobbyists:* Eric Lichtblau, "Across from White House, Coffee with Lobbyists," *New York Times,* June 24, 2010, www.nytimes.com/2010/06/25/us/politics/25caribou.html?pagewanted=all&_r=1&.

195. *"the White House wants to enlist their help. . .":* "Jim VandeHei on the White House and Lobbyists," *POLITICO,* Morning Joe Video, February 24, 2011, http://videoshare.politico.com/singletitlevideo_chromeless.php?bcpid=3090457

26001&bckey=AQ~~,AAAAAETmrZQ~,EVFEM4AKJdT-Wv9cQWadwt8
FUbtX2ID_&bctid=801293820001.

196. *In a Bloomberg article titled:* Mike Dorning, "Obama Alumni Join Unlob-
byist Ranks Selling Washington Wisdom," Bloomberg, March 21, 2014, www
.bloomberg.com/news/2014-03-21/obama-alumni-join-ranks-of-unlobbyists-
selling-washington-wisdom.html.

196. *In a sign of the times, in 2013:* Dave Levinthal, "American
League of Lobbyists Changes Name," The Center for Public Integrity, November 18, 2013, www.publicintegrity.org/2013/11/18/13789/
american-league-lobbyists-changes-name.

196. *"[I]t's time to have a bipartisan look . . . ":* William J. Clinton, "Interview with
Larry King," January 20, 1994, Online at The American Presidency Project,
www.presidency.ucsb.edu/ws/?pid=50243.

197. *it costs $1.5 million to win a House seat:* Russ Choma, "Election 2012: The
Big Picture Shows Record Cost of Winning a Seat in Congress," Center for
Responsive Politics, June 19, 2013, www.opensecrets.org/news/2013/06/2012
-overview.html.

197. *your task will be to recruit around fifty new donors:* Note that $100 is a hypo-
thetical figure. The average donation to President Obama's 2012 re-election
campaign was $65.89, and the average contribution, through early 2012, to
Elizabeth Warren's 2012 Senate campaign was $65. Byron Tau, "Obama Cam-
paign Final Fundraising Total: $1.1 Billion," *POLITICO*, January 19, 2013,
www.politico.com/story/2013/01/obama-campaign
-final-fundraising-total-1-billion-86445.html; Steve LeBlanc, "Warren
Raising Bulk of Campaign Funds Out of Mass.," Boston.com, February 3,
2012, www.boston.com/news/local/massachusetts/articles/2012/02/03/
warren_raising_bulk_of_campaign_funds_out_of_mass.

198. *were told to expect nine- to ten-hour workdays:* Ryan Grimm and Sabrina
Siddiqui, "Call Time for Congress Shows How Fundraising Dominates Bleak
Work Life," *Huffington Post*, January 9, 2013, www.huffingtonpost
.com/2013/01/08/call-time-congressional-fundraising_n_2427291.html.

198. *"They're no sooner elected and they're . . . ":* Ibid.

199. *"usually, staff reviews the voting schedule to see if . . .":* Interview with former
Senate chief of staff, February 10, 2014.

199. *limit the amount of money a member can raise:* "Contribution Limits, 2013-
2014," Federal Election Commission, www.fec.gov/pages/brochures/
contriblimits.shtml.

201. *local donations up to $175 are matched with public funds, six to one:* "Match-
ing Public Funds," New York City Campaign Finance Board, www.nyccfb.info/
candidates/candidates/publicmatchingfunds.aspx.

201. *"There is nothing I am so anxious about . . . ":* "To Form a Government: A Bipartisan Plan to Improve the Presidential Appointments Process," The Brookings Institution, April 5, 2001, www.brookings.edu/~/media/research/files/papers/2001/4/05governance/0405governance.pdf.

CONCLUSION

203. *"man or woman, whether a political foe or friend . . .":* Century of Service, transcript, March 21, 2012, Washington, DC, Transcript produced by Federal News Service, http://bipartisanpolicy.org/sites/default/files/document/files/Baker-Dole%20Century%20of%20Service%20Event%20Transcript.pdf.

203. *Baker's courage, including his decision to support the Panama Canal Treaty:* Century of Service, transcript, March 21, 2012, Washington, DC, Transcript produced by Federal News Service, http://bipartisanpolicy.org/sites/default/files/document/files/Baker-Dole%20Century%20of%20Service%20Event%20Transcript.pdf.

207. *only half the public disapproved:* "Congress and the Public," Gallup, www.gallup.com/poll/1600/congress-public.aspx.

Index

About the Author

Jason Grumet is the founder and president of the Bipartisan Policy Center, which promotes practical solutions to the country's public policy challenges. He previously directed the National Commission on Energy Policy and is respected on both sides of the aisle for his innovative approach to improving government effectiveness. He has a BA from Brown University and a JD from Harvard University. He lives in Washington, DC.